2.50

Discourse

Discourse
PURPOSES AND PROBLEMS

Cleanth Brooks and Robert Penn Warren;
S. I. Hayakawa;
Philip G. Penner and David Macaree

LONGMANS CANADA LIMITED

Preface

This book is intended for high-school students in their final year of English. Underlying the editors' choice of material, therefore, are assumptions that such students will profit by a systematic examination of the principles of effective expression, and from discussion of the relationship between language and purpose in communication.

This approach to the study of language is expressed in the following excerpts from the prefaces of the texts from which this book is drawn:

> . . . Good writing cannot be learned—or cannot readily be learned —by a process of blind absorption, trial and error, or automatic conditioning. It is learned as the student becomes aware of the underlying principles. If, in the practical, day-to-day business of writing, the student can be made constantly aware of the principles underlying what he is trying to do, then he comes to a deeper realization of the workings of his own mind and feelings and, through that realization, to a greater skill in expressing himself.
>
> —CLEANTH BROOKS AND ROBERT PENN WARREN:
> *Modern Rhetoric*

> . . . To understand how language works, what pitfalls it conceals, what its possibilities are, is to understand what is central to the complicated business of living the life of a human being. To be concerned with the relation between language and reality, between words and what they stand for in the speaker's or the hearer's thoughts and emotions, is to approach the study of language as both an intellectual and a moral discipline.
>
> —S. I. HAYAKAWA: *Language in Thought and Action*

We have selected and edited appropriate sections of C. Brooks' and R. P. Warren's *Modern Rhetoric* and S. I. Hayakawa's *Language in Thought and Action,* the one for its lucid account of the writer's problems in communicating effectively, the other for its readable analysis of the relationship, in a variety of contexts, between aim and expression. At the same time, recognizing that some students are deficient to a degree in certain writing skills, we have supplied a writers' handbook as a reference guide to various aspects of the process of communication.

The handbook contains, among other things, a glossary of terms commonly used in dealing with written expression, a review of common errors in sentence construction, and guides to structure and punctuation. The handbook also contains a brief outline of bibliographical style as part of a discussion of the writing of a term paper, and an analysis of the main fallacies used in argument. The first section of the handbook merits particular attention, for it contains a brief résumé of strategy and tactics for the young writer in the practice of his art, and it should be required reading with all composition assignments.

The text, we feel, lends itself to various approaches. The above-average student should be able to work through considerable parts of it on his own; other students may need more direct guidance; all should, however, be invited to look on the expression of ideas not as a burdensome task but as a craft that may approach the level of an art.

P. G. PENNER

D. MACAREE

Contents

PART ONE
Special Problems of Discourse

CHAPTER ONE

The Paragraph and the Sentence

Most of us do not write by painfully building up sentences into paragraphs and the paragraphs in turn into larger wholes. Few of us think out our compositions in that fashion. We write in large units of thought and *revise* by paragraph and sentence. It is easier to deal with the shaping principles of composition when one keeps the larger architecture in view. Nevertheless, the smaller elements should be studied apart from the whole composition. As a unit of thought, for example, a paragraph has a certain structure, achieved through unity, coherence, and emphasis. As a part of the larger structure, the total composition, the paragraph contributes to the unity, coherence, and emphasis of the whole.

The Paragraph as a Convenience to the Reader

A paragraph, mechanically considered, is a division of the composition, set off by an indentation of its first sentence or by some other conventional device, such as extra space between paragraphs. In manuscript it may be marked by the sign ¶. Paragraph divisions signal to the reader that the material so set off constitutes a unit of thought.

For the reader this marking off of the whole composition into segments is a convenience, though not a strict necessity. A truly well-organized, well-written piece of prose would presumably be no worse as a piece of prose if it were printed with no paragraph divisions whatsoever. Printed thus, it would say precisely what it said before. But the reader would certainly be irritated, and rightly so, because the writer had failed to provide these pointers to the organization of his thought. Since communication of one's thought is at best a difficult business, it is the part of common sense (not to mention good manners) to mark for the reader the divisions of one's thought and thus make the thought structure visible upon the page.

Where should these divisions occur? How long should a paragraph be? In answering these questions, let us again begin by adopting the position of the reader. For him, a composition consisting of one- or two-sentence paragraphs might as well be printed without paragraph divisions at all. Segmentation on this scale would tell the reader little more about organization than the segmentation already given by the division into sentences.

Common sense dictates that the length of the normal paragraph will lie between the extremes of very short paragraphs and no paragraphs at all. But this is not to say that an *occasional* very short paragraph—even a paragraph of only one sentence—may not tell the reader a great deal. The shortness of the paragraph emphasizes its importance. Similarly, an occasional long paragraph does no damage and may serve to emphasize the unity of a long passage, always provided, of course, that the long passage actually constitutes a unit. We may sum up, then, by saying that there is no formula for ascertaining the length of paragraphs. Only common sense and the requirements of the occasion can determine how long any paragraph ought to be.

The Paragraph as a Unit of Thought

Paragraphing, obviously, can be of help to the reader only if the indicated paragraphs are genuine units of thought—not faked units nor mere random bits of writing arbitrarily marked off as units. *A paragraph undertakes to discuss one topic or one aspect of a topic.* Nevertheless, any realistic definition must be rather loose and general. Fortunately, we do not construct paragraphs by applying definitions. In his actual writing, the student will find his best approach is to remind himself that the paragraph is a *part* of the composition. A paragraph thus has its "part" to play, its own particular job to do, in the larger structure of meaning.

THE STRUCTURE OF THE PARAGRAPH

The paragraph, however, has its own structure, and there are various ways of indicating that structure. One of these ways is to build the paragraph around one sentence, the *topic sentence,* which states the central thought of the whole paragraph. We may think of the topic sentence as a kind of backbone, or spine, which supports the body of the paragraph and around which the rest of the structure is formed. Here is an example:

> *The reader of a novel—by which I mean the critical reader—is himself a novelist; he is the maker of a book which may or may not please his taste when it is finished, but of a book for which he must take his own share of the responsibility.* The author does his part, but he cannot transfer his book like a bubble into the brain of the critic; he cannot make sure that the critic will possess his work. The reader must therefore become, for his part, a novelist, never permitting himself to suppose that the creation of the book is solely the affair of the author. The difference between them is immense, of course, and so much so that a critic is always inclined to extend and intensify it. The opposition that he conceives between the creative and the critical task is a very real one; but in modestly belittling his own side of the business he is apt to forget an essential portion of it. The writer of the novel works in a manner that would be utterly impossible to the critic, no doubt, and with a liberty and with a range that would disconcert him entirely. But in one quarter their work coincides; both of them make the novel.　　　　　　—PERCY LUBBOCK: *The Craft of Fiction*

In this paragraph the first sentence is the topic sentence. It states the thesis, which the paragraph as a whole develops. It is frequently said that every paragraph contains a topic sentence, stated or *implied.* A more accurate statement, however, is that some paragraphs have topic sentences and that others do not; for an "implied" topic sentence is one which the reader must construct for himself as a way of summarizing the paragraph in question. Obviously any piece of composition possessing even a minimum of unity may be summed up in some kind of sentence. The "implied" topic sentence, therefore, is an abstraction—a kind of ghost sentence. In the pages that follow we shall mean by *topic sentence* only an actual sentence. Nevertheless, though insisting that every paragraph have unity, we shall admit the existence of paragraphs that do not embody a topic sentence.

We have just looked at a paragraph that begins with a topic sentence. Here follows a paragraph in which the topic sentence concludes the paragraph:

The artistic temperament is a disease that afflicts amateurs. It is a disease which arises from men not having sufficient power of expression to utter and get rid of the element of art in their being. It is healthful to every sane man to utter the art within him; it is essential to every sane man to get rid of the art within him at all costs. Artists of a large and wholesome vitality get rid of their art easily, as they breathe easily or perspire easily. But in artists of less force, the thing becomes a pressure, and produces a definite pain, which is called the artistic temperament. Thus, very great artists are able to be ordinary men—like Shakespeare or Browning. There are many real tragedies of the artistic temperament, tragedies of vanity or violence or fear. *But the great tragedy of the artistic temperament is that it cannot produce any art.*

—G. K. CHESTERTON: "On the Wit of Whistler", *Heretics*

The last sentence of this paragraph makes a generalized statement of the point developed in the preceding sentences. The topic sentence serves, in this instance, as a kind of summary. Although the beginning and the end of a paragraph constitute emphatic positions for the topic sentence, it may, in fact, occur at any place in the paragraph.

■ Applications

Construct several paragraphs, each of which will incorporate one of the following statements as its topic sentence:

1. A person can become accustomed to almost anything.
2. Hockey still remains our national sport.
3. Television is the death of the imagination.
4. Television is the hope of the arts.
5. Modern man grows increasingly dependent upon his machines.
6. Familiarity breeds contempt.

Methods of Paragraph Organization

With or without a topic sentence, there is always the problem of arranging the material of a paragraph. What are the typical organizational principles? We can answer by saying that they are, by and large, the same as those that govern the composition as a whole. Exposition, for example, uses such methods of organization as classification and division, comparison and contrast, illustration, and definition. These methods can determine the make-up of the smaller as well as the larger units of composition. Thomas Henry Huxley's "The Herring" is a good instance of the use of illustration, and this instance constitutes, as it happens, a single paragraph:

> If anyone wants to exemplify the meaning of the word "fish", he cannot choose a better animal than a herring. The body, tapering to each end, is covered with thin, flexible scales, which are very easily rubbed off. The taper head, with its underhung jaw, is smooth and scaleless on the top; the large eye is partly covered by two folds of transparent skin, like eyelids—only immovable and with the slit between them vertical instead of horizontal; the cleft behind the gill-cover is very wide, and, when the cover is raised, the large red gills, which lie underneath it, are freely exposed. The rounded back bears the single moderately long dorsal fin about its middle.
>
> —THOMAS HENRY HUXLEY: "The Herring"

We can say that in general the more complex methods of exposition and argument, such as functional analysis, chronological analysis, causal analysis, and deductive reasoning, rarely determine the structure of a single paragraph. Their very complexity prevents their doing so, for the structure of the paragraph is usually simple. It consists of the statement and elaboration of a point, or of a contrast made between two points, or of the illustration of an argument, or of the application of some principle.

Some paragraphs, however, do have a rather explicit logical structure in which the topic sentence states a conclusion which follows from premises stated in the body of the paragraph. Here is a paragraph so constructed:

> A really great pitcher must have control. Charles Ramsey had wonderful speed and a curve that broke as sharply as any that I have ever seen. He dazzled opposing batters with his fireball or made them break their backs reaching for pitches that broke sharply away from the plate. Charles had nearly everything—he even fielded his position brilliantly—but he lacked control. Even on his best days his control was less than certain. Shrewd batters learned this, and waited him out, frequently successfully, for a base on balls. On his worst days he simply couldn't find the plate. A pitcher without control cannot win close games. For this reason I do not consider Ramsey a great pitcher.

This is a rather simple paragraph on a simple subject; yet it is characterized by a logical structure. We can see this plainly by stating its argument in the form of a conclusion deduced from premises:

A great pitcher must have control. (major premise)

Charles Ramsey lacks control. (minor premise)

Therefore Charles Ramsey is not a great pitcher. (conclusion)

In narration and description, simpler kinds of organization, such as time sequence or the sequence of objects arranged in space, are commonly used. The following description of a cathedral provides a simple illustration of the paragraph built round the objects beheld as the observer looks upward:

> And so, taking care not to tread on the grass, we will go along the straight walk to the west front, and there stand for a time, looking up at its deep-pointed porches and the dark places between their pillars where there were statues once, and where fragments, here and there, of a stately figure are still left, which has in it the likeness of a king, perhaps indeed a king on earth, perhaps a saintly king long ago in heaven; and so higher and higher up to the great mouldering wall of rugged sculpture and confused arcades, shattered, and grey, and grisly with heads of dragons and mocking fiends, worn by the rain and swirling winds into yet unseemlier shape, and coloured on their stony scales by the deep russet-orange lichen, melancholy gold; and so, higher still, to the bleak towers, so far above that the eye loses itself among the bosses of their traceries, though they are rude and strong, and only sees, like a drift of eddying black points, now closing, now scattering, and now settling suddenly into invisible places among the bosses and flowers, the crowd of restless birds that fill the whole square with that strange clangour of theirs, so harsh and yet so soothing, like the cries of birds on a solitary coast between the cliffs and sea.
>
> —JOHN RUSKIN: *The Stones of Venice*

The following descriptive paragraph by T. E. Lawrence is organized on the movement of the observer through a mountain pass:

> Our path took us between the Sakhara and the Sukhur by a narrow gorge with sandy floor and steep bare walls. Its head was rough. We had to scramble up shelves of coarse-faced stone, and along a great fault in the hill-side between two tilted red reefs of hard rock. The summit of the pass was a knife-edge, and from it we went down an encumbered gap, half-blocked by one fallen boulder, which had been hammered over with the tribal marks of all the generations of men

who had used this road. Afterwards there opened tree-grown spaces, collecting grounds in winter for the sheets of rain which poured off the glazed sides of the Sukhur. There were granite outcrops here and there, and a fine silver sand underfoot in the still damp water-channels. The drainage was towards Heiran.

—T. E. LAWRENCE: *Seven Pillars of Wisdom*

There are other ways in which descriptions of a scene may be organized. They may be keyed to the senses; that is, to hearing, touch, sight, taste or smell; they may be dominated by a special mood or focused upon a particular detail; and so on. All these methods of describing a scene apply to descriptive paragraphs as well as to the larger units of description.

Unity, Coherence, and Emphasis

By the very fact of discussing the typical ways in which paragraphs may be organized, we have assumed that a paragraph has unity, for a formless blob of writing would require no organization at all. Organization implies a unifying purpose; and unity implies coherence. Coherence imposes its own problems upon the inexperienced writer, for even when he has carved out a paragraph that relates to *one* idea and does *one* job within the composition, the parts of it may not actually hang together. It is possible for a paragraph to have an ascertainable unity and yet lack coherence.

Brief discussion should not omit all mention of the third member of the triad—emphasis. In general, emphasis is a function of coherence; that is, only when we have made our thought truly coherent can we expect a proper scale of emphasis. Two places in a paragraph, the beginning and the end, tend to be those of greatest emphasis. It is no accident that topic sentences tend to occur at the beginning or the end of the paragraph.

Summary

There is no formula by which the length or structure of a paragraph may be determined. The student must use his best judgment, his common sense, and his taste. Unless he is very sure of his ground, he will tend to employ paragraphs of medium length and to use the more conventional paragraph structures. But in following these common-sense rules he must not conceive of paragraphs as mechanical units of even length and of homogeneous make-up. He should feel free, on occasion, to formulate paragraphs of "felt unity", relying upon his own impression of the "rightness" of the structure. For the student must never forget that the paragraph is a part—a meaningful part—of a larger structure and therefore cannot be formulated mechanically any more than can the larger structure of which it is a part.

■ Applications

What structural principles are to be found in each of the following paragraphs? If you judge that the paragraph has no real structure, say so and indicate why.

1. To tell when the scythe is sharp enough this is the rule. First the stone clangs and grinds against the iron harshly; then it rings musically to one note: then, at last, it purrs as though the iron and stone were exactly suited. When you hear this, your scythe is sharp enough; and I, when I heard it that June dawn, with everything quite silent except the birds, let down the scythe and bent myself to mow.

—HILAIRE BELLOC: "The Mowing of a Field", *Hills and the Sea*

2. The heart is a complicated mechanism. Essentially it is a muscular pump composed of four chambers and their incoming and outgoing blood vessels. The action of these chambers is co-ordinated and controlled by an intricate nervous mechanism. The chambers are paired into a right half and a left half. The upper chamber on each side is called the auricle; the lower, the ventricle. Each auricle is separated from its ventricle by a muscular valve which permits the flow of blood downward but prevents the leakage of blood backward.

—LOUIS I. DUBLIN: *The Problem of Heart Disease*

3. It happened one day about noon, going towards my boat, I was exceedingly surprised with the print of a man's naked foot on the shore, which was very plain to be seen in the sand. I stood like one thunderstruck, or as if I had seen an apparition: I listened, I looked around me, but I could hear nothing, nor see anything. I went up to a rising ground, to look farther; I went up the shore and down the shore, but it was all one; I could see no other impression but that one. I went to it again to see if there were any more, and to observe if it might not be my fancy;

but there was no room for that, for there was exactly the print of a foot, toes, heel, and every part of a foot; how it came thither I knew not, nor could I in the least imagine; but, after innumerable fluttering thoughts, like a man perfectly confused and out of myself, I came home to my fortification, not feeling, as we say, the ground I went on, but terrified to the last degree; looking behind me at every two or three steps, mistaking every bush and tree, and fancying every stump at a distance to be a man. Nor is it possible to describe how many various shapes my affrighted imagination represented things to me in, how many wild ideas were found every moment in my fancy, and what strange unaccountable whimsies came into my thoughts by the way. —DANIEL DEFOE: *Robinson Crusoe*

LINKING PARAGRAPH WITH PARAGRAPH

Since paragraphs are parts of a whole work—that is, elements in an ordered sequence—it is important that they be properly linked. Obviously there must be an intrinsic continuity: what one section, paragraph, or sentence presents must bear some relation to the whole subject and to what has just preceded. But even when there is this intrinsic continuity, the writer may have to help the reader by using certain devices of connection and transition, by giving him links or signposts. The judicious use of transitional words and phrases, such as *therefore, consequently, hence, thus, accordingly, on the contrary, however, nevertheless, furthermore, finally, in the same way,* and *moreover,* constitutes one way of helping the reader. The writer may also make use of the co-ordinate conjunctions *for, and, but, or,* and *nor* as signs of the connection between paragraphs. Since, however, we ordinarily use these conjunctions to join the parts of a sentence, or to join sentence with sentence, we employ them less frequently to tie a paragraph to a preceding paragraph.

If we do provide the reader with transitional words as signposts, obviously we must use them accurately. We must not begin a paragraph by writing "In the same way" unless what follows *is* "in the same way"; we must not write "Consequently" unless what follows is a consequence of the preceding paragraph.

An effective device for linking paragraphs is the repetition of a key word or phrase. It is a useful device, especially if we wish to avoid the formality of style suggested by the employment of transitional words and abruptness occasioned by the use of *and, but* or *or*. The following paragraphs from *Time* magazine illustrate the use of this device of repetition:

> *A buzzard coasting* high in the air over Central America last week would have seen nothing unusual. The mountainous, forest-matted isthmus lay quietly in the greasy November sun. Among the many human realities invisible to the buzzard were the boundary lines—the imaginary but very actual barriers that said: "This is Costa Rica; this is Guatemala; this is Nicaragua."
>
> For below the *coasting buzzard*, in the gray-green jungles of northern Nicaragua, more was stirring than his great bird's-eye view could catch. Snaking through the scrub, *guerrilla riflemen made short, sharp little raids* against government outposts. In and out of the piny mountain country on Nicaragua's northern flank, armed, machete-toting *men filtered mysteriously*. In Guatemala and Costa Rica dusty little *companies*, in faded denim and khaki, *marked time in the tropic heat*.
>
> *All this scattered activity* added up to one gathering purpose. That purpose called itself the Caribbean Legion.

Here is a series of three paragraphs from Dorothy Sayers' *The Mind of the Maker*:

> It is for this reason that I have prefixed to this brief study of the creative mind an introductory chapter in which I have tried to make clear the difference between *fact* and *opinion*, and between the so-called "laws" based on *fact* and *opinion* respectively.
>
> In the creeds of Christendom, we are confronted with a set of documents which purport to be, not expressions of *opinion*, but statements of *fact*. Some of these *statements* are historical, and with these the present book is not concerned. Others are theological—which means that they claim to be statements of fact about the nature of God and the universe; and with a *limited number of these I propose to deal*.
>
> *The selected statements* are those which aim at defining the nature of God, conceived in His capacity as Creator. They were originally . . . .

Another obvious device for linking paragraphs is the use of the demonstrative pronouns *this* (*these*) and *that* (*those*); but these words must be used with care. We are frequently tempted to employ them vaguely, hoping that the idea or object to which they refer will be clear from the context. Frequently it is not clear, and, instead of a tight and neat coupling of the two paragraphs, we have only the vague and clumsy suggestion of a tie. For example, consider the problem of making a transition between the following paragraphs:

A table is put in a garden, and on the table a piece of blue cardboard is placed, on which there is a watch-glass containing a drop of syrup. After a short while bees come to the syrup and suck up some of it. The bees then fly to their hive and give the syrup to other bees in the hive to make honey. Then they return to the feeding-place which they have discovered. We let the bees go on doing this for a while, after which we take away the blue cardboard with the syrup on it. Instead of this card we now put on the table a blue card on the left side of the first feeding-place, and a red card to the right of the first feeding-place. These new cards have no syrup on them but only an empty watch-glass lying on each. Thus, the blue card is on the left, the red card on the right, and there is nothing where the first blue feeding-card used to be. After we have arranged these new cards, we have not long to wait. Very soon bees arrive again, and it can be seen that they fly straight to the blue card; none go to the red card.

This behavior of the bees seems to indicate two things. The first is that the bees remember that blue means syrup and so they fly to the blue. Since they did not go to the place on the table where the syrup used to be, but flew to the blue card which had been placed on the left, it really was the blue card that attracted them, not the place where the syrup had previously been. We have trained the bees to come to the blue card. And the second thing our experiment seems to mean is that bees can tell blue from red.

—H. MUNRO FOX: "The Colors That Animals Can See",
The Personality of Animals*

We might be tempted to begin the second paragraph with: "This seems to indicate two things. The first is. . . ." But what the author wrote was: "This behavior of the bees seems to indicate two things. . . ." A little reflection will indicate that his judgment was sound. The author intends to state clearly a process of proof. He has been wise therefore to state very precisely what "this" refers to. The mistake of vague and indefinite reference is so common in student themes that the student should check each composition he writes to make certain that "this" or "that" standing at the beginning of a paragraph or at the beginning of a sentence refers unmistakably to some specific noun.

* "The Colors That Animals Can See", from *The Personality of Animals* by H. Munro Fox. Copyright 1940. Reprinted by permission of the author and Penguin Books, Ltd.

Specialized Paragraphs

As parts of a larger structure, paragraphs often have specialized functions. The opening paragraph (or paragraphs), for example, must introduce the whole essay; the final paragraph (or paragraphs) must bring it to a suitable conclusion. Within the essay itself, there may be many paragraphs of specialized function: one paragraph may state a particular argument; another may provide an illustration; still another may effect a transition between two sections of the essay.

These part-to-whole relationships cannot be studied by considering the paragraph in isolation. Here, too, the student will learn most by studying whole essays. Study of the paragraph, therefore, always leads us back to the general problems of composition.

■ Application

Analyze the transition between paragraphs in the following student theme:

Why I Chose . . . . . . College

Before I decided on coming here to . . . . . . College, I had to do a lot of arguing with myself and with my family and some friends. But first, I had better say what the argument was about. All my family are doctors, all the men, that is—my father, two uncles, and a first cousin—and all of them are good at the business. When I was a kid, it just never crossed my mind to be a policeman or cowboy. It was doctor all the way, to use the language of the race track where my father takes me now and then when he gets any time off. He once said to me that it was just as well that being a doctor takes so much time, for otherwise he might be a tout.

My marks in school were good enough for me to have some choice in the college I could go to. Naturally the first thing I wanted to know about any college was whether you could get good pre-med work. Everybody knows that you can get good pre-med training at Harvard or the other big universities, and I am aiming at the Harvard Medical School, but a smaller college like this one has to be investigated. I did, and I found out that in the last ten years, 22 per cent of the graduates of . . . . . . College have gone into medicine, and most of them have studied at medical schools in the top ten or so. Only two men failed to finish, and one of them had a physical breakdown. This record seems to settle the case for . . . . . . College as a good place for pre-med. I knew, too, that a lot of older men from here had become very successful doctors.

On the faculty here, too, is one famous biologist. In a small place like this you can work pretty close to a big man and watch how he does things and thinks about problems. You see, I think I have learned a lot already, just hearing my father and the family talk about cases and medical problems, and I calculated that the same process of what you might call learning by osmosis (I had high school biology and know about osmosis) could continue for me in a smaller college better than in a big one.

This last paragraph sounds as if I were tied to my family and dependent on them. I admire them, but I don't want to be dependent. That is one reason I didn't go to college near home, or to Stanford, where my family all went and are well remembered for studies and athletics. I wanted to get far away and be on my own so that I would become grown-up. A doctor has to learn responsibility early, or he is no good. The senior honors course here at . . . . . . also teaches responsibility, because it requires you to work out a big problem on your own.

There was another reason why I chose . . . . . ., in addition to its good pre-med record and the distance from home. It has a well-known English department. I don't mean this to sound like flattery, because everybody knows it is true. When I mentioned this reason to my cousin, Dr. Bob Mathews, he laughed at me and said I had better leave that English alone and get in some extra science. "Son", he said, "all the writing you will have to do if you are a good doctor is filling out prescriptions and signing your income tax return." I know that my cousin sort of laughs, too, at Uncle Bob, his father, in a friendly way and kids him for reading so much and writing a lot of articles, some of them not straight-through professional, but just for the layman.

I asked my uncle about Cousin Bob's point of view, and he said about Cousin Bob: "That's what you can expect from a surgeon. A surgeon is like a car mechanic. He just goes into the machine and patches it up. Except for what is wrong with the mechanism, every patient looks alike to him. That may be all right for a surgeon, but you plan to be a general practitioner. I'm one myself, and I wouldn't be anything else. It's the kind of medicine that has the human quality in the fullest way."

My father says, too, that in general practice human nature plays a big part. You have to understand the patient all the way through, not just the patient as a machine with a broken part. He says that you have to know who the driver of the machine is, and when he says that, he touches his forehead. "Lots of times it is bad driving that busts the axle, no fault in the steel."

My father agrees with my uncle and says that literature is one way of studying human nature—and a good way. But he winked at me, then, and said, "But don't forget poker. That's a pretty good way, too. Why do you think I strip all these lawyers around here in my biweekly game? Hell, they're being so logical about everything, and I'm just looking at their faces for symptoms." My father kids a lot, but he is supposed to be one of the best poker players in Santa Barbara, as well as one of the best doctors.

To sum up, I had to know that . . . . . . is a good place for pre-med work, that it is a good place for me to try to be independent, and that it is a good place for me to study literature for the purpose I have in mind (though I mean to study it, too, because I like it, and a doctor needs some sort of relaxation, such as my father's racing and occasional poker).

RHETORIC AND GRAMMAR OF THE SENTENCE

Having applied the principles of rhetorical organization to the composition as a whole and to its parts (the paragraphs), we next apply them to the smallest rhetorical unit, the *sentence*.

With this smallest rhetorical unit, however, we encounter another problem—the problem of grammar. In the composition as a whole, we can take the problem of grammar for granted; for, since the larger units of a composition are made up of sentences, we can assume that the demands of grammar have been met. But now, although we shall still be primarily concerned with how to make our sentences effective (the rhetorical problem), we shall have to touch upon specifically grammatical problems, which concern the rules and conventions that govern English sentence structure.

The basic distinction between grammar and rhetoric might be illustrated from the game of football. The "grammar" of the game would be the rules and conventions that determine the conduct of the game, including the system of scoring. The "rhetoric" of the game would be the knowledge of strategy and manoeuvre that leads to effective play and a winning game. To play the game correctly would not *necessarily* be to play it effectively, though effective play would certainly have to conform to the rules of the game. Let us consider the sentence, then, in both its rhetorical and grammatical aspects.

The sentence most frequently used in writing is the *full statement sentence,* or *subject-predicate sentence.* This description is not necessarily accurate for sentences in conversation, nor for sentences that ask questions, nor for those that make requests. The full statement sentence is the one most frequently used in writing, and demonstrates the three basic principles of rhetorical structure: unity, coherence, and emphasis. A sentence that makes a statement obviously has an independent subject-predicate combination, and its parts *cohere* (that is, are related to one another in special ways so as to produce unity). The term *emphasis* is applicable, for every good complete sentence must have a special focus, a specific centre of emphasis, around which the parts cohere. This centre of emphasis is most often the verb.

The Normal Word Order of the English Sentence

We all make sentences that are unique—unlike any others. Yet each of these unique sentences can be understood because, to be English, it must be based on an English pattern. The number of patterns is very limited. English depends heavily for expressing its meaning upon the position that words occupy in these sentence patterns. In some instances, change of position makes a radical change in meaning. Thus "The boy hit the ball" means something very different from "The ball hit the boy." Most of the shifts of meaning accomplished by rearrangement of words and word groups within sentences are far less drastic than that in the example just cited. Yet, even the slight alterations and shadings to be gained by manipulations of word order are important if we value the clarity and force of our writing.

Normal Order

The *normal* pattern of the English sentence gives us a subject (noun, pronoun or noun substitute) followed by a finite verb, the verb agreeing with its subject in person and number:

Birds fly. A bird flies. I am here. (noun, verb)

If the verb requires a complement (noun or nouns, adjective or adverb) the complement normally follows the verb.

Birds eat worms. (noun, verb, noun)
Birds give their babies food. (noun, verb, noun, noun)
Birds are singers. (noun, verb, noun)
The birds are hungry. (noun, verb, adjective)
The birds are here. (noun, verb, adverb)

Note that, if there are two nouns in the complement, they have a *fixed* position. We do not write, "The mother bird gave a worm her babies."

This, then, is the normal, or natural, word order of the English sentence:

$$\text{Noun Verb} \left\{ \begin{array}{l} \text{noun} \\ \text{noun, noun} \\ \text{adjective} \\ \text{adverb} \end{array} \right.$$

Each of these parts can have modifiers; you can say: "The old mother bird in our apple tree feeds her hungry babies big fat worms." But the basic pattern is still:

Bird feeds babies worms. (noun, verb, noun, noun)

Shifts in Word Order

Even though variety in sentence structure is desirable, the student should not strive to avoid normal order. The normal patterns need not be monotonous, for changes in the modifiers and the ordering of the modifiers, as well as changes in the length of the sentences themselves, will afford plenty of variety. A return to the normal word order of English is frequently the most direct way out of a tangled sentence.

A shift from the normal always calls attention to itself. The shift is thus justified only when such emphasis is justified. Consider the following instance:

A bigger fool I have never seen. [*Fool* is the direct object, and the shift of position, a direct reversal of the normal pattern, is very emphatic.]

In addition to the simple method of putting the complement before the subject and verb, illustrated above, we have another important device for stressing what would be in the natural word order the direct object of the verb. Thus, instead of

The guardsman struck the boy. (noun$_1$, verb, noun$_2$)

we may write:

The boy was struck by the guardsman. (noun$_2$, be, past participle of verb, by, noun$_1$)

And if we do not know who did the striking or if, for the moment at least, we are not interested in the agent, we may write:

The boy was struck. (noun$_2$, be, past participle of verb)

What the student should note, in the first place, is that this construction, the "passive" construction, has the effect of altering the normal word order in English; and, in the second place, that though on occasion it is effective, it is not to be over-used or to be used without a good reason. If the writer drifts into this kind of construction lazily and unthinkingly, he will exhibit the kind of woolly and flaccid writing that causes authors of grammar handbooks to warn against the "weak passive". For example, consider these "weak passives":

The problem of how to give people a proper sense of the perils of the atomic bomb without at the same time immobilizing them with terror *was discussed*.

The matter *has been taken* under advisement and at the proper time *will be acted upon*.

The whole panorama—exciting, splendid, and yet awe-inspiring— *was seen* by me.

English has other devices for shifting word order. Sometimes we use the "filler" or "dummy" word *there*:

A bird is in the tree. (noun, verb, adverb)

can become:

There is a bird in the tree.

A great river flowed through the land. (noun, verb, adverb)

can become:

There flowed through the land a great river.

We also use a "dummy" *it* to delay a subject for emphasis:

To see such poverty and misery made him heartsick.

can become:

It made him heartsick to see such poverty and misery.

The rigid word order of the pattern with two objects, as in:

The mother bird brought her babies food.

can be broken by making the first object (indirect object) into a *to* or *for* phrase, which becomes a movable:

The mother bird brought food to [for] her babies.
To her babies, the mother bird brought food.

Similarly, we can sometimes change the noun-verb-adverb pattern by putting the adverb first:

I *am here* can be *Here I am* or *Here am I.*

Each order gives a different emphasis to the message.

Position of the Modifiers

We now need to consider the position in the sentence occupied by the various modifiers—by the adjectives and adverbs, and by the phrases and clauses which function either as adjectives or adverbs. The position of some of these modifiers is rather rigidly fixed; that of others is optional, and since there is no prescribed position for them, the ordering of these "movable" modifiers is a matter of taste, emphasis, and expressiveness. We can say that the fixed modifiers are placed largely in accordance with grammatical rules; the position of the movable modifiers is assigned largely in terms of rhetorical considerations.

Fixed modifiers

Let us consider first the fixed modifiers. These include most adjectives, and phrases and clauses which have the function of adjectives. Relative clauses, adjectival phrases, and adjectival infinitives *follow* the substantive* which they modify. We must write, for example:

* A substantive is any word, phrase or clause used as a noun.

The man *to see* is Jim.
The man *I knew* was Jim.
The man *whom I mentioned* was Jim.
The house *in the country* was for sale.

We cannot write:

The *to see* man is Jim.

or:

The *I knew* man was Jim.

Single adjectives, on the contrary, just reverse this rule. The normal position of a single adjective is *before* the substantive that it modifies. For example, we would normally write:

A *bright* day dawned.
A *long black* automobile rounded the corner.
He gave an *extended, involved,* and *tortuous* argument.

Predicate adjectives, of course, do not come under this rule. We say that they modify the substantive "through the verb", and they normally come after the verb. Consider these illustrations.

The rose was *red.*
The third night seemed *long.*
The house was *for sale.*

On occasion, however, we do reverse the normal positions. Examples will readily occur to the student. Here are a few:

Comrades *all!*
Chapter *ten.*
John the *Baptist.*
A car, *long* and *black,* rounded the corner.
A small face, *dirty,* appeared at the window.
Black is my true love's hair.

As we have seen earlier, variation from the norm is emphatic, and in all these illustrations the reversal of normal position has the effect of emphasizing the modifiers used.*

We observed earlier that thoughtless use of emphatic position or over-use of emphatic position defeats its own ends. The principle applies to modifiers. John Bunyan, in his *Pilgrim's Progress,* used the phrase "the house beautiful". In the context provided by Bunyan the expression is well used. But, with it as model, the advertisers nowadays produce such absurdities as "the memorial park beautiful", "the body beautiful", and "the hair-do glamorous". Variation from the normal position of the adjective, like other emphatic devices, ought to be used sparingly and cautiously.

To sum up, the position of most adjectival modifiers is definitely fixed. The student's real problem here is to avoid clumsiness and absurdity through a careless placing of such modifiers.

In this connection, relative clauses (which we must remember are adjectival modifiers) call for a further word. Relative clauses may be *unlinked* as in the sentence "The man I knew was Jim" or *linked* as in "The man whom I knew was Jim." The *link* words are the pronoun *who* (*whom*), restricted to human beings; *which,* restricted to animals and inanimate objects; and *that,* unrestricted. A relative clause which *immediately* follows the substantive modified requires no link word; otherwise it does, and the choice of the proper link word may be necessary for clarity. Compare:

The man in the automobile that I recognized was Jim.

with:

The man in the automobile whom I recognized was Jim.

---

* One qualification of this principle, however, must be made. Some of the examples seem to represent, not an emphatic variation, but the normal pattern: e.g., *chapter ten* and *John the Baptist.* But in expressions of this sort, as a little reflection will show, the modifier is important and normally requires stress. Furthermore, there are other expressions in which we normally encounter the adjective following the noun: first, certain fossilized expressions derived from French law, such as "body politic" and "heir apparent"; and second, expressions such as "the day following", "the funds available", which actually represent elliptical expressions which we would have to fill out as follows: "the day following (this day)", "the funds available (to us)". These classes of exceptions, however, do not affect the general rule, that an adjective normally *precedes* its substantive, and that the reversal of this position throws emphasis upon the adjective.

The first sentence is ambiguous, whereas the second sentence is not.

Relative clauses occasion difficulty in still other ways. We may make a clumsy reduplication of clauses:

The man who had just come in whom I had never met was a Mr. Rogers.

Better to write:

The new arrival, whom I had never met, was a Mr. Rogers.

or:

A Mr. Rogers, whom I had never met, had just come in.

Sometimes we carelessly make a relative clause modify a general idea which is implied but not expressed. Thus:

She had been hurt and bitterly disappointed, which accounted for her strange conduct.

Better to write:

Her hurt and bitter disappointment accounted for her strange conduct.

or:

She had been hurt and bitterly disappointed, a fact which accounted for her strange conduct.

Movable modifiers

The position of adverbial modifiers is far less rigidly fixed than that of adjectival modifiers. For example, consider the variety of positions occupied by adverbial modifiers in the sentences that follow:

There, at ten o'clock, I arrived *as I had been told to do.*
At ten o'clock, I arrived *there, as I had been told to do.*
There, as I had been told to do, I arrived *at ten o'clock.*

The first sentence tends to stress the place as the most important matter; the second sentence stresses the time of arrival; the third sentence emphasizes the place and suggests that the instructions had been principally concerned with designating it. Control of the shadings of meaning is the mark of a skillful writer. Thus the fact that adverbial modifiers can be shifted about does not mean that we are at liberty to place them at random but, on the contrary, that if we are to write well, we must exercise great care in placing them.

Caution: Unless adverbs such as *merely, just, only, almost* are placed immediately before the words that they modify, the meaning may become ambiguous.

> You *only* live once.
> You *just* have one bullet left.
> I *merely* asked for what was left.

Most of us fall into such sentences in daily speaking, and the inflections with which we say them can usually be counted upon to make the meaning clear. But, in writing, where inflection cannot help, we should be more precise; we should make unmistakably clear that *only* modifies *once* and that *just* modifies *one*. Therefore the proper sequences are "only once" and "just one". Does *merely* indicate that I requested rather than demanded, or is the writer trying to say that he asked for nothing in excess of what was left? With this last instance, we are led to the problem of "squinting constructions".

In such constructions the modifier looks two ways, and it is not clear which of the two possibilities is intended. For example:

> The winner of the match tomorrow plays in the final round.

Does the sentence mean that:

> The winner of the match plays in the final round tomorrow.

or does it mean:

> The winner of the match to be played tomorrow goes into the final round.

In the following sentence, *often* is ambiguous:

> The pitcher that goes to the well often gets broken.

Dangling phrases

There is, however, one kind of adjectival modifier that is freely movable, the participial or verbal adjective. Thus, one may write:

> *Smoking a cigarette,* James sauntered down the street.
> James, *smoking a cigarette,* sauntered down the street.
> James sauntered down the street, *smoking a cigarette.*

All three sentences are perfectly good English. There is no one correct position for the participial phrase, and where we place it is dictated largely by considerations of taste.

The fact that the participle, though an adjectival modifier, has this character of movability makes it all too easy for the student to confuse it with the other movable modifiers, the adverbial modifiers. The confusion results in the so-called dangling participle. (The participle, having no substantive to modify, is said to dangle.) For example:

Walking down the street, a barber shop came into view.

What is meant is obviously:

Walking down the street, I saw a barber shop. [participle modifies I]

or:

As I walked down the street, a barber shop came into view. [adverbial clause substituted for the participle]

Consider some further instances of the dangling participle:

Throwing to either side a band of hissing foam, we felt the boat shudder under us as we turned on full power.
Based upon statistics, he should not die for some years.

Other verbals than the participle may be left dangling by the careless writer. In this example a gerund phrase dangles:

On peering into the darkness, the shape disappeared.

Evidently the writer meant to say:

On peering into the darkness, he found that the shape had disappeared.

Here an infinitive phrase dangles:

To hold it properly, the handle must be grasped.

The writer evidently meant to say:

To hold it properly, one must grasp the handle.

Obviously, in order to avoid falling into absurdities we need to consider with some care the relationship between the modifier and the rest of the sentence; and, as the above examples indicate, verbals call for special care.

Absolute constructions

An absolute construction is a phrase, usually consisting of a noun or pronoun modified by a participle and having only a very general relation to the rest of the sentence.

> *The mission having been carried out,* the force received orders to return.
> *The principal danger once passed,* they threw off their fears.

Some authorities also classify as absolute constructions such phrases as the following:

> *To judge from his face,* he can't be very old.
> *Remembering the unpredictability of the weather and of human nature,* everything else portends a fine game on Saturday.
> *Taking all the evidence into account,* the decision was a just one.

It may not be altogether easy to see just how these expressions escape being dangling modifiers. An argument sometimes urged, that they escape dangling because they designate a *general* truth, is not altogether convincing. Perhaps we shall do best simply to say that such expressions are idiomatic; i.e., that English simply does permit us, not altogether logically, to say:

> *To judge from his face,* he can't be very old.

and does not require us to expand this to:

> *To judge from his face,* I can't believe that he is very old.

■ Applications

I Convert the following sentences to normal word order; that is, re-establish the pattern of *subject, verb, inner* and *outer complements.*

1. Icebergs, he could see wherever he looked.
2. There was a man once that was bored with his life.
3. The arrival of five cruisers and twenty destroyers was reported.
4. The great bear was surrounded by a horde of yapping, excited dogs.

5. It was a great bear that was surrounded by the horde of yapping, excited dogs.
6. Ways and means for handling the peak late-afternoon traffic through Westville and Lakeville were discussed.

II In the following sentences, some of the adjectival modifiers are improperly placed. Rearrange the modifiers, and, where necessary, rewrite the sentences to improve clarity and effectiveness.

1. A two-storey house was for sale with green shutters.
2. A man in the army I served with gave me this book.
3. It was the man I knew whom I now saw.
4. The lady whom I knew from Boston has not returned.
5. Boy is missing in first pair of long pants.
6. Slowly filling with water, we saw the ship go down.

III The following sentences contain dangling participles. Remove them (a) by rewriting the sentence so that the participle is given some word to modify and (b) by rewriting the dangling participle into a subordinate clause. For example:

Ringing the doorbell, the house answered us with silence.

Correct to (a) "Ringing the doorbell, we could hear from the house only the answer of silence." Or (b) "Although we rang the doorbell, the house answered us with silence."

1. Hurrying and out of breath, scurrying up the depot stairs, the 9:01 for Grand Central swept past us.
2. The afternoon drowsed on to an end, sipping lemonade and listening to records.
3. Reading the thrilling ghost story, the grandfather clock ticked insistently in our ears.
4. Hanging on for dear life, the car careened to the edge of the road.
5. Walking up the last steps of the drive, the first mutterings of thunder were heard.

IV Some of the following sentences include dangling modifiers. In others, the modifiers have been shifted out of the order in which they were originally written. Remove dangling modifiers, and rearrange the italicized modifiers so as to improve the clarity and effectiveness of each sentence.

1. Though the Greek scientist Eratosthenes had, *with only a small error,* calculated the distance of the sun from the earth and the earth's circumference at the equator, his theory of a global world was received by men of common sense *with polite scorn.*
2. Singing merrily and happily, our music put the whole company in a jolly mood.
3. In myriad private hotel rooms of myriad hotels the Alumni Weekly Lunch is, *today,* being celebrated, *as every day.*
4. *Because their maxims would not have expressed their hearts,* they would not have been perfect moralists *then, even if their theory had been correct* (which, I think it was, *though not in statement,* in intention).
5. Thinking as hard as we could, the answer still could not be found.
6. Eight men were drowned, *however,* and *from that memory* my grandfather *at intervals all his life* suffered and never read anything but the shipwreck of St. Paul *if asked to read the family prayers.*
7. There can be no miracles *unless there exists something else which we may call the supernatural, in addition to Nature.*

General Principles of Sentence Structure

Parallelism

Thus far we have considered the structure of the sentence from one point of view: that of the arrangement of its basic constituents and of the various kinds of modifiers. But other principles may determine the structure of a sentence. One of these is *parallelism,* a method of adjusting grammatical pattern to rhetorical pattern. In its simplest terms, parallelism means no more than that elements of like meaning should be put in like constructions.

The very richness of English tempts us to violate parallelism. For example, we have two noun forms of the verb. We can use the infinitive *to swim* or the gerund *swimming.* Consequently, the careless writer may blunder into a sentence like this: *"To swim* and *hunting* are my favourite sports."* But the distinction between infinitive and gerund awkwardly distracts the reader from what is a co-ordinate relation. We ought to write: *"Swimming* and *hunting* are my favourite sports."* Or: *"To swim* and *to hunt* are my favourite sports."*

It is our great variety of movable modifiers, however, that most tempts us into violations of parallelism. We may write, for example: *"Being lazy by nature* and *because I am clumsy,* I have never liked tennis."* Such violations of parallelism easily creep into first drafts —even into the first drafts of a good writer. Careful rewriting is the remedy.

In learning to avoid these blunders, we must not forget, however, that the principle of parallelism is a positive one. It is, in fact, a powerful rhetorical device. By using parallel construction, we emphasize parallel ideas, and we can thus play off one sort of meaning against the other. Sentences constructed on this principle are sometimes called "balanced sentences". Here are two examples:

1. As the hart panteth after the water brooks, so panteth my soul after Thee, O God.
2. He was sick of life, but he was afraid of death; and he shuddered at every sight or sound which reminded him of the inevitable hour.

The parallel elements may be represented in the following scheme:

1.	as	so
	hart	soul
	panteth	panteth (repetition)
	water brooks	Thee
2.	sick	afraid
	life	death

Co-ordination and subordination

Co-ordination may be regarded as an aspect of parallelism. We have seen that elements of like meaning should be put in like constructions. Conversely, we must not link as equal, elements that are not of equal importance. A less-important element must be made subordinate to a more important one. Consider the following sentence: "I stayed at home; I was ill." What is the relation between the two statements? The writer has merely associated them. He has not defined the relation of one to the other. He might define the relationship in various ways:

Because I was ill, I stayed at home.
While I was staying at home, I was ill.
Although I stayed at home, I was ill.
Feeling ill, I stayed at home.
I stayed at home, quite ill.

Simple, uncritical writing, such as that of a child, tends to present a succession of co-ordinate units: "Then the bear got hungry. He came out of his den. He remembered the honey tree. And he started walking toward the honey tree." The mature and discriminating writer indicates the relation of his statements, one to another, by subordinating, thus:

Having done this, she thought it prudent to drop a few words before the bishop, letting him know that she had acquainted the Puddingdale family with their good fortune so that he might perceive that he stood committed to the appointment.

The writer who points up relationships, instead of leaving them to be inferred by the reader, obviously makes the reader's task easier. He gives not only facts but an interpretation of facts: the very pattern of subordination is an interpretation. When, however, the writer, by using subordination, assumes this burden of interpretation, he must not falsify his interpretation by careless and thoughtless subordination. He must think through the relation of part to part. Unless he does so, he may write sentences like this: "My head was feeling heavy when I took an aspirin." In this sentence the motive for the act is treated as though it were the matter of importance; the act itself has been relegated to the subordinate position. Rather than confuse the reader with a subordination which inverts the real relationship, the writer would have done better simply to have written: "My head was feeling heavy; I took an aspirin." But it is obvious, of course, that the proper subordination would be: "Because my head was feeling heavy, I took an aspirin." Or: "When my head began to feel heavy, I took an aspirin."

Here are two further examples of improper subordination:

The workman snored loudly and he had a red face.

Alter to:

The workman, who had a red face, snored loudly.

or to:

The red-faced workman snored loudly.

Mr. Jones is our neighbour and he drove by in a large automobile.

Alter to:

Mr. Jones, who is our neighbour, drove by in a large automobile.

or to:

Mr. Jones, our neighbour, drove by in a large automobile.

Though subordination is important as a means for tightening up a naïve and oversimple style, the student ought not to be browbeaten into constant subordination. In certain contexts a good writer might prefer:

The workman snored loudly. He had a red face.

This form of the statement does bring into sharp focus the detail of the red face. It might even suggest a leisurely observer, looking on with some amusement.

Summary

Grammatical subordination must conform to the rhetorical sense. It is an important means for securing economy. Careful subordination tends to give the sense of a thoughtful observer who has sifted his ideas and arranged them with precision.

Loose sentences and periodic sentences

We can view sentence structure in still another way. We can distinguish between those sentences in which the sense of the sentence is held up until almost the end (*periodic sentences*) and those in which it is not held up (*loose sentences*). Holding up the sense creates suspense: we do not know how the sentence is "coming out" until we have reached, or nearly reached, the end of it. Here is an example:

> It was partly at such junctures as these and partly at quite different ones that with the turn my matters had now taken, my predicament, as I have called it, grew most sensible.   —HENRY JAMES

If we convert the sentence to loose structure, we get something like this:

> With the turn my matters had now taken, my predicament, as I have called it, grew most sensible, partly at such junctures as these and partly at quite different ones.

The loose sentence is the "normal" sentence in English; the structure of the periodic sentence is "abnormal". As we noted above, deviation from the norm always tends to be emphatic. The periodic sentence, in skillful hands, is powerfully emphatic. By inversion, by use of the "It was" construction, or by interposition of movable modifiers between subject and predicate, the sentence and its primary statement are made to end together. But like all deviations from the norm, the periodic sentence—and the balanced sentence—are somewhat artificial. Over-used, such sentences soon weary the reader.

Sentence length and sentence variation

How long should a sentence be? It may be as short as one word. "Go!" is a perfectly good sentence; it has a predicate with subject implied. On the other hand, a sentence may be forty or fifty words long. In fact, by tacking together elements with *and*'s and *but*'s, we can construct sentences of indefinite length. These are the possible extremes. But with the sentence, as with the paragraph, common sense and taste set reasonable limits. A succession of very short sentences tends to be monotonous. Extremely long sentences tend to bog down the reader in a quagmire of words.

This is not, of course, to say that the writer should not feel free to use a one-word sentence whenever he needs it or even a succession of short sentences to gain special effects. Notice how the short sentences in the following extract from James Joyce's short story "Two Gallants" keep the reader's attention focused on one character and in the character's relation to the action.

> He was hungry, for, except for some biscuits which he had asked two grudging curates to bring him, he had eaten nothing since break-

fast-time. He sat down at an uncovered wooden table opposite two work-girls and a mechanic. A slatternly girl waited on him.

"How much is a plate of peas?" he asked.

"Three halfpence, sir," said the girl.

"Bring me a plate of peas," he said, "and a bottle of ginger beer."

He spoke roughly in order to belie his air of gentility, for his entry had been followed by a pause of talk. His face was heated. To appear natural he pushed his cap back on his head and planted his elbows on the table. The mechanic and the two work-girls examined him point by point before resuming their conversation in a subdued voice. The girl brought him a plate of grocer's hot peas, seasoned with pepper and vinegar, a fork and his ginger beer. He ate his food greedily and found it so good that he made a note of the shop mentally. When he had eaten all the peas he sipped his ginger beer and sat for some time thinking of Corley's adventure. In his imagination he beheld the pair of lovers walking along some dark road: he heard Corley's voice in deep energetic gallantries, and saw again the leer of the young woman's mouth. This vision made him feel keenly his own poverty of purse and spirit. He was tired of knocking about, of pulling the devil by the tail, of shifts and intrigues. He would be thirty-one in November. Would he never get a good job? Would he never have a home of his own? He thought how pleasant it would be to have a warm fire to sit by and a good dinner to sit down to. He had walked the streets long enough with friends and with girls. He knew what those friends were worth: he knew the girls too. Experience had embittered his heart against the world. But all hope had not left him. He felt better after having eaten than he had felt before, less weary of his life, less vanquished in spirit. He might yet be able to settle down in some snug corner and live happily if he could only come across some good simple-minded girl with a little of the ready.

—JAMES JOYCE: "Two Gallants", *Dubliners**

By the same token, he ought to feel free to use very long sentences to gain special effects. The following sentence from Lytton Strachey's *Queen Victoria* will illustrate:

Perhaps her fading mind called up once more the shadows of the past to float before it, and retraced, for the last time, the vanished visions of that long history — passing back and back, through the cloud of years, to older and ever older memories — to the spring woods at Osborne, so full of primroses for Lord Beaconsfield — to Lord Palmerston's queer clothes and high demeanour, and Albert's face under the green lamp, and Albert's first stag at Balmoral, and Albert in his blue and silver uniform, and the Baron coming in through a doorway, and Lord M. dreaming at Windsor with the rooks cawing in the elm-trees, and the Archbishop of Canterbury on his knees in the dawn, and the old King's turkey-cock ejaculations, and Uncle Leopold's soft voice at Claremont, and Lehzen with the globes, and her mother's feathers sweeping down towards her, and a great old repeater-watch of her father's in its tortoise-shell case, and a yellow rug, and some friendly flounces of sprigged muslin, and the trees and the grass at Kensington. —LYTTON STRACHEY: *Queen Victoria*

Strachey is imagining what may have passed through the old Queen's dying mind as she slipped from consciousness. He imagines the succession of memories as going backward in time, from those of adult life to those of youth, and on back to the memories of childhood. The loosely linked series of phrases which constitute the sentence can be justified on two counts: the memories are presented as those of a dying mind, and, as the memories go backward in time, they become those of a child. Thus dramatically considered, the jumping from scene to scene (as suggested by the dashes) and the loose tacking on of additional scenes (by *and*'s) are justified. This sentence, which closes Strachey's book with what amounts to a recapitulation of Victoria's life, is thus used to gain a special effect.

The normal limitations and requirements of the human mind dictate how much can be taken in satisfactorily "at one bite". Unless the writer is striving for some special effect, he ought to regard with suspicion very short and, especially, very long sentences. The human mind also requires variety: the sentences should not all be monotonously of the same length.

Alternation of long and short sentences is but one means, however, by which to secure variety. Another, and a most important, means consists in varying the structure of the sentence. Sentences that repeat a pattern become monotonous. Here is an example:

I was twenty that April and I made the glen my book. I idled over it. I watched the rhododendron snow its petals on the dark pools that spun them round in a swirl of brown foam and beached them on a tiny coast glittering with mica and fool's gold. I got it by heart, however, the dripping rocks, the ferny grottos, the eternal freshness, the sense of loam, of deep sweet decay, of a chain of life continuous and rich with the ages. I gathered there the walking fern that walks across its little forest world by striking root with its long tips, tip to root and root to tip walking away from the localities that knew it once. I was aware that the walking fern has its oriental counterpart. I knew also that Shortia, the flower that was lost for a century after Michaux found it *"dans les hautes montagnes de Carolinie"*, has its next of kin upon the mountains of Japan. I sometimes met mountain people hunting for ginseng for the Chinese market; long ago the Chinese all but exterminated that herbalistic panacea of theirs, and now they turn for it to the only other source, the Appalachians.

The "I was—I idled—I gathered" formula is relieved somewhat by the long descriptive phrases and relative clauses. Even so, it is irritatingly monotonous. Here is the way in which Donald Culross Peattie actually wrote the passage:

> The glen was my book, that April I was twenty. I idled over it, watching the rhododendron snow its petals on the dark pools that spun them round in a swirl of brown foam and beached them on a tiny coast glittering with mica and fool's gold. But I got it by heart, the dripping rocks, the ferny grottos, the eternal freshness, the sense of loam, of deep sweet decay, of a chain of life continuous and rich with the ages. The walking fern I gathered there, that walks across its little forest world by striking root with its long tips, tip to root and root to tip walking away from the localities that knew it once, has its oriental counterpart; of that I was aware. And I knew that Shortia, the flower that was lost for a century after Michaux found it, *"dans les hautes montagnes de Carolinie"*, has its next of kin upon the mountains of Japan. Sometimes I met mountain people hunting for ginseng for the Chinese market; long ago the Chinese all but exterminated that herbalistic panacea of theirs, and now they turn for it to the only other source, the Appalachians.
>
> —DONALD CULROSS PEATTIE: *Flowering Earth*

There are many ways in which to vary sentence structure. Nearly everything said earlier in this chapter can be brought to bear on this problem. We can invert the normal pattern, or rearrange the pattern to throw emphasis on what is normally the subject or complement; we can subordinate severely or rather lightly. Most of all, we can dispose the modifiers, particularly the movable modifiers, so as to vary the pattern almost indefinitely. The effort to secure variety should never be an overriding consideration. A sentence should take the structure best adapted to its special job. The writer will usually find that he is thoroughly occupied in discharging this obligation.

Yet it is well to remind ourselves here again of the claims of the whole composition. We never write a "collection of sentences"; we write an essay, a theme, a total composition. The good sentence honours the claims exerted upon it by the total composition. And in our writing, and especially in our *rewriting*, we need to see that we have avoided monotony of sentence length or of sentence structure.

■ Applications

I Try to determine which of the following sentences are periodic in structure and which are loose. Rewrite the periodic sentences into loose sentences, and the loose into periodic. Pick out the balanced sentences, if any.

1. Peace cannot be secured without armies; and armies must be supported at the expense of the people. It is for your sake, not for our own, that we guard the barrier of the Rhine against the ferocious Germans, who have so often attempted and who will always desire, to exchange the solitude of their woods and morasses for the wealth and fertility of Gaul.   —EDWARD GIBBON

2. The night, the earth under her, seemed to swell and recede together with a limitless, unhurried, benign breathing.

—KATHERINE ANNE PORTER

3. If we begin with certainties, we shall end in doubts; but if we begin with doubts, and are patient in them, we shall end in certainties.   —FRANCIS BACON

4. The mania for handling all the sides of every question, looking into every window, and opening every door, was, as Bluebeard judiciously pointed out to his wives, fatal to their practical usefulness in society.   —HENRY ADAMS

5. Bubbling spontaneously from the artless heart of a child or man, without egoism and full of feeling, laughter is the music of life.

—WILLIAM OSLER

6. Every night I pulled my flag down and folded it up and laid it on a shelf in my bedroom, and one morning before breakfast I found it, though I had folded it up the night before, knotted around the bottom of the flagstaff so that it was touching the grass.   —W. B. YEATS

7. The hunger and thirst for knowledge, the keen delight in the chase, the good-humoured willingness to admit that the scent

was false, the eager desire to get on with the work, the cheerful resolution to go back and begin again, the broad good sense, the unaffected modesty, the imperturbable temper, the gratitude for any little help that was given—all these will remain in my memory, though I cannot paint them for others.

—F. W. MAITLAND

II Look back to the paragraphs quoted from *Time* magazine on page 12. *Time* style is celebrated for its inversion of, and its drastic departures from, normal sentence order. The motive, presumably, is a desire for condensation and emphasis. Rewrite these paragraphs so as to restore normal sentence order. Can you justify the departures from normal order? Is emphasis intelligently used? Or does too much emphasis result in no emphasis?

III The following paragraph is from Ring Lardner's *You Know Me, Al,* which purports to be a series of letters from Jack, the rookie pitcher, to his friend. As a revelation of character and of speech "in character", it is quite perfect. But rewriting it may provide us with a useful exercise in sentence structure and proper subordination. Put it into formal English.

We was to play 2 games here and was to play 1 of them in Tacoma and the other here but it rained and so we did not play neither 1 and the people was pretty mad a bout it because I was announced to pitch and they figured probily this would be there only chance to see me in axion and they made a awful holler but Comiskey says No they would not be no game because the field neither here or in Tacoma was in no shape for a game and he would not take no chance of me pitching and may be slipping in the mud and straneing myself and then where would the White Sox be at next season. So we been laying a round all the p.m. and I and Dutch Schaefer had a long talk to gether while some of the rest of the boys was out buying some cloths to take on the trip and Al I bought a full dress suit of evening cloths at Portland yesterday and now I owe Callahan the money for them and am not going on no trip so probily I wont never get to ware them and it is just $45.00 throwed a way but I would rather throw $45.00 a way then go on a trip a round the world and leave my family all winter.

CHAPTER TWO

Diction

Good diction is the choice of the right words. Accurate, effective expression obviously requires the right words: the words which will represent—not nearly, not approximately, but exactly—what we want to say. This is a simple rule; but to apply it is far from simple. The good writer must choose the right words, yes; but how does he know which are the right words?

Diction would be no problem if there existed for each object and each idea just one word which denoted specifically that object or idea—if there were one name and one name only for each separate thing. But language is not like that. Most words are not strictly denotative; that is, they do not merely point to a specific object. Some words in English, it is true, particularly scientific words, do represent the only name we have for a specific object or substance. *Lemming,* for example, is the only name we have for a certain mouse-like rodent; *purine* is the only name of a compound the chemical formula of which is $C_5H_4N_4$. The language of science ideally is a language of pure denotation. But scientific language constitutes a special case, and its problems are different from those of more ordinary language.

PRIMARY MEANING AND IMPLIED MEANING

Actually, instead of one word and only one word for each thing, the writer finds competing for his attention a number of words, all of which denote exactly or approximately the same thing. Moreover, even those words which have exactly the same denotation, that is, those which explicitly refer to the same thing, may have different connotations—different shades of meaning.

For example, *brightness, radiance, effulgence,* and *brilliance* may be said to have the same general denotation, but there is a considerable difference in what they connote. *Radiance* implies beams radiating from a source, as the words *brilliance* or *brightness* do not. *Brilliance,* on the other hand, suggests an intensity of light which *effulgence* and *brightness* do not. Again, *brightness* is a more homely, everyday word than are *radiance, brilliance,* and *effulgence.* These are only a few suggested contrasts among the connotations of these words, all of which describe a quality of light.

Varying connotations in words with the same denotation may also be illustrated from words which refer to concrete objects. Compare the simple words *bucket* and *pail.* The primary meanings are much the same. We might apply either word to naming the same vessel. But in most of present-day America *bucket* is more likely to be the ordinary word, with associations of everyday activity; whereas *pail* will seem a little more old-fashioned and endowed with more "poetic" suggestions. It connotes for some readers a bygone era of pretty milkmaids in an idyllic setting. But *bucket,* too, may have sentimental associations, someone will exclaim, remembering the song, "The Old Oaken Bucket". For words change in meaning from period to period, and their associated meanings change, as a rule, much more rapidly than do their primary meanings.

The process of growth and decay in language is so strong that many words in the course of generations have shifted not only their associations but their primary meanings as well; some have even reversed their original meanings.

The history of word change is interesting in itself, but we are concerned here with the light that it throws upon the nature of words. Words shift meaning because they are not static but are dynamic. The secondary and associated meanings of a word are powerful, and it is not surprising that sometimes one of them becomes the new primary meaning. It behooves the writer to take into account these important associated meanings of a word as well as its precise denotation. Indeed, the writer has the task of controlling both dimensions of his language. Thus in a romantic tale one might appropriately use the word *steed* rather than *horse.* But in ordinary contexts one certainly would not say or write, "Saddle my steed", unless he were being deliberately playful or ironic. On the other hand, there are still other contexts in which, instead of the rather neutral word *horse,* it might be appropriate to use words like *plug* or *nag,* terms which are as derisive or humorous in tone as *steed* is poetic and "literary".

GENERAL AND SPECIFIC; ABSTRACT AND CONCRETE

A *general* word refers to a group, a class; and a *specific* word refers to a member of that class. *Tree* is a general word, but *oak, elm, poplar* are specific. We must remember, however, that the terms *general* and *specific* are relative, not absolute. *Coat,* for example, is more specific than *garment,* for a coat is a kind of garment. But *coat,* on the other hand, is more general than *hunting jacket,* for a hunting jacket is a kind of coat. So with our trees above. *Oak* is more specific than *tree* but more general than *black oak* or *water oak* or *white oak.*

The specific word tends to give colour and tang, tends to appeal to the imagination. Suppose we write: "He saw a ship on the horizon." What can our reader's imagination do with that? It can put some sort of floating object, large, man-made, and designed for transportation, on the imagined horizon. But what is the shape of the object? Will there be a smudge of smoke or the glint of white sail? The word *ship* is a general word and, therefore, cannot give a vivid image in that split second in which the reader's eye rests upon the sentence. Suppose we substitute *liner, schooner, brig, tanker, sloop, junk,* or some other specific word. Then there is something for the imagination to seize on. There is no blur on the horizon; there is a shape.

But suppose, one may object, that we write *brig* and that the reader does not know what rig such a craft carries. Does he then have a shape on the horizon? Most readers would get the glint of sail and not the smudge of smoke, for their information might go that far. The specific word, however, does more than give, or appeal to, information. The mere fact of the use of the specific word gives some sort of nudge to the imagination, gives some sense of knowingness, makes the reader kid himself a bit. If we use the word *brig,* even the reader totally ignorant of nautical matters, as most of us are, feels, just for a moment, a little like an old salt.

There is another distinction which is important in our choice of words. It has to do with concreteness and abstraction. *Peach, pear, quince, apple,* and *apricot* are concrete words. The word *peach* implies certain qualities: a certain shape, a certain colour; a certain kind of sweetness. But *peach* implies these qualities as "grown together", as we should actually find them embodied in a peach. (The Latin word from which *concrete* derives means literally "grown together".) We can, of course, *abstract* (this word literally means "take away") these qualities from the actual peach and refer to them in isolation: *sweetness, fuzziness, softness.* Isolating these qualities in such fashion, we get a set of *abstract* words. *Sweetness* isolates a quality common to peaches, and of course, to many other things; the quality is thought of as an idea in its own right.

Words that refer to ideas, qualities, and characteristics *as such* are usually abstract. Words that name classes of objects and classes of actions are usually general. Words that refer to particular objects and particular actions are usually both concrete and specific. These are, on the whole, our most vivid words; they reflect immediately the world of things known to our senses. This comment is not meant to imply that concrete and specific words are somehow "better" than abstract and general words. For some purposes they are indeed better, but for others, not. The world of ideas and concepts requires its terms just as urgently as does the world of particular things.

■ Applications

I Make a list of the concrete words in the following passage of description:

> The late afternoon sun that still came over the brown shoulder of the mountain showed the bridge dark against the steep emptiness of the gorge. It was a steel bridge of a single span and there was a sentry box at each end. It was wide enough for two motor cars to pass and it spanned, in solid-flung metal grace, a deep gorge at the bottom of which, far below, a brook leaped in white water through rocks and boulders down to the main stream of the pass.
>
> The sun was in Robert Jordan's eyes and the bridge showed only in outline. Then the sun lessened and was gone and looking up through the trees at the brown, rounded height that it had gone

behind, he saw, now that he no longer looked into the glare, that the mountain slope was a delicate new green and that there were patches of old snow under the crest.

Then he was looking at the bridge again in the sudden short trueness of the little light that would be left, and studying its construction. The problem of its demolition was not difficult. As he watched he took out a notebook from his breast pocket and made several quick line sketches. As he made the drawings he did not figure the charges. He would do that later. Now he was noting the points where the explosives should be placed in order to cut the support of the span and drop a section of it back into the gorge. It could be done unhurriedly, scientifically and correctly with a half dozen charges laid and braced to explode simultaneously; or it could be done roughly with two big ones. They would need to be very big ones, on opposite sides and should go at the same time.

—ERNEST HEMINGWAY: *For Whom the Bell Tolls**

Make another list of the concrete words in the following passage:

Thanks to this universality of athletic sports, English training is briefer and less severe. The American makes, and is forced to make, a long and tedious business of getting fit, whereas an Englishman has merely to exercise and sleep a trifle more than usual, and this only for a brief period. Our oarsmen work daily from January to July, about six months, or did so before Mr. Lehmann brought English ideas among us; the English varsity crews row together nine or ten weeks. Our football players slog daily for six or seven weeks; English teams seldom or never "practice" and play at most two matches a week. Our track athletes are in training at frequent intervals throughout the college year and are often at the training table six weeks; in England six weeks is the maximum period of training, and the men as a rule are given only three days a week on the cinder track. To an American training is an abnormal condition; to an Englishman it is the consummation of the normal. —JOHN CORBIN: *An American at Oxford*

Which passage tends to use the greater proportion of concrete words? Why?

II Assume that, in an account of a motor trip through the Atlantic provinces, you have written the following paragraphs:

We stopped the car beside the stone wall near the gate that had led to the farmhouse door. The house was grey and unpainted. It must have been unlived in for years. Some of the windows were broken. The roof was in disrepair.

The house was set in what had been a thriving apple orchard, and now on this October day, the old trees were worth looking at. A majority of them were filled with fruit. The sun was shining, and the sight was very pretty, even though some of the trees were rotted. A lot of them had vines growing up their trunks, and Jim said it was poison ivy.

Rewrite this passage so as to make the reader see the scene. Your revision will certainly call for changes in diction, but do not hesitate to make more extensive changes.

The misuse of abstract and general words

Much writing that is woolly and clouded, difficult to read, clogged and ineffective, is writing that is filled with general and abstract words. For example:

Quite significantly, the emphasis is being placed upon vocational intelligence, which is based upon adequate occupational information for all pupils in secondary schools. . . . This emphasis upon vocational guidance for the purpose of making young people intelligent concerning the world of occupations and the requirements for entering occupations need not conflict seriously with other views of guidance that take into account everything pertaining to the education of the pupil.

There are a number of things wrong with this flabby statement, among them, the large number of abstract words. The author might have written:

High schools today insist that the student learn enough about jobs to choose his own job wisely. The student needs to learn what various jobs pay, what training they require, and what kinds of people find them interesting. He can learn these things while he is learning the other things that schools are supposed to teach. Both kinds of learning are preparations for life, and one need not interfere with the other.

The rewritten version still makes use of general and abstract words (*training, preparation,* and so on); but some of the cloudiest of the abstractions (*vocational intelligence, occupational information*) have been removed, and the rewritten version is not only simpler but has more force.

Many subjects, however, require general and abstract words. For example, compare these two ways of saying the same thing:

A child needs sympathy.
A child does not like frowns. Cold looks cow him. He is fearful when he hears harsh words.

The second account is long-winded; even so, the concrete words do not convey fully the meaning of the one abstract word *sympathy*.

The writer cannot, and need not try to, avoid abstract and general words. But he ought not to fall into the slovenly habit of using them without thought. In any case, he should remember that a sprinkling of concrete and specific words can be used to lighten the numbing weight of piled-up abstractions. To illustrate, compare:

1. A child needs sympathy. Tolerance of his mistakes and the sense of understanding and comradeship provide the proper stimulus for his developing personality. Conversely, an environment defective in sympathy and understanding can be positively thwarting; it can lead to repressions and thus lay the foundation for ruinous personality problems.
2. A child needs sympathy. He didn't intend to smash the vase or to hurt the cat when he pulled its tail. Tolerance of mistakes and some understanding is necessary if he is to feel that he is a comrade. Acceptance as a comrade stimulates him to become a better comrade. He grows and develops toward responsibility. But he finds it hard to grow normally in a cold and repressive atmosphere. The meaningless spanking—meaningless to him, since he had no intention of breaking the vase—drives him in on himself. He becomes confused and repressed. Some of these confusions and repressions may linger into adult life.

In choosing his words, the overriding consideration, of course, will always be the particular effect that the writer wishes to obtain. Description and narration, for example, thrive on the concrete and the specific. Note the number of concrete and specific terms in the following passage:

He knew the inchoate sharp excitement of hot dandelions in young Spring grass at noon; the smell of cellars, cobwebs, and built-on secret earth; in July, of watermelons bedded in sweet hay, inside a farmer's covered wagon; of cantaloupe and crated peaches; and the scent of orange rind, bitter-sweet, before a fire of coals.

—THOMAS WOLFE: *Look Homeward, Angel*

Exposition and argument, on the other hand, by their very nature, call for a diction in which general and abstract words are important.

> Marx's interpretation of the past is explicit and realistic; his forecast of the future seems to me vague and idealistic. I have called it utopian, but you object to that word. I do not insist on it. I will even surrender the word "idealistic". But the point is this. Marx finds that in the past the effective force that has determined social change is the economic class conflict. He points out that this economic class conflict is working to undermine our capitalistic society. Very well. If then I project this explanation of social changes into the future, what does it tell me? It seems to tell me that there will be in the future what there has been in the past—an endless economic class conflict, and endless replacement of one dominant class by another, an endless transformation of institutions and ideas in accordance with the changes effected by the class conflict.
> —CARL BECKER: "The Marxian Philosophy of History",
> *Everyman His Own Historian: Essays on History and Politics*

LANGUAGE GROWTH BY EXTENSION OF MEANING

We have said that a word has not only a specific meaning but also implied meanings. The implied meanings are obviously less definite than the specific meaning, and therefore less stable and more amenable to change. In scientific language the specific meanings are rigidly stabilized, and the hazy and shifting implied meanings are, in so far as possible, eliminated. In a colourful and racy use of everyday language, just the reverse is the case. The implied meanings are rich and important. We are often tempted to use a word, not *literally* (that is, adhering strictly to the specific meaning), but *figuratively,* stressing the associations of the word. It is through such a process that words have shifted their meanings in the past; but this process of extension of meaning is constantly at work even in our own time. Let us consider an illustration of the process.

The casual and unthinking view of language sees each word as fastened neatly and tightly to a certain specific object: *weasel* means a certain kind of small, furry mammal of slender body, that moves furtively, preys on birds, rats, and rabbits, sucking their blood, and occasionally also sucking eggs; *cooking* means the preparation of food by exposing it to heat; *spade* means an instrument for digging in the earth. But words are not actually so neatly fastened to the objects for which they stand. Even when we are determined to speak forthrightly and "call a spade a spade", we rarely do so. It is against the nature of language that we should be able to do so.

For example, Bob, who is determined to call a spade a spade, says: "Well, Joe has weaseled out on us again. Yesterday when I told him the Collins deal was finally cooking, he pretended he had never heard of it and said he wouldn't buy a pig in a poke." But obviously one is not calling a spade a *spade* when he attributes to another human being the actions of a weasel, describes the preparation of a business deal as a piece of cookery, and makes the agreement to be signed the purchase of a pig enclosed in a bag.

Weasel and *cooking*—not to mention the pig—are not being used literally here; their meanings have been extended through analogy. In the case of *cooking* the extension of meaning is very easy to grasp: one sort of preparation—cooking—is extended to mean another and more general sort of preparation. *Weaseling* is more difficult. There may be some implication of "weasel words", that is, words that have had the substance sucked out of them, like eggs sucked by a weasel; but the more probable analogy here is that between Joe's wriggling out of his promise and the weasel's bodily movements as it glides through apparently impossibly small apertures.

But the point to be made here does not concern the basis for the analogy, whether of physical resemblance (the *jaws* of a vise), similarity of function (the *key* to a puzzle), similarity of effect (a *shining* example), or anything else. The point to be made is, rather, that people normally use words in this way, extending, stretching, twisting their meanings, so that they apply to other objects or actions or situations than those to which they originally applied. This is the *metaphorical* process, about which we shall have more to say in the next chapter. The essence of metaphor inheres in this transfer of meaning, in the application of a word that literally means one thing to something else.

Thus far we have taken our illustrations from common words. But less common words and learned words will illustrate the same process of extension of meaning. Indeed, most of our words that express complex ideas and relationships have been built up out of simpler words. For example, we say, "His generosity caused him to over-look my fault." *Overlook* here means to "disregard or ignore indul-gently". But *overlook* is obviously made up of the simple words *look* and *over*. To look over an object may imply that one does not let his gaze rest upon that object: his eyes pass over it without noticing it. *Overlook,* then, in the sense of "disregard" is an extension and specialization of one of the implied meanings of *look over.* We have said "one of the meanings", for *look over* obviously implies other possible meanings. Consider the nearly parallel expression "to see over". From it we get the word *oversee.* This word normally means today *to direct, to supervise*—something quite different from "over-look". *Supervise* is built out of the same concepts as *oversee,* for *super* in Latin means "over", and -*vise* comes from the Latin verb *videre* (past participle *visus*) which means "to see". A bishop, by the way, is literally an *overseer.* For *bishop* comes originally from two Greek words: *epi,* which means "over", and *skopein,* which means "to look". Thus such diverse words as *overlook, oversee, supervise,* and *bishop* represent particular extensions of much the same primitive literal meaning.

The Dictionary: A Record of Meanings

The etymology (that is, the derivation and history) of a word is often highly interesting in itself, but knowledge of word origins is also of great practical usefulness. The full mastery of a particular word frequently entails knowing its root meaning. Possessing that meaning, we acquire a firm grasp on its various later meanings, for we can see them as extended and specialized meanings that have grown out of the original meaning.

As an example, here is the entry in *Webster's Collegiate Diction-ary* for the word *sad*:

sad (săd), *adj.;* SAD′DER (-ẽr); SAD′DEST. [AS. *sæd* satisfied, sated.]
1. *Archaic.* Firmly established. **2.** Affected with or expressive of grief; downcast; gloomy. **3.** Characterized by or associated with sorrow; melancholy. **4.** Afflictive; grievous. **5.** Dull; somber; — of colors. **6. a** Shocking; wicked; — often playfully. **b** *Slang.* Inferior.

The word is an adjective (*adj.*). The forms of the comparative and superlative degrees are given; then its derivation (from Anglo-

Saxon *saed*). Next, the dictionary lists seven meanings of this word, one of which it designates as archaic (1) and another as slang (6*b*).

Even so brief an account as this suggests a history of shifting meanings. Inspection of a larger dictionary, such as *Webster's New International Dictionary* or the *Oxford English Dictionary* (also known as *A New English Dictionary*), with its fuller information as to the derivation of the word and its finer discrimination of meanings (including the various earlier meanings), enables us to make out a detailed history of the meanings of the word.

Sad is closely related to the German word *satt* ("full to repletion") and to the Latin word *satis* ("enough"), from which we get such modern English words as *satiate* and *satisfied*. But a man who has had a big dinner is torpid and heavy, not lively or restless, and so *sad* came to carry the suggestion of *calm, stable, earnest*. Shakespeare frequently uses it to mean the opposite of "trifling" or "frivolous". But a person who seems thus sober and serious *may* be so because he is grieved or melancholy, and the word thereby gradually took on its modern meaning of "mournful" or "grieved". But we must not end this account without mentioning other lines of development. The sense of *torpid* or *heavy* was extended from animate beings, which can eat to repletion, to inanimate things which cannot— to bread, for example, that fails to rise, or to a heavy laundry iron. In this connection the student should look up the word *sadiron*.

Meaning 5 (dull; somber;—of colors) represents still another such extension. It means the kind of colour which a sobersides (as opposed to a gay and sprightly person) would wear, that is, dull, sober colours.

Has the process of extension now ceased? Hardly. Meaning 6*a* represents a fairly late instance of it. In mock deprecation, a young fellow might be called "a sad young dog", as though his conduct caused horror and grief. Meaning 6*b* is a later extension still, one that has not yet been approved by careful speakers as "good English". In such a phrase as "sad sack" this meaning of *sad* had temporarily gained wide currency (though in formal American English we tend to prefer the word *sorry*: a sorry team, a sorry outfit, a sorry job). If meaning 6*b* ever established itself in standard English, the dictionary will remove the characterization "slang". (Some terms which began as slang have found their way into the language and into good usage; but a vastly greater number have enjoyed a brief popularity, have been discarded, and are now forgotten or remembered only by scholars.)

The definition of a word is, then, a somewhat more complex business than one might suppose. It consists frequently not just of *the* meaning, but of interrelated sets of meanings, some of which are current and some of which are not, and some of which have been accepted into good society and some of which are merely clinging to the fringes of society. A word which is appropriate in one context obviously might be grossly out of place in another.

■ Applications

I Following are entries for the word *sad* from the *American College Dictionary** and *Webster's New World Dictionary of the American Language*:†

sad (săd), *adj.*, sadder, saddest. 1. sorrowful or mournful: *to feel sad*. 2. expressive of or characterized by sorrow: *sad looks*. 3. causing sorrow: *a sad disappointment*. 4. (of color) somber, dark, or dull. 5. *Often Humorous.* deplorably bad; shocking: *a sad attempt*. 6. *Dial.* soggy or doughy: *sad bread*. 7. *Archaic.* firm or steadfast. [ME; OE *sæd*, c. G *satt*, Goth. *saths* full, sated; akin to L *sat*, *satis* enough, *satur* sated, Gk. *hádēn* enough] —**sad·ly** (săd′lĭ), *adv.*
—Syn. 1. unhappy, despondent, disconsolate. SAD, DEPRESSED, DEJECTED, MELANCHOLY describe states of low spirits. SAD, the general term, varies in its suggestion from a slight, momentary unhappiness to deep-felt grief, or to a continuous state of combined pensiveness, wistfulness, and resignation: *sorrowful and sad, sad and lonely*. DEPRESSED refers to a temporary lapse in natural buoyancy because of fatigue, unhappiness, a sense of being unable to change unsatisfactory conditions, or the like: *depressed by a visit to the slums*. DEJECTED, though also referring to a temporary state of discouragement caused by some definite event or circumstance, implies lower spirits, being cast down by disappointment, frustration, and the like: *dejected over losing one's position*. MELANCHOLY describes a state caused rather by temperament and a chronically gloomy outlook than by any external reason: *habitually melancholy*.

sad (sad), *adj.* [SADDER (-ĕr), SADDEST (-ist)], [ME.; AS. *sæd*, sated, full, hence having feelings associated with satiety; akin to G. *satt*, satisfied (with food, etc.); IE. base *sā-, satisfied, sated, seen also in L. *satis*, enough (cf. SATISFY, SATIETY)], 1. having, expressing, or showing low spirits or sorrow; unhappy; mournful; sorrowful. 2. causing or characterized by dejection, melancholy, or sorrow. 3. dark-colored; dull. 4. [Colloq.], very bad; deplorable: often used as an intensive. 5. [Dial.], heavy,

compact, or soggy: said of earth, pastry, etc. 6.
[Archaic], sober; trustworthy; firm; constant.
SYN.—**sad** is the simple, general term, ranging in implication
from a mild, momentary unhappiness to a feeling of intense
grief; **sorrowful** implies a sadness caused by some specific loss,
disappointment, etc. (the death of his dog left him *sorrowful*);
melancholy suggests a more or less chronic mournfulness or
gloominess, or, often, merely a wistful pensiveness (his *melancholy* thoughts about the future); **dejected** implies discouragement or a sinking of spirits, as because of frustration; **depressed**
suggests a mood of brooding despondency, as because of fatigue
or a sense of futility (the novel left him feeling *depressed*); **doleful** implies a mournful, often lugubrious, sadness (the *doleful*
look on a lost child's face).—*ANT.* happy, cheerful.

Compare these entries with the one previously quoted from
Webster's Collegiate Dictionary. (If you are using some other
dictionary, look up *sad* in it.) How do the entries vary in (1)
the information they include and (2) the manner in which this
information is presented? Which entry do you find most satis-
factory?

II Look up the origins of the following words:

nostril	Bible	fast (*adj.*)
thrilling	fine (*adj.*)	sympathetic
gerrymander	infant	malaria
urbane	silly	melancholy

Does knowledge of its origin clarify the meaning of any one of
these words? Does it enable you to understand the relationship between current discrepant meanings (that is, "He made a
fast trip", and "The boat was made *fast* to the pier"; or "This
fine print hurts my eyes" and "He was a big, *fine,* upstanding
man"). Does knowledge of the origin of the word help account
for such uses as "legal *infant*" and "the *Book*" (as applied to
the Bible)?

III With the help of the dictionary, discriminate as carefully as
you can among the words in the following groups:

1. sulky, petulant, peevish, sullen, morose, crabbed, surly
2. sceptic, infidel, atheist, freethinker, agnostic
3. reasonable, just, moderate, equitable, fair-minded, judicial
4. belief, faith, persuasion, conviction, assurance, reliance
5. brave, daring, courageous, fearless, valiant, dauntless

Does a knowledge of the origin of the word throw light upon
the special connotations of any of these words?

THE COMPANY A WORD KEEPS: COLLOQUIAL, INFORMAL, AND FORMAL

Earlier, in discussing the implied meanings of words, we touched briefly upon the way in which these meanings may determine the appropriateness of a word for a particular context (page 39). The word *steed,* we saw, would be proper for some contexts, *nag* for others, and *horse* for still others. But the problem of appropriateness is important and deserves fuller treatment.

In the first place, there is what may be called the dignity and social standing of the word. Like human beings, a word tends to be known by the company it keeps. Words like *caboodle* and *gumption* are good colloquial words and perfectly appropriate to the informal give-and-take of conversation. But they would be out of place in a dignified and formal utterance. For example, a speech welcoming a great public figure in which he was complimented on his "statesman-like gumption" would be absurd. To take another example, many of us use the slang term *guy,* and though, like much slang it has lost what pungency it may once have had, its rather flippant breeziness is not inappropriate in some contexts. But it would be foolish to welcome our elder statesman by complimenting him on being a "wise and venerable guy". The shoe, it is only fair to say, can pinch the other foot. Certain literary and rather highfaluting terms, in a *colloquial* context, sound just as absurd. We do not praise a friend for his "dexterity" or for his "erudition", not, at least, when we meet him on the street or chat with him across the table.

The fact that words are known by the company they keep does not, however, justify snobbishness in diction. Pomposity is the worst of all faults. Words must be used with tact and common sense. But the comments made above do point to certain areas of usage of which most of us are already more or less aware. The various kinds of diction (and their necessary overlappings) are conveniently represented in the accompanying diagram.*

Modern slang, for example, falls into segment *e*—and possibly *d*. It would be properly available for colloquial and informal writing. (But segments *d* and *e,* of course, include more than slang: they

---

* From *The American College Dictionary,* ed. by Clarence L. Barnhart, copyright, 1956, by Random House, Inc.

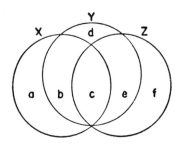

The three circles X, Y, Z, represent the three sets of language habits indicated above.

X—formal literary English, the words, the expressions, and the structures one finds in serious books.

Y—colloquial English, the words, expressions, and the structures of the informal but polite conversation of cultivated people.

Z—illiterate English, the words, the expressions, and the structures of the language of the uneducated.

b, c, and e represent the overlappings of the three types of English.

c—that which is common to all three: formal literary English, colloquial English, and illiterate English.

b—that which is common to both formal literary English and colloquial English.

e—that which is common to both colloquial English and illiterate English.

a, d, and f represent those portions of each type of English that are peculiar to that particular set of language habits.

include colloquial terms of all kinds that do not occur in formal literary English.) Segment *a* includes the terms that occur only in formal literary English, but the overlap of formal literary English with colloquial and illiterate English is large—so large that most of the words used in writings of the most formal style are to be found in writings at the other extremes of style.

It would be misleading, therefore, to suggest that there is a mechanical rule for selecting the diction that one uses in an informal essay, or in a formal treatise, or to express the dialogue of "low characters" in a novel. The degrees of elevation of style and shadings of formality and informality are so many—and vary so much even within one work—that we cannot hope to find our appropriate diction segregated for us in one compartment. But our chart should make plain that in this matter of levels of diction, the dictionary can be of real help. It marks, as such, colloquial words, slang, technical words, and so on. Yet recourse to the dictionary is not a substitute for the student's developing a feeling for language. The dictionary can help, but wide reading and practice in writing can help even more.

The student already has a more sensitive feeling for language than he realizes. It would not occur to the student—except as a joke—to say to a friend: "I am trying to ascertain the assignment for next week in English. The amiable pedagogue who directs our labours was inaudible to me, though I think he must have mumbled something. Can you advise me?" Even though the student is not likely to err in the direction of the pompous and the ornate, he may very well be tempted into a colloquial and slangy style. He *might* write for his history instructor:\ "I think that C. D. Howe got a raw deal from Parliament. He was a pretty cantankerous customer, I have to admit, and mighty stubborn. Lots of people just didn't like the cut of his jib. But I think he was honest as the devil."

■ Applications

I   Rewrite the short passage about C. D. Howe above to make it more formal.

II Rewrite the following sentences, removing (a) any stilted diction and (b) any slang or illiterate diction. In general try to make the diction fit an informal standard.
1. We approached Emporium City from Route 60, driving like a bat out of hell.
2. Miss Warner was a young creature of patrician elegance and of disdainful hauteur but really pretty dumb.
3. It sure was picturesque! Titanic vistas solicited our view. It was all mighty grand.

III The following passages are quite informal—even colloquial—in diction and expression. Rewrite them so as to make them as formal as possible.

A I could recognize big changes from Commerce down. Beaver [THE] Dam Rock was out in the middle of the river now, and throwing a prodigious "break"; it used to be close to the shore, and boats went down outside of it. A big island that used to be away out in mid-river has retired to the Missouri shore, and boats do not go near it any more. The island called Jacket Pattern is whittled down to a wedge now, and is booked for early destruction. Goose Island is all gone but a little dab, the size of a steamboat. The perilous "Graveyard", among whose numberless wrecks we used to pick our way so slowly and gingerly, is far away from the channel now, and a terror to nobody. One of the islands formerly called the Two Sisters is gone entirely; the other, which used to lie close to the Illinois shore, is now on the Missouri side, a mile away; it is joined solidly to the shore, and it takes a sharp eye to see where the seam is—but it is Illinois ground yet, and the people who live on it have to ferry themselves over and work the Illinois roads and pay Illinois taxes: singular state of things!   —SAMUEL L. CLEMENS: *Life on the Mississippi*

B Educationally, Exeter is a great school but its teachings went deeper than ancient history or Latin (which was compulsory when I was there). It taught virtue, an old-fashioned word, that was instilled like art appreciation. If you don't catch the students pretty young, they will never learn virtue any more than they will ever learn Latin.

Today I think there should be a course in every prep school (and in every high school) called Virtue 1, which would teach simple honest, candor, courage and conviction. I am alarmed not only at the prevalence of cheating in the nation's schools but, most importantly, at the fact that no one considers it wrong. No wonder it's so hard to find an honest cop. It's fashionable to say that the cops are on the take because they're poorly paid and I'm sure low pay is part of the answer. But you could pay every cop in the land $50,000 a year and, if virtue has not been inculcated in him at a fairly early age, he'll still be on the take because a fellow can always use a few extra bucks.

—JOHN CROSBY: "Old School Tie"*

HOW ASSOCIATIONS CONTROL MEANINGS

Thus far we have seen how associated meanings determine what may be called the social tone of a word. But we must go on to consider the very important way in which these meanings actually determine, though sometimes subtly, the effect of the word; that is, the way in which they actually determine meaning. In our time especially, propaganda and advertising have made this whole matter very important.

A group of words that points to more or less the same thing may range in their associations from highly favourable to highly unfavourable. For example, we may call an agriculturist a "farmer", a

---

* From John Crosby, "Old School Tie", *New York Herald Tribune,* October 21, 1960.

"planter", a "tiller of the soil", or, in more exalted fashion, "the partner of Mother Nature"; but we can also refer to him as a "rube", a "hayseed", or a "hick". Few of our words merely *name* something. They imply a judgment about its value as well. They make a favourable or an unfavourable evaluation. Consider, for example, the following table of rough synonyms:

FAVOURABLE	NEUTRAL	UNFAVOURABLE
highest military leadership	general staff	army brass
motor sedan, cabriolet, convertible	automobile	jalopy
secret agent	informant	stool pigeon
cherub	child	brat
Democratic (or Republican) statesman	party leader	political boss
self control	discipline	regimentation

By choosing terms with the appropriate associations, we can easily colour our whole account of a man or an event or an idea. Much of the effectiveness of this method depends upon the fact that the writer ostensibly is only pointing to certain things, only naming them: the damaging (or ennobling) implications are, as it were, smuggled in surreptitiously. Notice how heavily the following passage from an essay by H. L. Mencken leans upon this device. (The italics are supplied by the present authors.)

> "The Ride of the Valkyrie" has a certain intrinsic value as pure music; played by a competent orchestra it may give civilized pleasure. But as it is commonly performed in an opera house, with a *posse* of fat *beldames* throwing themselves about the stage, it can produce the effect of a dose of ipecacuanha. The sort of person who actually delights in such spectacles is the sort of person who delights in plush furniture. Such half-wits are in a majority in every opera house west of the Rhine. They go to the opera, not to hear music, not even to hear bad music, but merely to see a more or less obscene *circus*.
>
> —H. L. MENCKEN: "Opera", *Prejudices: Second Series*

As a matter of fact, Mencken has clearly expressed his attitude. But this attitude is certainly given point and vividness by the implications of such a phrase as "posse of fat beldames". The effect depends upon implications as well as upon denunciation.

The power of association is also illustrated by our recourse to *euphemisms*. Certain words, even necessary words, which refer to unpleasant things, are avoided in favour of softening expressions or indirect references. In many contexts "bastard" is felt to be too brutal; so "illegitimate" is substituted for it. Even a word like "died" may be shunned in favour of "deceased", or "passed away", or "went to his reward". Undertakers have taken to calling themselves "morticians", and butchers in some parts of the country prefer to be known as "meat-cutters". Whatever one may think of the substitutions, they at least testify to the power of past associations and the desire of men to avoid words with unpleasant or disparaging associations.

Here follows the account of an incident as it might be reported by a relatively impartial writer:

> Liberal (or Conservative) Senator Briggs expressed surprise at being met by reporters. He told them that he had no comment to make on the "Whitlow deal". He said that he had not known that Whitlow was in the employ of General Aircraft and observed that the suggestion that he had received favours from Whitlow was an attempt to discredit him.

How might a hostile reporter describe the incident? He would perhaps give an account something like this:

> Senator Briggs, Liberal (or Conservative) wheelhorse, was obviously startled to find himself confronted by newspapermen. He stubbornly refused to comment on what he called the "Whitlow deal" and professed not to have known that Whitlow was a lobbyist. The Senator complained that he was being smeared.

The second account seems to be substantially the same as the first. The "facts" are not appreciably altered. But the emotional colouring, and, with it, the intended effect on the reader, have been sharply altered. The senator is now a "wheelhorse", with its suggestions of a hardened and (probably) calloused political conscience. Whitlow is a "lobbyist", and again suggestions of political corruption are insinuated. Moreover, the senator's actions and speech ("obviously startled", "stubbornly refused", "professed not to have known", and "complained") are made to suggest guilt.

Now the point in this comparison of the two accounts is not to indicate that the drier, more objective account is necessarily "truer" and therefore to be preferred. Our estimable fictitious senator may, in fact, be quite guilty, and the writer of the second account may have given us the more accurate account of what actually happened in the interview. (It is even conceivable that the first account was written by a reporter who was pretty certain of the senator's guilty conduct but whose editor had ordered him to play down any suggestion of guilt. In that event, the first account would have to be regarded as biased.) The point to be made is this: The colouring of attitudes in a piece of writing is extremely important and is, indeed, an integral part of its "meaning".

■ Applications

I For the following words, try to find synonyms (or generally synonymous words or phrases) of opposite associations:

rebellion	harsh	dictator
tycoon	reformer	liberal
elegant	conventional	ward leader
discrimination	diplomacy	theoretical

II Alter the diction of the following passages in order to gain (a) a more favourable tone; (b) a less favourable tone. (The sample sentence, with its optional terms, will illustrate the kind of alteration required.)

The veteran (*still-youthful, aging*) movie star walked (*swept, minced*) into the strong (*brilliant, harsh*) light and paused for a moment to look at (*glance at, ogle*) the crowd.

1. The old woman walked up to the counter and priced the scarf. She hesitated, seemed to think for a moment, and then opened her black purse, and extracted a five-dollar bill. She laid it on the counter and began to finger the bright piece of cloth.

2. The mayor, a stocky man of middle age, stepped forward to the microphone with a sheaf of papers in his hand. He placed these on the lectern and cleared his throat. His face was serious as he began his speech.

3. The two boys, fifteen and seventeen, were ill at ease when they appeared before Judge Baker, who regarded them impersonally from the bench. An atmosphere of tension

prevailed in the courtroom as lawyers began shuffling their papers.

WORN-OUT WORDS AND CLICHÉS

We began this chapter by saying that the problem of diction is that of finding the right words, the words which will say exactly what the writer wants to say. But we have seen that exactness in language cannot be attained mechanically, that the exactness required works on a number of levels and in a number of different ways. Words are not static. They have a history; they have biographies; and even have, one is tempted to say, personalities. Most of all, since they are not changeless and inflexible, but to some extent plastic, changing their shape a little under the pressure of the context in which they occur, they offer a continual stimulus and challenge to the imagination of the writer.

Language, as we have seen, changes, develops, grows and, by the same token, language wears out. We are not thinking, however, of the normal sloughing off of words that have died natural deaths and now either do not occur in a modern dictionary at all or, if they do occur, are marked *obsolete* (*shoon* for *shoes*) or *archaic* (*e'en* for *even*). We are thinking rather of words that have been thoughtlessly used in certain contexts so often that they have lost nearly all their force. Whether we call these threadbare expressions "trite" or "hackneyed" or term them "stereotypes" and "clichés" is of little importance.

Common Stereotypes, Including Slang

A jargon made up of stereotypes and clichés is produced by writers who do not think out what they want to say but find a worn groove in the language down which they let their thoughts slide. Books on rhetoric sometimes supply lists of threadbare expressions against which the student is warned: "the more the merrier", "last but not least", "to trip the light fantastic toe". Hackneyed phrases of this sort have probably by now become too literary, too old-fashioned, to offer much temptation to a modern student—even to a lazy one. But stereotyping continues, and much of the writing and conversation to which we are constantly exposed is a tissue of trite expres-

sions. The sports page, for example, will yield stereotypes in abundance. Mr. Frank Sullivan amusingly exhibits some of these in
question-and-answer form:

Q If [the teams] don't roll up a score what do they do?
A They battle to a scoreless tie.
Q What do they hang up?
A A victory. Or, they pull down a victory.
Q Which means that they do what to the opposing team?
A They take the measure of the opposing team, or take it into camp.
Q And the opposing team?
A Drops a game, or bows in defeat.
Q This dropping, or bowing, constitutes what kind of blow for the
losing team?
A It is a crushing blow to its hopes of annexing the Eastern champion-
ship. Visions of the Rose Bowl fade.
Q So what follows as a result of the defeat?
A A drastic shakeup follows as a result of the shellacking at the hands
of Cornell last Saturday.
Q And what is developed?
A A new line of attack.
Q Mr. Smith, how is the first quarter of a football game commonly
referred to?
A As the initial period.   —FRANK SULLIVAN: "Football is King"

Society-page editors have their own brand of stereotypes: "social
function", "society bud", "gala affair". To come still closer home,
there is slang. Some slang expressions may once have been pungent
and colourful. The sportswriter who first described the strike-out of
a slugging batter by saying "he made three dents in the atmosphere"
conveyed the scene sharply and humorously. When slang is thus
"tailor-made" for the occasion, it may be bright and perceptive,
though, if it is still fresh and vivid, it is a question whether it ought
to be viewed as "slang" at all. But, as most of us use it, slang is a
worn and impoverished language, not bright and irreverent and
lively, but stale and dead: "the party was a washout"; "I'm fed up";
"he crabbed a lot"; "he blew his top". The real sin committed here
is not so much that of bringing slang's flippant associations into a
serious context. We do not often commit this fault. The real sin in
using slang consists in using a thin and inexpressive language—slang
that has lost the edge of slang.

JARGON: THE DEGENERATIVE DISEASE OF PROSE

We have to step up, however, to a somewhat more exalted plane to find the stereotypes which most damage modern prose and which are likely to do the student most harm. These stereotypes are such expressions as "along the lines of", "in the last analysis", "socio-economic considerations", "the world of business affairs", "according to a usually reliable source". Such locutions puff out many an official document, many a political speech, and it must be admitted, many a professor's lecture or article.

In the following excerpt Malcolm Cowley discusses an example of academic jargon.

An example that comes to hand is the central idea of an article by Norman E. Green, printed in the February, 1956, issue of the *American Sociological Review*. In English his argument might read as follows:

"Rich people live in big houses set farther apart than those of poor people. By looking at an aerial photograph of any American city, we can distinguish the richer from the poorer neighborhoods."

I won't have to labor over a sociological expression of the same idea, because Mr. Green has saved me the trouble. Here is part of his contribution to comparative linguistics. "In effect, it was hypothesized," he says— a sociologist must never say "I assumed," much less "I guessed"—"that certain physical data categories including housing types and densities, land use characteristics, and ecological location"—not just "location," mind you, but "ecological location," which is almost equivalent to locational location—"constitute a scalable content area. This would be called a continuum of residential desirability. Likewise, it was hypothesized that several social data categories describing the same census tracts, and referring generally to the social stratification system of the city, would also be scalable. This scale could be called a continuum of socio-economic status. Thirdly, it was hypothesized that there would be a high positive correlation between the scale types on each continuum."

Here, after ninety-four words, Mr. Green is stating, or concealing, an assumption with which most layman would have started, that rich people live in good neighborhoods. He is now almost ready for his deduction, or snapper:

"This relationship would define certain linkages between the social and physical structure of the city. It would also provide a precise definition of the commonalties among several spatial distributions.

By the same token, the correlation between the residential desirability scale and the continuum of socio-economic status would provide an estimate of the predictive value of aerial photographic data relative to the social ecology of the city."

Mr. Green has used 160 words—counting "socio-economic" as only one—to express an idea that a layman would have stated in thirty-three. As a matter of fact, he has used many more than 160 words, since the whole article is an elaboration of this one thesis. Whatever may be the virtues of the sociological style—or Socspeak, as George Orwell might have called it—it is not specifically designed to save ink and paper.

—MALCOLM COWLEY: "Sociological Habit Patterns in Linguistic Transmogrification"*

Whether we call such verbiage officialese, when it emanates from some government bureau, or gobbledygook (a term invented by a former Congressman, Maury Maverick), or simply jargon, its empty wordiness is characteristic. Here are two samples culled from *College English*—a fact which should warn us that anyone can fall prey to jargon, even those who undertake to teach others how to write effective English.

(1) If we start at one of the extremes of the continuum, we shall find a grouping around a point of great vitality and wide appeal. Keenly aware of the painstaking scholarship and of the high creative effort that over the centuries has accumulated the body of subject matter we call "English," a group of our ablest teachers conceive their role to be to transmit this product of human endeavor, this hard-won store of learning and of art, this rich portion of man's heritage of culture, to the oncoming generations, and to imbue them with some perception of its worth.

(2) But whether we are trained statisticians or not, we can improve the results of our examination speeches and themes. First of all, we can, without great difficulty, develop better controlled problems. There are various degrees of control possible in examination speeches and themes, and, within reasonable limits, it would seem as though the greater the control the more meaningful the test results. Complete freedom of choice of topic and material puts a premium upon accidental inspiration and upon glibness rather than thoughtfulness. A single assigned topic is palpably unfair since it may strike the interest and experience of some and yet leave others untouched.

* "Sociological Habit Patterns in Linguistic Transmogrification", *The Reporter,* September 20, 1956.

These two passages have been somewhat unfairly taken out of context. Moreover, the topics discussed are not precisely colourful and exciting. Is it fair to condemn their authors for having written jargon? How else could either writer have said what he had to say?

It is true that we have torn the passages out of context and that the subject matter is difficult. Yet, even so, the symptoms of jargon are present. Consider the second excerpt: Both "puts a premium upon" and "palpably unfair" are clearly stereotypes. Moreover, what does the author gain by specifying "without great difficulty" and "within reasonable limits"? Are these specifications necessary? Could they not be assumed? Has not the writer put them in for rhetorical purposes, that is, to "dress up" his statement rather than to make necessary qualifications?

Jargon: Some Antidotes

Jargon, of course, involves more than stereotypes. Jargon is nearly always compounded of clusters of general and abstract words. Though there is no certain prescription against jargon, it is easy to state one or two practical antidotes.

1. The student should try to use words that are as specific and concrete as possible; that is, he should never use a word more general and indefinite than he has to. Hazy and indefinite expressions represent the easy way out for a writer who is too timid to commit himself or too lazy to think through what he wants to say.

2. The student should avoid stereotypes of all kinds—prefabricated phrasings which come easily to mind but which may not represent precisely his own ideas and emotions. But note this carefully: He should never avoid an *individual* word because it seems simple and common. If the sense calls for a simple, common word, it is generally best to repeat the word, if necessary, again and again. There is little to be said in favour of what is sometimes called *elegant variation,* that is, the substitution of some synonym in order to avoid repetition. Here is an example: "Mr. Jones was a powerful *financier.* As a *tycoon* he had a deep suspicion of socialism. He shared the feelings of his associates who were also *bankers.*" The variations are irritating and can be confusing. Either recast the sentences or repeat *financier.*

On the other hand, the student should try to avoid *words strung together*—that is, phrasings—which are common and, for that very reason—probably stereotyped. He cannot avoid all common expressions, nor should he try to avoid them, but he should learn to inspect them carefully before he decides to use them. If he really needs to say "along the lines of", or if something is really "in consideration of" something else and an emphasis on *consideration* is relevant, then let him use the expression by all means. But it is a good rule to remember that though he need never shy away from an individual *word* because it is common, he ought to be very shy of *phrases* that are common.

3. The student should try to use live words, remembering that finite verbs are the most powerful words that we have. We can find an instance of the failure to do so in the second sentence of the excerpt from *College English* quoted on page 61.

> Keenly aware of the painstaking scholarship and of the high creative effort that over the centuries has accumulated the body of subject matter we call "English," a group of our ablest teachers conceive their role to be to transmit this product of human endeavor, this hard-won store of learning and of art, this rich portion of man's heritage of culture, to the oncoming generations. . .

This sentence is packed with ideas, but the only finite verb in it (aside from *has accumulated* and *call,* in the two relative clauses) is the verb *conceive.* A participle, *aware,* is made to carry the weight of the first twenty-six words; and the whole latter part of the sentence hangs from two successive infinitives, "to be" and "to transmit". The sentence has so little stamina that it sprawls. It sprawls because the writer has starved it of finite verbs. The author might better have written:

> Our ablest teachers realize what effort has gone into the making of that body of subject matter we call "English". They know it is a precious thing, for it embodies the effort of painstaking scholars and of great poets and novelists. They want to transmit this heritage of culture to the oncoming generations.

Finite verbs are more powerful than strings of participles, gerunds or infinitives. Moreover, a specific verb is usually stronger than a more general verb qualified by modifiers. Compare "He walked along slowly" with "He strolled", "He sauntered", "He dawdled", "He lagged". Frequently, it is true, we need the qualifiers. But we ought not to forget the wealth of concreteness which the English language possesses in its great number of verbs which name specifically, and therefore powerfully, certain modes of action.

4. Finally, the student ought to remember that simple sentences in normal sentence order rarely degenerate into jargon. An essay so written may be childishly simple, and it can become monotonous; but it will seldom collapse into the spineless flabbiness of jargon.

Jargon, however, is not to be dealt with summarily. It is our most pervasive kind of "bad" style, and, like style in general, it is the product of the interplay of many elements. We shall have to recur to this topic in some of the chapters that follow, especially in the discussion of metaphor.

■ Applications

I The following passage is badly infected with jargon. Try to determine what the author means to say, and then put it into English for him. (You might apply the four antidotes to jargon previously described.)

The chemical age gives every highly technical nation a choice between self-sufficiency and trade on whatever barter or bargaining basis it desires, thus upsetting time-honoured geographical alignments of monopolies of certain natural products and altering the whole concept of imperialism. This is an entirely new situation for agriculture. For centuries the threat of eventual scarcity of food and land hung over the world. Within a few decades the march of science has brought about a complete reversal. On the one hand the chemist and the technologist have made possible the production of greater and greater quantities of products on less and less land, resulting in enormous surpluses of acreage, crops, and labour. At the same time, ironically enough, the chemist is removing one product after another from the soil into the laboratory, throwing still more land out of cultivation and further reducing the amount of labour needed.

II Lancelot Hogben, the author of the following passage, is attempting to treat with some sprightliness a subject which for most people is abstruse and painfully dry. Is he successful? If so, how does his choice of diction contribute to his success? How many concrete words does Hogben use? How many abstract words? How does Hogben avoid the sense of formality? Illustrate from his choice of diction. What are the connotations of *bowling, petrol, car, tank,* and *motorcycle*? What are the connotations of *Greeks, abacus,* and *counting frame*? Does Hogben actually want the contrast between the associations of the two groups of words? What purpose does it serve? Do the associations of *Good Friday* and *All Fools' Day* clash? What purpose is served by this clash?

[Euclid] was limited by the social culture in which he lived. The Greeks did not live in a world of interest and petrol consumption and bowling analysis. Ratios were not familiar quantities. They represented a process of division which was carried out with a very stiff instrument, the abacus. Proportion did not sit lightly on Euclid's pupils. You can easily see the difficulty of Euclid's pupils. Suppose I know that the petrol consumption of a car is 35 miles to the gallon. I can get the number of miles I can run before filling up by multiplying the number of gallons in the tank by 35. I can get the number of gallons I require by dividing the number of miles I intended to run by 35. The two processes are equally easy in our arithmetic. The arithmetic of the counting frame is different. Multiplying one proper number by another always gives you an exact result which you get by repeated addition. Dividing one proper number by another means finding how many times you can take one away from the other. Usually you have some beads left over on the counting frame. You rarely get an exact answer. So division was a much more difficult process to grasp when people thought that all real numbers were proper numbers. Euclid had to devote a whole book (Book V) to illustrate the simple rules of proportion which are all summed up in the diagonal rule given in the last chapter. Draw two right-angled triangles, one with the two shorter sides 3 and 4 centimetres long, the other with the two shorter sides of 1½ and 2 inches; compare them, and you will see without difficulty that two triangles having corresponding sides whose lengths are in the same ratio is a situation no more difficult to grasp than the fact that a motorcycle has the same petrol consumption on Good Friday and All Fools' Day.

—LANCELOT HOGBEN, *Mathematics for the Million**

* Reprinted from *Mathematics for the Million* by Lancelot Hogben, by permission of W. W. Norton & Company, Inc. Copyright 1937, 1940 by the publishers.

CHAPTER THREE

Metaphor

In metaphor there is a transfer of meaning—the Greek word from which metaphor is derived means "to transfer". A word that applies literally to one kind of object or idea is applied by analogy to another. Thus a ray of sunshine *cuts* the gloom (as if it were a knife); a ship *courses* the seas (its motion likened to that of a greyhound); a man *weasels* out of his promise (as a ferret-like animal wriggles through a small hole).*

Language normally grows by a process of metaphorical extension; we extend old names to new objects. (In fact, someone has happily called metaphors "new namings".) But when, in this process of extension, a metaphor is really absorbed into common language, like the *bed* of a river, it loses its metaphorical force; it becomes a dead metaphor. Compare, for example, "the bed of a river" with "the dance of life". The first phrase carries no suggestion that the bed is a place of repose or that the river is sleepy! We use "the bed of a river" as a pure denotation from which the associated meanings that apply to *bed* in its usual senses are quite absent. But it is very different with the phrase "the dance of life". This metaphor is still alive. The suggestions (of something rhythmic, of patterned movement, even, perhaps, of gaiety and happiness) are meant to be associated with life.

---

* In this chapter we have used *metaphor* in the largest and most inclusive sense. We have not distinguished metaphor proper from *simile* (an *explicit* comparison, usually introduced by *like* or *as*: "she glided into the room *like a swan*", "he was bald *as an egg*"), or *metonymy* (the use of a part to designate the whole: "he employed twenty *hands* on his farm"), or other such specializations of the metaphoric principles. Such classifications are, in our considered opinion, of little practical importance to the writer.

The term "dead metaphor" can itself illuminate the problem now being considered. With "dead" metaphors, we can say, *rigor mortis* has set in: they have no flexibility, no force; they have stiffened into one meaning. Metaphors that are still alive prove that they are alive by their flexibility; and because they are still alive, they can be used to give colour and life to a piece of writing. They are concrete and particular; they reflect the world of the senses. They can still excite the imagination.

In metaphors that are still recognizably metaphoric, there are, of course, varying degrees of life. The following examples are not very lively, but they do show that metaphor is a perfectly normal and important part of our normal speech: we say, for example, "John is a good egg"; "Jane is a peach"; "He ran out on the deal"; "That remark threw him for a loss." Such expressions are rather worn and faded. But their original metaphorical character is plain enough, and we still think of them, and use them, as metaphors. The list of expressions that are badly shopworn but are still recognizably metaphors could be extended almost indefinitely: "hot as the devil", "independent as a hog on ice", "lazy as a dog", "crazy as a bat", and so on.

METAPHOR IN EVERYDAY LANGUAGE

Our preference for the concrete and the particular, as these examples show, is not only normal; it is deeply and stubbornly rooted in the human mind. Consider the following situation: It is a hot day. We can say, "It is hot" or "It is very hot", or, piling on the intensives, we can say, "It is abominably and excruciatingly hot." But most of us, afflicted with the heat, will resort to metaphor of some kind: "It's hot as hell", or more elaborately, "It's hot as the hinges of hell." Evidently metaphor is felt to add forcefulness, and evidently the forcefulness has some relation to sharpness of detail and concreteness of expression.

That is one point, then: in metaphor, force and sharpness of detail, especially of sensory detail, tend to go together. Indeed, we are usually attracted to metaphor in the first place because ordinary language seems worn and abstract. A second point to be made is this: metaphor tends to accompany the expression of emotions and attitudes. A strictly scientific purpose would find entirely adequate expression in the statement that it is now 97.6 degrees Fahrenheit and that the humidity is 88.

Let us consider another simple case. Suppose we feel a special kind of happiness and try to express our feelings. We can say, "I feel happy." Or we can try to find a word which more accurately hits off this special feeling: *merry, gay, ecstatic, cheerful, glad, jolly, or joyous.* There are many synonyms for *happy,* as the dictionary will quickly reveal, and they differ in their shades of meaning. For example, *jolly* suggests heartiness and the good humour that go with comfortable living; *ecstatic* suggests an elevating rapture; *gay* suggests sprightliness, a nimble lightheartedness. We shall do well to consult the dictionary to learn (or remind ourselves of) the wealth of resources at our disposal. Even so, we rarely find an adjective which exactly expresses our feelings. We tend to resort to metaphor. We say "I'm happy as a June bug", or "I feel like a million dollars", or "I'm walking on air this morning", or "I feel like a colt in springtime."

If a feeling is very special or complex, we are usually *forced* to resort to metaphor. Here is the way a writer of fiction expresses the happiness of a young soldier when the brilliant woman who has dazzled him shows him a small attention:

> She regarded him with her kindly glances, which made something glow and expand within his chest. It was a delicious feeling, even though it did cut one's breath short now and then. Ecstatically he drank in the sound of her tranquil, seductive talk full of innocent gaiety and of spiritual quietude. His passion appeared to him to flame up and envelop her in blue fiery tongues from head to foot and over her head, while her soul appeared in the centre like a big white rose . . . .

> —JOSEPH CONRAD: "The Warrior's Soul", *Tales of Hearsay*

The author tries to do justice to the emotion that the young soldier feels, and in doing so, he twice resorts to metaphor. The first is a rather simple and even conventional metaphor of a feeling of warmth within his chest—something that seems to "glow" and "expand". The second attempts to interpret as well as present the quality of the emotion—the lady is encircled in flame, but the flames, though fierce ("blue fiery tongues"), do not injure her and may even be said to protect her. The white rose, which in his ecstatic vision stands for her soul, is not scorched or shriveled.

■ Application

Choose metaphors which will describe *how you feel* in the following situations. Do not necessarily take the first metaphor which comes to mind; try to avoid worn-out metaphors; try to find a metaphor which describes as accurately as possible your own feelings.

1. On getting an A when you would have been happy to settle for the grade of C.
2. On getting well splashed by a passing car when on your way to an appointment.
3. On your first experience of stage fright.
4. On seeing a serious accident.
5. On first discovering that a close friend has betrayed your friendship.
6. On coming to realize that you have been guilty of a serious fault.

Slang as Metaphor

In connection with metaphor it may be profitable to consider again two abuses of language, slang and jargon, which have already been touched upon in the preceding chapter. The impulse to use slang springs from our preference for the concrete and the particular. Slang expressions are originally metaphoric, and the problem of the misuse of slang cannot properly be solved apart from the more general problem of the use and abuse of figurative language. That is why it does very little good for the instructor to tell the student—or for the student to tell himself—not to use slang, for this advice is essentially negative. The student is right in wanting to make his writing warm, colourful, and lively. What he needs to do, therefore, is not to discard figurative language in favour of abstract expressions; but rather to inspect all his figurative language, *including slang,* in order to improve it as metaphor. He will try to eliminate all metaphors that are worn and trite, or that seem pretentious, or that are discordant with the rest of the composition. The practical result, of course, will be that in this process most of the slang will be sloughed off, but sloughed off *because it proves to be poor and ineffective metaphor,* not because it is figurative. The writer will scarcely be able to avoid the use of metaphor even if he tries. But he wants it to be alive rather than dead, responsible and controlled rather than irresponsible and wild.

Jargon and Worn-out Metaphor

But why recur to the second general abuse of language, jargon, in this chapter on metaphor? What possible connection can jargon have with metaphor? The first answer to this question can be put simply: There is an important negative relation. It is the very lack of concrete words and of metaphorical vividness and particularity that makes jargon cloudy and ineffective. A primary way to avoid jargon, then, is to use concrete language, including its extension into metaphor. The spinelessness of jargon is in part the result of the writer's timid avoidance of vigorous metaphor. Even the most timid writer, however, is not actually able to avoid all metaphor; and with this observation we can give a second answer to the question. Jargon characteristically involves stereotypes of all kinds, including stereotyped, and therefore lifeless, metaphor. This connection of jargon with secondhand metaphor is forcefully put by the British writer, George Orwell:

> Prose (nowadays) consists less and less of *words* chosen for the sake of their meaning, and more and more of *phrases* tacked together like the sections of a prefabricated henhouse. . . . There is a huge dump of worn-out metaphors which have lost all evocative power and are merely used because they save people the trouble of inventing phrases for themselves. . . . Modern writing at its worst . . . consists in gumming together long strips of words which have already been set in order by someone else.

The student will observe that Orwell himself uses metaphor very effectively: "sections of a prefabricated henhouse", "dump of worn-out metaphors", "gumming together long strips of words". Orwell thus vividly suggests his two points of indictment: the lazy and careless craftsmanship of the writer of jargon and the secondhand quality of the materials he uses.

Confused Metaphor and Half-dead Metaphor

Orwell has hardly exaggerated, and the faults which he points out are found just as frequently in America as in Great Britain. The writer of the passage that follows is attempting to describe the effect of "comic books":

> They defy the limits of accepted fact and convention, thus amortizing to apoplexy the ossified arteries of routine thought. But by these very tokens the picture-book fantasy cuts loose the hampering debris of art and artifice and touches the tender spots of universal human desires and aspirations, hidden customarily beneath long accumulated protective coverings of indirection and disguise.

But can one defy a limit? One can, of course, defy another person to set a limit. The comic books may break across boundaries, may exceed limits, and their authors may defy authorities to set any limits that they will respect. But here it is the comic books that are made to "defy limits", probably because the author was looking for a strong metaphor, and was willing to accept, without asking too many questions of it, the first strong metaphor that he found. The defiance hinted by the comic books has violent results. The comic books amortize the "ossified arteries of routine thought". To "amortize" is to cancel a mortgage. And "amortize", like "mortgage", is related etymologically to Latin *mors,* death. Even so, how can a defiance extinguish a mortgage on the arteries of thought—to the point of apoplexy? People who suffer from hardening of the arteries are subject to strokes of apoplexy. Perhaps the writer is trying to say that the outrageous breaking of the conventions drives certain readers to apoplexy. But he has his apoplectic stroke affect the creaky and antiquated thoughts themselves. The result is a rather amazing mix-up.

In the next sentence, the comic books, having by their defiance ruptured the arteries of conventional thought, proceed to cut loose the "debris of art and artifice". Or rather, it is the fantasy which cuts this debris loose. But "debris" means a scattered mass of materials. Can one cut a person loose from debris? Does one not rather dig a victim out of the debris which has fallen upon him? And how can such debris be *worn,* as is evidently the case here, as a "protective covering"? The cutting loose of wreckage, the pulling off of a disguise, and the removal of a protective shell are here thoroughly scrambled. The confusion is not helped when we remember that the debris in question is composed of "art and artifice" and that the agent which cuts it loose is fantasy—something which one usually regards as associated with both art and artifice.

The instance of mixed metaphor that we have just examined was published in a "quality" magazine, and that fact should constitute a warning to the student writer. Try to think out what you want to say. Then be sure that your metaphors are consistent with it, and when they are closely connected, are consistent with one another.

■ Application

The following passages are taken from articles in reputable magazines. Make a criticism of the use of metaphor in these passages. Where the metaphors seem garbled or inappropriate, rewrite the passage, substituting consistent or appropriate metaphors.

1. As his fame was slowly ascending, partly because of this social skill of his, in to more illustrious circles, so was it trickling down among the more numerous obscure.

2. The emancipation of the slaves withdrew the Negroes from the maternal wing of the plantation system and threw them into the labour market.

3. Therefore, when he championed his middle class, he instinctively set his face against everything that threatened to substitute quantity for quality—against the encroachments of commerce and the new imperialism which the progressively minded among both Whigs and Tories were imbibing from Chatham. And the caveat against the dangers lurking in materialistic panaceas is not without implications that carry beyond the time and the place.

THE FUNCTION OF METAPHOR

Thus far we have given our attention to some of the abuses of figurative language. It is high time to give a more positive account of metaphor and to show some of the uses of figurative language. After all, why do we use metaphor? What purpose does it serve? We have already assumed in earlier pages that it has its value in contributing colour and liveliness, but if we are to understand why it is one of the great resources of the writer, we shall need to define more clearly what its function is. This is all the more necessary since the conventional account of the uses of metaphor is calculated to mislead. For example, we are in the habit of saying that the purpose of metaphor is to illustrate or to embellish; but these terms can easily suggest that figurative language is a kind of "extra" which may be usefully or gracefully "added on" to a statement, but which is never essential to the statement, never a direct part of what is being said. In accordance with this conventional view, the practical function of metaphor is to give a concrete illustration of some point which has been put more abstractly. Metaphor provides a pleasing decoration, like an attractive wallpaper pasted onto the wall or like a silk ribbon tied around a box of candy. But the trouble is that, in either case, the figure of speech seems to be something which can be left off; and if we misconceive the purposes of metaphor by thinking of it as something external and additional, we shall never come to understand why an understanding of metaphor is absolutely essential to good writing—and to good reading too.

Scientific Statement and Metaphor

Let us begin by disposing of a special kind of writing in which metaphor is indeed unnecessary and is merely an addition. If we wish to say "$2 + 2 = 4$" or that "the square of the hypotenuse of a right triangle is equal to the sum of the squares of the other two sides", we shall not require metaphor. Metaphor would be in the way. Such statements as these, however, are very special; the terms used in them are (or aspire to be) pure denotations. As we pointed out in the preceding chapter, if such terms have associations at all, the associations are surely irrelevant. Thus the "words" employed are not being used as words in the usual sense; for most words are capable of metaphorical extension. These scientific terms are, by contrast, rather special symbols, and the purest scientific statements are able to dispense with words altogether: thus $2 + 2 = 4$, or $H_2SO_4 + Fe \rightarrow FeSO_4 + H_2\uparrow$.

But important as such statements are, they represent a stringently specialized discourse. Most of the discourse which interests us as human beings and which we must use as writers goes far beyond abstract relationships of this kind. Most of our discourse has to do with the "full" world of our human experience, not with the colourless, soundless, abstract world of modern physics, say, or of mathematics.*

Metaphor as Illustration

It ought to be noted, however, that even the scientific writer very often needs to go beyond this stringently limited abstract discourse, and for him too, metaphor, though frankly employed as illustration, may be highly necessary and useful. The following passage from Bertrand Russell's *The Scientific Outlook* will illustrate this point. The book is addressed to a general audience, and Russell is attempting to convince his reader that "what is actually experienced is much less than one would naturally suppose". He proceeds to analyze a typical experience for us—what happens scientifically when we "see" someone:

> You may say, for example, that you see your friend, Mr. Jones, walking along the street: but this is to go far beyond what you have any right to say. You see a succession of coloured patches, traversing a stationary background. These patches, by means of a Pavlov conditioned reflex, bring into your mind the word "Jones", and so you say you see Jones; but other people, looking out of their windows from different angles, will see something different, owing to the laws of perspective: therefore, if they are all seeing Jones, there must be as many different Joneses as there are spectators, and if there is only one true Jones, the sight of him is not vouchsafed to anybody. If we assume for a moment the truth of the account which physics gives, we shall explain what you call "seeing Jones" in some such terms as the following. Little packets of light, called "light quanta", shoot out from the sun, and some of these reach a region where there are atoms of a certain kind, composing Jones's face, and hands, and clothes. These atoms do not themselves exist, but are merely a compendious way of alluding to possible occurrences. Some of the light quanta, when they reach Jones's atoms, upset their internal economy. This causes him to become sunburnt, and to manufacture vitamin D. Others are reflec-

---

* This is not, of course, to question the importance or the reality of such worlds. The scientist can deal with his material only in this abstract way. His language is neither more nor less real than the language of the poet or the novelist. It is merely different. In this connection, the student might reread the discussion of abstract and concrete words in Chapter 2.

ted, and of those that are reflected some enter your eye. They there cause a complicated disturbance of the rods and cones, which, in turn, send a current along the optic nerve. When this current reaches the brain, it produces an event. The event which it produces is that which you call "seeing Jones". As is evident from this account, the connection of "seeing Jones" with Jones is a remote, round-about causal connection. Jones himself, meanwhile, remains wrapped in mystery. He may be thinking about his dinner, or about how his investments have gone to pieces, or about that umbrella he lost; these thoughts are Jones, but these are not what you see.

—BERTRAND RUSSELL: *The Scientific Outlook**

The passage may be regarded as an instance of the expository method of illustration. Notice that Russell has completed his analysis with the last statement of the passage; yet apparently he felt that the account might prove too technical and that his reader might fail to understand. Therefore he adds the following statement: "To say that you see Jones is no more correct than it would be, if a ball bounced off a wall in your garden and hit you, to say that the wall had hit you. Indeed, the two cases are closely analogous." Most readers will be grateful for this illustration. Most minds find abstractions so alien to them that they need a concrete statement such as the analogy provides. This is a truth which the writers of all books of scientific popularization know. Even if the writer is able, as Bertrand Russell is able here, to state his analysis directly, the extra illustration—the concrete analogy drawn from daily experience—is helpful.

■ Applications

I The author of the following passage originally supplied illustrative or summarizing comparisons to make clearer or more emphatic what he had to say. Here, however, the summarizing comparison has been omitted. Try to supply an appropriate comparison.

An insect, therefore, is not afraid of gravity; it can fall without danger, and can cling to the ceiling with remarkably little trouble. It can go in for elegant fantastic forms of support like that of the daddy-long-legs. But there is a force which is as formidable to an

* From *The Scientific Outlook* by Bertrand Russell, by permission of George Allen and Unwin, Ltd.

insect as gravitation to a mammal. This is surface tension. A man coming out of a bath carries with him a film of water of about one-fiftieth of an inch in thickness. This weighs about a pound. A wet mouse has to carry about its own weight of water. A wet fly has to lift many times its own weight and, as everyone knows, a fly once wetted by water or any other liquid is in a very serious position indeed. An insect going for a drink is in as great danger as. . . .

—J. B. S. HALDANE: "On Being the Right Size", *Possible Worlds*

II In the following passage the author has made much use of illustrative metaphor. Try to restate what is said in language as unmetaphorical as you can devise. Do not be surprised if you find that the rewritten version requires a good many more words than the original passage.

We, then, the animals, consume those stores in our restless living. Serenely the plants amass them. They turn light's active energy to food, which is potential energy stored for their own benefit. . .

Animal life lives always in the red; the favorable balance is written on the other side of life's page, and it is written in chlorophyll. All else obeys the thermodynamic law that energy forever runs down hill, is lost and degraded. In economic language, this is the law of diminishing returns, and it is obeyed by the cooling stars as by man and all the animals. They float down its Lethe stream. Only chlorophyll fights up against the current. It is the stuff in life that rebels at death, that has never surrendered to entropy, final icy stagnation. It is the mere cobweb on which we are all suspended over the abyss.

—DONALD CULROSS PEATTIE: *Flowering Earth**

Metaphor as Essential Statement

In the strict scientific statement, then, metaphor would seem to have no place, and in less strict scientific discussion it would seem to be auxiliary and optional. But we shall make a serious mistake if we conclude that in other kinds of writing metaphor is a device of as little fundamental importance. The truth is quite to the contrary! In most of the writing with which we are concerned—political speeches, articles on international affairs, letters to friends, expressions of opinion, attempts to persuade and convince, essays in which we invite other people to share our experiences and evaluations of

* From *Flowering Earth by* Donald Culross Peattie. Copyright 1939 by Donald Culross Peattie. Courtesy of G. P. Putnam's Sons.

life—in these and in nearly all the writing that we shall do, metaphor is a primary device of expression.

The common misconception of metaphor makes it, as we have seen, a mere ornament, and therefore an inessential part of expression. But metaphor is not a mere decoration, an "extra". It often represents not only the most compact and vigorous way of saying a thing—it represents sometimes the only way in which the particular thing can be said at all. This last remark holds especially true when "the thing to be said" involves an interpretation or evaluation. Metaphor is indeed an indispensable instrument for interpreting experience.

Let us illustrate. In the sentence that follows, Helen Keller describes what tactile sensation means to a person who has always been blind and deaf: "The immovable rock, with its juts and warped surface, bends beneath my fingers into all manner of grooves and hollows." The rock, of course, does not literally bend; it is "immovable". But under her sensitive fingers, which do duty for eyes, the rock itself seems to respond dynamically to her touch. For what is being described is not the fumbling of an ordinary person who is blindfolded. We are, rather, being let into Helen Keller's "world", a world of exciting qualities which most of us do not know at all. Metaphor here is the only means by which it may be made known to us, since this world does not exist in our experience and cannot be pointed to; it can only be created for us.

Consider what metaphor does in the following passages. In the first passage Arthur Koestler is describing Western Europe. But he is doing more than that—he is interpreting its state of mind:

> Western Europe is a patient in an iron lung. American economic and military aid provide it with oxygen, but it cannot live and breathe by itself. The sickness which paralyses it is not of an economic nature. Nor is it social strife; nor the Communist phantom creed. These are symptoms of the disease, but not its cause. The cause is both deeper and simpler: Europe has lost faith in itself.
>
> —ARTHUR KOESTLER: *The Trail of the Dinosaur**

Note how much work the iron-lung comparison does. The social

* From *The Trail of the Dinosaur* by Arthur Koestler. Copyright 1947, 1948, 1951, 1953, 1955 by Arthur Koestler. Reprinted by permission of The Macmillan Company.

and economic structure of Western Europe is able to function mechanically just as the polio victim's body is able to do, but the impulses have to come from without—the process is not self-sustaining. There is a paralysis of the will, so Koestler argues, that parallels the paralysis of the chest muscles of the iron-lung patient. Try to say all that this paragraph says without using Koestler's comparison, and you will begin to see how much the comparison accomplishes.

Consider this passage from a student theme:

> Off yonder, beyond the glitter of the water where the sun still struck, you could see the cloud piling up like a cliff, black and slate-coloured, streaked with purple. I said like a cliff, but it was like a cliff that somehow, momentarily, grew taller while you looked at it, looking awfully solid but somehow swelling and coiling upward at the same time.

The comparison to a swelling and coiling cliff enables the reader to visualize what the storm cloud looked like as it boiled up. But it does more; it goes far to suggest the awe and fright that the storm cloud excited in the mind of the girl who describes it.

One more example, this one selected to combat the conventional notion that metaphor is somehow "literary". Here is the way in which "Bugs" Baer describes the collapse of a prize fighter: "Zale folded as gracefully as the Queen's fan and fell on his battered face alongside the ropes. His seconds carried him to his corner like three window-dressers packing a melted dummy off during a heat wave on the sunny side of Broadway." This description may be judged to be good writing or bad, but it is easy to see why Baer used figurative language. He was not trying to "tell" us about the scene; he was trying to make us *see* the scene, vividly, freshly, fully, as a somewhat cynical but highly interested observer might have seen it.

The nature and function of metaphor can be further illustrated from passages of description. Here we are struck by the number of metaphors and also by the *amount of work* that the metaphors actually do. For example:

Heat "like a drawn sword" (T. E. Lawrence)
"Mr. Chadband moves softly and cumbrously, not unlike a bear who has been taught to walk upright." (Charles Dickens)
Miss Emily, whose eyes are like "two small pieces of coal pressed into a lump of dough" (William Faulkner)

In the following passage Helen Keller gives an account of her sense of touch:

> When I think of hills, I think of the upward strength I tread upon. When water is the object of my thought, I feel the cool shock of the plunge and the quick yielding of the waves that crisp and curl and ripple about my body. The pleasing changes of rough and smooth, pliant and rigid, curved and straight in the bark and branches of a tree give the truth to my hand. The immovable rock, with its juts and warped surfaces, bends beneath my fingers into all manner of grooves and hollows. The bulge of a watermelon and the puffed-up rotundities of squashes that sprout, bud, and ripen in that strange garden planted somewhere behind my finger tips are the ludicrous in my tactual memory and imagination.
>
> —HELEN KELLER: *The World I Live In*

We must admit that the world of Helen Keller's experience is a special world which can be conveyed to us only through suggestion and analogy. Yet, a little reflection will show us that the world of experience belonging to each of us is far more special than we may think, for our world is to a great extent determined by our values, moods, and emotional biases. If we are to communicate our experience with any accuracy, figurative language is frequently the only way by which it can be conveyed. By means of metaphor we grasp not only the experience as an entity but its "meaning", its value to us as well.

What Makes a "Good" Metaphor?

In judging the value of a metaphor, the importance of the physical similarity of the items compared is easily over-estimated. In many effective comparisons the degree of physical similarity is not very great. Some element of resemblance there must be, of course. But a good comparison is not necessarily one in which there is close resemblance, since "illustration", as we have seen, is not the primary purpose of metaphor. Moreover, even a great deal of dissimilarity does not necessarily render the comparison strained or forced.

The Element of Similarity in Metaphor

To realize this last point, let us consider one of the tritest comparisons of all: "Her eyes were like stars." Far from seeming strained or over-ingenious, the comparison will seem to most of us entirely too simple and easy. Yet even in this well-worn analogy the objects compared are really very dissimilar. Certainly the human eyeball and the flaming mass of elements that make up the stars have very little in common. If this examination, which compares the two objects as scientifically considered, seems somewhat unfair, we can go on to point out that the eyes, even those of a lovely woman, do not much resemble the glinting points of light which are the stars as we see them. The truth of the matter is that what supports this oldest and most hackneyed of comparisons is not the physical resemblances so much as the associations: the associations of stars with brilliance, with the high and celestial. It is these associations which make the stars seem "like" the glances of the eyes of someone loved.

Thus, every comparison has a very important subjective element in it; its proper task is to interpret, to evaluate—not to point to physical analogies. Its proper function is, as we have said, to define attitude.

Let us consider one of the celebrated comic comparisons in English literature. In his satire "Hudibras", Samuel Butler describes the rosy sky of dawn:

And like a lobster, boyl'd, the morn
From black to red began to turn.

We think of this as an absurd comparison, and so it is—appropriately so—for "Hudibras" is a humorous poem. Yet it is worth asking why the comparison strikes us as absurd. We are likely to say that it is absurd because the dawn does not in the least resemble a boiled lobster. But the colours to be seen in the shell of a boiled lobster may very closely resemble the exact shade of red to be seen on some mornings. The absurdity does not come from the lack of physical resemblance; it comes from the absurd contrast of the small with the large, the commonplace and homely with the beautiful and grand, the grotesque creature in the steaming pot with the wide, fresh expanse of the dawn sky. Butler has, for humorous effect, deliberately played them against each other.

Contrast in Metaphor

We think of metaphors (and related figurative expressions) as "comparisons", and yet it is plain that we might as accurately refer to them as "contrasts". For the elements of dissimilarity between the terms of a metaphor may be of just as much importance as the elements of likeness. One can go further still: in an effective metaphor there must be a *considerable degree of contrast.* If we say "the river roared like a flood" or "the dog raged like a wild beast", we feel that the metaphor in each case is weak or nonexistent. A river is too much like a flood, and a dog, though a tame beast, too much resembles a wild beast. If, on the other hand, we say, "the fire roared like a flood" or "the fire raged like a wild beast", we feel that these are metaphors, even though actually rather poor metaphors. Fire and flood or fire and beast are sufficiently dissimilar for us to feel that some metaphorical transfer occurs; in these cases there are the "new namings" which constitute metaphor.

We are inclined to reject what we rather awkwardly call "far-fetched" comparisons. (The term is awkward because it suggests that the terms of a good comparison are close together, though we have seen that even "eyes" and "stars" are not really very close.) But if comparisons must not be too "farfetched", neither must they be too "nearly fetched". They have to be fetched some distance if we are to have a recognizable metaphor at all.

■ Applications

I The following metaphors are primarily *illustrative,* that is, the metaphor makes something plain by comparing it with a simpler or more familiar thing. But are they *merely* illustrative? Are any of the metaphors used to *state* a meaning as well as to *illustrate* a meaning? Test them on this point by trying to restate precisely "the thing said" in nonmetaphorical language.

A On each side of the bee's abdomen are four little waxpockets situated in the joints of the hard-surfaced body; and here the supply of wax may be seen issuing, the flat, light-coloured wax appearing somewhat like a letter which a man has tucked up under his waistcoat.

—CHARLES D. STEWART: "The Bee's Knees"

B Intellectual assimilation takes time. The mind is not to be enriched as a coal barge is loaded. Whatever is precious in a cargo is taken carefully on board and carefully placed. Whatever is delicate and fine must be received delicately, and its place in the mind thoughtfully assigned.

—ARLO BATES: "Reading on the Run",
Talks on the Study of Literature

C Bed is the perfect laboratory—just the right degree of withdrawal from the world, yet with the comforts at hand, and errands delegated to someone else. The toast crumbs, accumulating among the sheets, set up the irritation inside the shell and start the pearl growing.

—E. B. WHITE: "Peavy, Book and Guitar"

D This man was hunting about the hotel lobby like a starved dog that has forgotten where he had buried a bone.

—O. HENRY: "A Municipal Report", *Strictly Business*

II Do any of the following metaphors seem farfetched and extravagant? Do any seem tame and flat? What principle, if any, seems to determine the matter of acceptability? Are any of the passages ineffective because the metaphors are "mixed"? Is it possible to shift rapidly from one metaphor to another without producing confusion? Are we never to mix metaphors? What principle, if any, seems to determine this matter?

A The chickens he raised were all white meat down through the drumsticks, the cows were tended like children, and the big ram he called Goliath had horns with a curl like a morning-glory vine and could butt through an iron door. But Dan'l wasn't one of your gentleman farmers; he knew all the ways of the land, and he'd be up by candlelight to see that the chores got done. A man with the mouth of a mastiff, a brow like a mountain and eyes like burning anthracite—that was Dan'l Webster in his prime.

—STEPHEN VINCENT BENET: *The Devil and Daniel Webster*

B A smile lit the eyes of the expiring Kentuck. "Dying!" he repeated; "He's a-taking me with him. Tell the boys I've got the Luck with me now"; and the strong man, clinging to the frail babe as a drowning man is said to cling to a straw, drifted away into the shadowy river that flows forever to the unknown sea.

—BRET HARTE: "The Luck of Roaring Camp"

C Due to the great increase in the importance of social and economic problems during the past generation, philosophy is giving more attention than heretofore to the social and economic aspects of life. Also, esthetics is receiving greater consideration as the problem of civilization's goal becomes more pressing.

—JOHN GEISE: *Man and the Western World*

D And he shall be like a tree planted by the streams of water,
That bringeth forth its fruit in its season,
Whose leaf also doth not wither;
And whatsoever he doeth shall prosper.
The wicked are not so,
But are like the chaff which the wind driveth away.

—PSALM 1:3-4.

III What is the function of each of the following metaphors? Are any of them merely decorative? What does each metaphor "say"? Try to restate in nonmetaphorical language the exact shade of meaning that each conveys.

A The furnished room received its latest guest with a first glow of pseudo-hospitality, a hectic, haggard, perfunctory welcome like the specious smile of a demirep.

—O. HENRY: "The Furnished Room", *Strictly Business*

B A late moon had cut a round, white hole in the sky off to the east, shedding enough light so that down below I could see the thin smoke-like scattered clouds floating halfway between me and the chromium-plated highway of the Potomac.

—BIERNE LAY, JR.: *I Wanted Wings*

C Her bones felt loose, and floated around in her skin, and Doctor Harry floated like a balloon around the foot of the bed. He floated and pulled down his waistcoat and swung his glasses on a cord.

—KATHERINE ANNE PORTER: "The Jilting of Granny Weatherall"

CHAPTER FOUR

Tone and Other Aspects of Style

TONE AS THE EXPRESSION OF ATTITUDE

Every piece of discourse implies a particular situation. A politician is attempting to convince a hostile audience; or a mother is attempting to coax a child into doing something which the child dislikes; or a legislator who can assume agreement on ends is trying to persuade his colleagues that certain procedures constitute the best means by which to secure these ends. Even technical treatises, which attempt no persuasion, imply a special situation; the writer assumes that he is writing for people whose interest in the truth is so absorbing that rhetorical persuasions would be unnecessary and even positively irritating.

Just as every discourse implies a situation in which the writer is related to his audience, so every discourse also implies a certain *tone*. This term "tone" is based frankly on a metaphor. We all know how important in speech the tone of voice may be in indicating the precise meaning of the words. For instance, the words "very well", uttered in a certain tone of voice, may imply enthusiastic agreement, but spoken in another tone of voice they may indicate nothing more than surly compliance. The "tone" of a piece of writing, in the same way, may show the writer's attitude, and in so doing may heavily qualify the literal meaning of the words.

The importance of tone is easily illustrated by the misunderstandings which personal letters so often provoke. In conversation, even a rather clumsy and inadequate knowledge of language can be so supplemented by the actual tone of the voice that little serious misunderstanding will occur. But when such a speaker writes a letter

—where, of course, the "tone of voice" has to be implied by the words themselves—all sorts of misunderstandings can, and frequently do, occur. The practiced writer, on the other hand, is able even in this medium to control what we have called the "tone".

All through this book we have been dealing with the problem of tone, although we have rarely used the word. For example, in the chapter on Diction, we touched upon the problem of tone when we discussed the associations of words and the way in which certain words are coloured by our attitude—the word *cop* used to refer to a police officer, or *rube* used to refer to a farmer. Again, we saw in the chapter on Metaphor the ways in which comparisons—"He's a good egg", "She's a peach"—express our attitudes. All such devices represent means for controlling tone. But tone is more than these devices; it is a pervasive thing which characterizes the whole composition, and it is a matter so important in its own right that it deserves special discussion.

The Importance of Tone

In most of our writing an important part of what we are trying to "communicate" is our attitude itself. This is certainly true of poetry and fiction, but it is also true of most essays, sermons, orations, and letters. It is even true of much of what we are inclined to regard as pure exposition. For even in expository writing the author is rarely content to give us mere facts, or mere propositions. He feels that to do this is to be painfully and technically "dry".

If we turn back to Bertrand Russell's paragraph on "scientific seeing" (page 74), we find a lively discussion couched in informal language of a subject that could have been dry and technical. Russell wants to encourage his reader to understand what he is explaining, rather than frighten him away with specialized scientific language. While he finds certain unfamiliar words and phrases unavoidable (*causal connection, compendious, traversing*), he tries to establish at the opening and maintain throughout the piece a familiar tone which will put the reader at ease—Mr. Jones walking along the street, thinking about his dinner or the umbrella he has lost.

Attitude Toward Subject

We are well acquainted, however, with subjects which scarcely permit informality of tone, even when being presented to intimates. To take an extreme case, here is a quotation from a sermon by the great seventeenth-century preacher John Donne:

> Make haste to have these spiritual graces; to desire them is to begin to have them: but make not too much haste in the way. Do not think thy self purer than thou art because thou seest another do some such sins as thou hast forborne.
>
> Beloved, at last, when Christ Jesus comes with his scales, thou shalt not be weighed with that man, but every man shall be weighed with God: *Be pure as your Father in heaven is pure,* is the weight that must try us all; and then, the purest of us all that trusts to his own purity must hear that fearful *Mene Tekel Upharsin,* Thou art weighed, thou art found too light . . . .

Donne addresses his congregation intimately and directly. He even calls them "beloved", but no matter how close a relation the preacher has with his congregation, the urgency of the subject forbids informality. He may, it is true, use simple and realistic language, but the seriousness of the subject pervades his language.

This is not to say, however, that humour or wit is not possible about serious subjects, even about death itself. When, in an old anecdote, the condemned man is being led out to the gallows in the cold dawn and asks for a handkerchief to put around his neck to keep from catching cold, we are not offended by the levity—we laugh. When Mercutio, in Shakespeare's *Romeo and Juliet,* makes a joke about his death wound and says that it is "not so deep as a well nor so wide as a church door: but 'tis enough, 'twill serve", we aren't offended. For one thing, both the condemned man and Mercutio are making light of their own distress, and we too feel a sense of release with them. Humour can work, and often does work, in both literature and life as a way of rising above distress, an antidote for self-pity. Humour thus employed works as a kind of understatement, undercutting the expected note of seriousness.

But we must remember that humour about a serious subject always requires tact and discrimination. The writer may understand this need for tact and discrimination if he thinks of the occasion of his writing as analogous to a social situation. What kind of reader can he assume? One who can respond to the humour or one who will be shocked by it? But perhaps the writer wants to shock. Then he should ask himself whether he wants to shock just to show off, or whether the shock is to make a point, to bring some new awareness. And always we can recognize that there are certain situations where levity can only be offensive and, worse, silly. To take a most extreme instance, it is hard to imagine a person who would show levity in discussing the Passion of Christ. Blasphemy would be, in a sense, comprehensible, for, in a backhand way, blasphemy always recognizes the seriousness of the thing blasphemed. It is like an inverted prayer, we might say. But levity here would be comprehensible only as an indication of a vain, silly, and unimaginative person.

If we turn from serious to light subjects, the same general principles apply. The light subject requires light treatment, not deadpan solemnity—unless, of course, that solemnity is indeed part of the joke. To look ahead, observe the serious, almost mock-heroic elements in the passage from "Farewell, My Lovely", Lee Strout White's essay on the Model T Ford (page 91). In this discussion we have concerned ourselves with two extremes: seriousness and levity. Needless to say, there are hundreds of shadings between these extremes. The possible variations of tone are almost infinite.

Attitude Toward the Audience

Until now we have, for the most part, emphasized tone as indicating the writer's attitude toward his subject, or the attitude which the subject might elicit from the writer. But the writer's attitude toward the audience is equally important. It is so important that, as we can see by the previous section, one can scarcely talk about the attitude toward the subject without drifting over into a discussion of the audience.

Let us suppose that we are writing in support of the American policy toward Red China. The subject itself would, of course, allow certain different kinds of tone. We know that there is no merely mechanical equation between subject and tone. But the subject is a serious one, and though humour and satire might enter, flippancy could not. The demands of the subject would, however, be only the beginning of the study of tone. The treatment for a friendly audience, one that assumed the basic policy to be correct and that merely wanted further clarification, would scarcely be adequate for a hostile audience. We might want to persuade the hostile audience and lead them bit by bit to agreement. We might want to find the common ground and try to show that once they recognize it, they will have to follow, step by logical step, to the present policy. We might want to shock them into an awareness of the necessity of the present policy. We might, in fact, try any number of approaches, and each approach, or combination of approaches, would imply a different tone. And each possible tone would, of course, be different from the merely explanatory tone taken toward the friendly audience.

Furthermore, considerations of friendliness and hostility are not the only ones that determine the writer's attitude toward his audience. The knowledge which a special audience possesses and its interests and concerns are also determining factors. Suppose that we are writing about China. It will make a difference if our essay is to appear in a technical journal edited for specialists in political science; or in *Fortune* magazine edited for prosperous businessmen; or on a newspaper editorial page; or in *Maclean's* magazine. It will make a difference if we read our paper before a college forum, or a California audience with its keen awareness of the Orient, or a Midwestern Chamber of Commerce dinner. The same tone would not serve for all. What is good for everything is not very good for anything.

The advertising page will furnish another kind of example of the way in which a writer's attitude toward his audience determines tone. Advertising puts a special premium upon catching and holding the interest of the reader. The advertising copy writer who did not understand some of the elementary principles of the control of tone would soon be on his way to the nearest government unemployment insurance office.

Here is an advertisement that depicts a young woman on a luxurious bed looking dreamily at a handsome blanket. The caption begins: "For you to whom beauty is a necessity. . . . Yours is a nature that thrives on beauty. . . . Seize it as a vital factor in your daily living. To you a blanket should be more than a source of warmth. Exquisite colours, luxuriously deep nap, rich, virgin-wool loveliness—these awaken in you an emotional response far beyond the material."

These statements, of course, are not addressed merely to the young woman pictured in the advertisement. They are addressed to the reader as well, and they make certain flattering assumptions about the reader: that she is a young woman of means who is at home with the luxurious and who has a soul which deserves and requires beauty as a necessity. Coarser natures may buy blankets simply for warmth, but you, dear and lovely reader, ought to have something more—even in a blanket.

■ Applications

I Select five advertisements from current magazines and state what is the primary basis of the appeal made to the reader. What attitude is taken toward the reader? What statements or devices in the advertisement suggest this attitude?

II Read the following student theme "Teachers I Have Known" and imagine that you are writing it for a teacher who you think probably knows something about his subject but who is quite dull in the classroom. Perhaps you might turn in this draft to him as it stands. Perhaps it will not hurt his feelings, or the hurt may actually be good for him. But with him in mind, could you render this theme more persuasive? Try rewriting some sections of it, particularly paragraphs 3 and 4, to see whether you can improve the tone as directed toward the special reader we have described.

Teachers I Have Known

In my twelve years at school, I have, of course known many teachers; I have made rather a hobby of studying my teachers because I hope one day to become a teacher myself. There are many kinds of teachers, but they can all be classified under one of two headings—good and bad. Fortunately for students there are many more teachers under the first heading than under the second.

Actually, it does not mean much to say that teachers are good or bad—the same can be said of people in any profession. A better way of separating the teachers that really teach from those that just stand up in front of a class is to ask how they got to be teachers in the first place: Did they become teachers because they were really interested in their subject and in young people, or did they just drift into the profession through indifference or necessity?

I should like to dispose of the second category first. There is little need to say much about such teachers; every student has known a few of them. Either they are indifferent toward their job, in which case the class is terribly boring, and the students fool around; or they actively hate teaching. Then watch out! The best thing to do in a class like that is to keep quiet and do just as much work as necessary to avoid the teacher's notice.

The other teachers are much more interesting, and there are many more kinds of them. Some become teachers because of an intense interest in their subject. They may be great teachers or well-known researchers; particularly in college, they may be outstanding men in their field. Some of them do not have the ghost of a notion how to put their subject across; they may not even try particularly, for students simply don't exist for them. All that matters is the subject. Even so, the student can get a lot out of their courses *if* he puts some effort into understanding them. Other teachers in this category do have a gift for organizing and communicating their subject. Their classes are a constant challenge—the teacher is not likely to make his subject easy!—and a delight.

Another variety of teacher with a purpose is the kind who is interested in his students. He is not a scholar; his main motivation is to help students. That is his mission in life. At the college level you probably find fewer of these teachers than in elementary or high school. I remember particularly my seventh-grade arithmetic teacher. It was a bad year for me; more than once I got into trouble with the school authorities. But this teacher was so decent to me that I became ashamed of myself; I started to behave better, and I even learned some arithmetic. Miss Jones may not have been a great mathematician, but she did me more good and taught me more than many other teachers I have had.

I should mention one other kind of interested teacher, a kind to be careful of. That is the teacher who wants to indoctrinate his students. He believes fanatically that all automobile engines should be limited to 60 horsepower, and he wants you to believe this, too. He is likely to spend lots of class time preaching about this *idée fixe,* and that time will be largely wasted for you. But otherwise he may be an excellent teacher. You should be tolerant and remember that the teacher is just a person, too.

TONE AS A QUALIFICATION OF MEANING

We began our discussion of tone with special emphasis upon tone as a reflection of the author's attitude—his specification as to how we are to "take" what he is saying. But it should be apparent by now that tone also represents a qualification of meaning—a shaping of what is to be said. Indeed, a little reflection will show that full meaning is rarely conveyed by merely literal statement. We constantly find that we must "read between the lines" in order to understand a letter; or that we must take into account the tone of voice and the facial expression if we are to understand fully a conversation with a friend. The importance of tone as a guide to meaning comes out particularly in essays that deal with our valuations and judgments.

For example, consider how important is the tone in the following passage describing the old Model T Ford:

I see by the new Sears Roebuck catalogue that it is still possible to buy an axle for a 1909 Model T Ford, but I am not deceived. The great days have faded, the end is in sight. Only one page in the current catalogue is devoted to parts and accessories for the Model T; yet everyone remembers springtimes when the Ford gadget section was larger than men's clothing, almost as large as household furnishings. The last Model T was built in 1927, and the car is fading from what scholars call the American scene—which is an understatement, because to a few million people who grew up with it, the old Ford practically *was* the American scene.

It was the miracle God had wrought. And it was patently the sort of thing that could only happen once. Mechanically uncanny, it was like nothing that had ever come to the world before. Flourishing industries rose and fell with it. As a vehicle, it was hard-working, commonplace, heroic; and it often seemed to transmit those qualities to the persons who rode in it. My own generation identifies it with Youth, with its gaudy, irretrievable excitements; before it fades into the mist, I would like to pay it the tribute of the sigh that is not a sob, and set down random entries in the shape somewhat less cumbersome than a Sears Roebuck catalogue.

The Model T was distinguished from all other makes of cars by the fact that its transmission was of a type known as planetary—which was half metaphysics, half sheer friction. Engineers accepted the word "planetary" in its epicyclic sense, but I was always conscious that it also means "wandering," "erratic." Because of the peculiar nature of this planetary element, there was always, in Model T, a certain dull rapport between engine and wheels, and, even when the car was in a state known as neutral, it trembled with a deep imperative and tended to inch forward. There was never a moment when the bands were not faintly egging the machine on. In this respect it was like a horse, rolling the bit on its tongue, and country people brought to it the same technique they used with draft animals.

LEE STROUT WHITE: "Farewell, My Lovely"*

To enjoy the passage just quoted one must be aware that the author laments the passing of the Model T with mock seriousness. The game that the author plays is to wreath literary allusions and sentimental clichés about a piece of machinery which seems to belong to a nonliterary and nonsentimental world. Suppose we remove the tone of mock lament and simply state the facts literally and directly. Here is what we might have if we treated the first paragraph in this fashion.

The new Sears Roebuck catalogue indicates that one may still purchase an axle for a 1909 Model T Ford. But this possibility, though interesting, does not mean that the Model T Ford is any longer an important factor in American transportation. The section of the catalogue devoted to Ford parts, once larger than that devoted to men's clothing, has now shrunk to a single page. No Model T's have been built since 1927, and this model is rapidly disappearing from the American highway.

The rewriting, by altering the tone, destroys the humour. It does even more. It destroys a good deal of what the passage says. For the real content of the passage is the presentation of a certain complex attitude toward some aspects of American life. The author's real concern is with American social history, but he presents that history not clinically and "sociologically", but affectionately and a little whimsically. The tone, then, is a most important element in "what" the author is saying. Lest the last example be thought a rather special case, consider the importance of tone in the following definition of a weed:

What is a weed? I have heard it said that there are sixty definitions. For me, a weed is a plant out of place. Or, less tolerantly, call it a foreign aggressor, which is a thing not so mild as a mere escape from cultivation, a visitor that sows itself innocently in a garden bed where you would not choose to plant it. Most weeds have natal countries, whence they have sortied. So Japanese honeysuckle, English plantain,

* From "Farewell, My Lovely" by Lee Strout White. Copyright 1936 The New Yorker Magazine, Inc. (formerly The F-R Publishing Corporation).

Russian thistle came from lands we recognize, but others, like gypsies, have lost all record of their geographic origin. Some of them turn up in all countries, and are listed in no flora as natives. Some knock about the seaports of the world, springing up wherever ballast used to be dumped from the old sailing ships. Others prefer cities; they have lost contact with sweet soil, and lead a guttersnipe existence. A little group occurs only where wool waste is dumped, others are dooryard and pavement weeds, seeming to thrive the more as they are trod by the feet of man's generations. Some prized in an age of simpler tastes have become garden *déclassés* and street urchins; thus it comes about that the pleasant but plebeian scent of Bouncing Bet, that somewhat blowsy pink of old English gardens, is now one of the characteristic odors of American sidewalk ends, where the pavement peters out and shacks and junked cars begin.

—DONALD CULROSS PEATTIE: *Flowering Earth**

We could describe a weed as follows:

A weed may be defined as a plant that, though growing in cultivated ground, is economically useless and is a detriment to the crop being cultivated. Yet, it must be conceded that this definition is somewhat subjective, for a plant considered useless by one person might be counted useful by another, and a plant ordinarily cultivated for its own sake might be regarded as a nuisance when found in a field planted to some other crop. But there is general agreement on most of the plants that we call weeds. Some examples would be dog fennel, dock, mullein, and ragweed.

This paragraph gives substantially the same definition as that given in the paragraph by Peattie. But it is relatively toneless. The author is not visualizing any particular person for whom he is writing, and he does not seem to have a particular attitude toward his subject. As a consequence, this paragraph is quite without personality.

Notice how much of the writer's personality comes through in the original passage. Peattie evidently possesses a great deal of botanical information. But the passage in question is not intended as technical description; rather it is a more desultory and amiable account of weeds. Peattie is a man of perception, with keen senses ("the pleasant but plebeian scent of Bouncing Bet", "the characteristic odors of American sidewalk ends"). He evidently has a sense of humour. He is aware of current politics ("foreign aggressor"). He has a sense of history.

Notice, too, how the diction unobtrusively but powerfully supports the variations of the basic metaphor. "Foreign aggressor" is pointed up by the use of the word "sortied". (A "sortie" suggests a military raid.) "Guttersnipe existence" sharpens the hint given by "others prefer cities". "Plebeian" and "somewhat blowsy" support and extend the suggestions made by "*déclassé*".

The diction, of course, does something more. Though Peattie is willing to use a technical term like *flora,* most of his words are specific and concrete. Moreover, he does not hesitate to use colloquial expressions like "knock about" and "peters out". Peattie is not at all like the fabled scholar who knew all the pedantic terms but could not address a dog in his own dialect. His diction is accommodated to the wholesome vulgarity of his subject. Peattie's paragraph illustrates the fact that a particular tone depends upon various factors—diction, metaphor, as well as the larger principles of composition. Tone, indeed, represents a kind of final integration of all the elements that go into a piece of writing. Writing that is toneless or confused in tone is usually bad writing.

■ Applications

I In the following description we get an impression of Jidda. It possesses a definite quality, a special atmosphere. What is the author's attitude toward this city? Does he loathe it? Admire it? Feel affection for it? Is his writing florid? Studiedly dry? What is the tone?

The style of architecture was like crazy Elizabethan half-timber work, in the elaborate Cheshire fashion, but gone gimcrack to an incredible degree. House-fronts were fretted, pierced and pargetted till they looked as though cut of cardboard for a romantic stage-setting. Every story jutted, every window leaned one way or other; often the very walls sloped. It was like a dead city, so clean underfoot, and so quiet. Its winding, even streets were floored with damp sand solidified by time and as silent to the tread as any carpet. The lattices and wall-returns deadened all reverberation of voice. There were no carts nor any streets wide enough for carts, no shod animals, no bustle anywhere. Everything was hushed, strained, even furtive. The doors of houses shut softly as we passed. There were no loud dogs, no crying children: indeed except in the bazaar, still half asleep, there were few wayfarers of any kind; and the rare people we did meet, all thin, and as it were wasted by disease, with scarred, hairless faces and screwed-up eyes, slipped past us quickly and cautiously, not looking at us. Their skimp, white robes, shaven polls with little skull-caps, red cotton shoulder-shawls, and bare feet were so same as to be almost a uniform.

The atmosphere was oppressive, deadly. There seemed no life in it. It was not burning hot, but held a moisture and sense of great age and exhaustion such as seemed to belong to no other place: not a passion of smells like Smyrna, Naples or Marseilles, but a feeling of long use, of the exhalations of many people, of continued bathheat and sweat. One would say that for years Jidda had not been swept through by a firm breeze: that its streets kept their air from year's end to year's end, from the day they were built for so long as the houses should endure.

—T. E. LAWRENCE: *Seven Pillars of Wisdom**

II For what audience is the following paragraph written? Has the audience been visualized by the writer? Could it be said that the writing is relatively "toneless"? If so, is its tonelessness a defect or a virtue?

Before intelligent criteria can be developed for the selection of superimposed leaders, the organization, through its professional staff, must first clearly define the objectives of its group program and establish qualifications for group leadership. Second, these objectives must be made clear to the leaders. In group work terminology the concept *socialization* appears as the central objective, but in the experience of the writer little effort has been made to define this concept so as to be understandable to the leader.

—FROM A MAGAZINE OF SOCIAL RESEARCH

Literal Statement and Ironical Statement

Irony always involves a discrepancy between the literal meaning of a statement and its actual meaning. On the surface, the ironical statement says one thing; in actuality it says something rather different. In the lighthearted, laughingly ironical statement, the literal meaning may be only partially qualified; in a bitter and obvious

* From *Seven Pillars of Wisdom* by T. E. Lawrence. Copyright 1925, 1935 by Doubleday & Company, Inc.

irony (such as that which we call sarcasm) the literal meaning may be entirely reversed. An example of rather lighthearted and affectionate irony occurs in the discussion of the Model T Ford by Lee Strout White (see page 91). The little car is treated in almost mock heroic style ("It was the miracle God had wrought . . . it was patently the sort of thing that could only happen once . . . before it fades into the mist, I would like to pay it the tribute of the sigh that is not a sob. . . ."). The informal essay frequently makes use of some form of gentle irony such as this.

A sample of ordinary sarcasm might be represented by a student's outburst at his roommate: "A fine friend you turn out to be, borrowing my car and taking my girl on a date." The literal meaning which proclaims the roommate to be a fine young man is just the opposite of what his now irate friend means to say about him.

Between the more delicate ironical qualifications and the sarcastic reversal there are a thousand shadings possible, and it is a pity that we do not have specific terms by which to describe them. Yet, on second thought, our lack of such terms may be no real handicap. We can develop these qualifications of meaning without in the least needing to give them a label. What is important is not that we have a glossary of terms, but that we be aware of the fact of ironical qualification. Here are two samples of ironical statement. The first is from a novel, Thackeray's *Vanity Fair*:

> Being an invalid, Joseph Sedley contented himself with a bottle of claret, besides his Madeira at dinner, and he managed a couple of plates full of strawberries and cream, and twenty-four little rout cakes, that were lying neglected in a plate near him, and certainly (for novelists have the privilege of knowing everything), he thought a great deal about the girl upstairs. "A nice, gay, merry young creature", thought he to himself. "How she looked at me when I picked up her handkerchief at dinner! She dropped it twice. Who's that singing in the drawing-room? Gad! shall I go up and see?"

This is rather obvious irony, but certainly not severely sarcastic. Thackeray tells us a good deal about Joseph Sedley's state of invalidism by describing his diet. But the joke is not so simple as this: Thackeray suggests something of Sedley's general character, and more economically than he might have done by giving a fully explicit description.

The second example is from *The Exurbanites*. Exurbia (from Latin *ex urbe,* meaning outside the city) is the name that the author assigns to those districts beyond the suburbs of New York City in which many people connected with the communications and entertainment industries live.

How do they spend their money?

Well, variously. In some cases, even as you and I. Being exurbanites, they hustle in to town, to see the latest play, or to hear the latest concert. They deal heavily in the metropolitan specialty shops and department stores: they average better than six charge accounts per family. There are bookstores, in this exurb, and these folks are highly literate: they buy books, some of which they may place in prominent positions on their coffee tables. They buy paintings, sometimes as investments; if they conceive it to be important to achieve status as hi-fi buffs, they buy expensive and intricate equipment, and subsequently records. (Standard classics, yes; plus some modern and off-beat classical types like Poulenc; Friml, no. Show tunes by Porter, Coward, etc., yes; Victor Herbert, no. Jazz, yes—if it's authentic; Liberace, no. And, importantly, a heavy play to off-color records, those for example, dubbed off the master on which the recording artist fluffed and in consequence, exchanged blue epithets with the boys in the band.)

—A. C. SPECTORSKY: *The Exurbanites*

The irony expressed in this passage is primarily an *irony of situation*; that is, the people described pretend to be interested in literature and music but are really concerned only with giving the impression of being highbrow. But this irony of situation is at least partially converted into an *irony of statement* by the way in which the writer describes the situation. It is as though he did not himself see the implications of such phrases as "sometimes as investments", "if they conceive it to be important to achieve status", and so on. The writer's refusal to make comments upon what he is depicting— his affecting not to see the implications of what he is describing—in itself constitutes irony.

■ Applications

I The scene described below is a British club in India, some decades ago. The orchestra has just played "God Save the King". What is the author's attitude toward his fellow countrymen? The passage is obviously ironic, but what is the precise shading of irony? Is the author indignant? Mocking? Bitter? Or what?

> Meanwhile the performance ended, and the amateur orchestra played the National Anthem. Conversation and billiards stopped, faces stiffened. It was the Anthem of the Army of Occupation. It reminded every member of the club that he or she was British and in exile. It produced a little sentiment and a useful accession of will-power. The meagre tune, the curt series of demands of Jehovah, fused into a prayer unknown in England, and though they perceived neither Royalty nor Deity they did perceive something, they were strengthened to resist another day. They poured out, offering one another drinks.
>
> —E. M. FORSTER: *A Passage to India*

II The student theme "Teachers I Have Known" (page 89) has some traces of irony in it. For example, the student asks: "Did they become teachers because they were really interested in their subject and in young people, or did they just drift into the profession through indifference or necessity?" But in general, the judgments are given directly and explicitly. Would there be any advantages in presenting the judgment against such teachers indirectly and ironically? Try rewriting this theme, making use of an ironical approach. Pretend, for example, that you are praising all teachers; or try to give a deadpan account of the teachers' faults as if you did not realize that they were faults.

Overstatement and Understatement

We have been occupied with a distinction between a literal and nonliteral (including the ironic) use of words. It is useful to consider the problem of tone in the light of another distinction, that between *overstatement* and *understatement*. Overstatement, as the term implies, is redundancy; but it is much more than mere repetition. The term connotes gushiness and floweriness—a straining after effects. The following passage consists of the last two paragraphs of Bret Harte's story, "The Outcasts of Poker Flat". In the story a gambler and a prostitute rise to heroism as they try to shelter and protect an innocent girl who has fallen into their company when the whole party is overtaken by a severe snowstorm in the mountains. The paragraphs that follow describe the last days of the two women, the innocent girl and the prostitute.

> The wind lulled as if it feared to waken them. Feathery drifts of snow, shaken from the long pine boughs, flew like white-winged birds, and settled about them as they slept. The moon through the rifted clouds looked down upon what had been the camp. But all human stain, all trace of earthly travail, was hidden beneath the spotless mantle mercifully flung from above.
>
> They slept all day that day and the next, nor did they waken when voices and footsteps broke the silence of the camp. And when pitying fingers brushed the snow from their wan faces, you could scarcely have told from the equal peace that dwelt upon them which was she that had sinned.

Here the author, in his anxiety to stress the pathos of the scene and the redemption of the fallen woman, is not content to let the scene speak for itself. The wind lulls the two women; the moon looks down upon them; a "spotless mantle" is "mercifully flung from above". The pseudopoetic language, the suggestion that nature mercifully hides "all human stain", the general absence of restraint and reserve—all indicate that the tone here is one of sentimentality; that is, emotion in excess of the occasion.

What was Bret Harte's own attitude? One has to conclude that either he himself was "soft" (that is, that he was taken in by his own attempt to "work up" an effect), or else he was cynically trying to seduce his reader into an emotional response which is not itself justified by the dramatic occasion that he provided. Whatever Harte's attitude, most readers will feel that the tone is sentimental. Sentimentality usually betrays itself by a straining to work up the reader's feelings. Of course, in a sense, any appeal to our emotions represents an attempt "to work up" an effect. But it is one thing to do this legitimately by presenting a scene with imaginative power, and it is quite a different thing to try to bully the reader into the desired emotional response. Readers may disagree on whether the response has been evoked legitimately or illegitimately (that is, sentimentally), but the principle involved is crucial. Otherwise any writer, however tawdry or mawkish, could demand our response simply by making a direct assault on our feelings.

We must not, however, associate overwriting merely with the softer emotions of love and pity. It can show itself in a strained attempt at humour or a hectic gaiety or a pretentious heartiness. Advertising copy will provide obvious instances.

Understatement does not constitute a true antithesis to over-statement. Though overstatement, as it is commonly used, is a term of adverse criticism, understatement is not. It does not necessarily mean statement that is starved and deficient, poor because of its meagreness. Instead it tends to mean statement of a calculated bare-ness or a studied dryness. Indeed, understatement is often a power-ful device for obtaining certain effects. One may illustrate by a pas-sage from *Seven Pillars of Wisdom* in which T. E. Lawrence des-cribes an incident that occurred in Arabia during World War I while he was serving with the Arabs in their revolt against Turkey. The incident took place while Lawrence was leading a raiding party of Arab tribesmen.

> My followers had been quarrelling all day, and while I was lying near the rocks a shot was fired. I paid no attention; for there were hares and birds in the valley; but a little while later Suleiman roused me and made me follow him across the valley to an opposite bay in the rocks, where one of the Ageyl, a Boreida man, was lying stone dead with a bullet through his temples. The shot must have been fired from close by; because the skin was burnt about one wound. The remaining Ageyl were running frantically about; and when I asked what it was, Ali, their head man, said that Hamed the Moor had done the murder. I suspected Suleiman, because of the feud between the Atban and Ageyl . . . but Ali assured me that Suleiman had been with him three hundred yards further up the valley gathering sticks when the shot was fired. I sent all out to search for Hamed, and crawled back to the baggage, feeling that it need not have happened this day of all days when I was in pain.
>
> As I lay there I heard a rustle, and opened my eyes slowly upon Hamed's back as he stooped over his saddle-bags, which lay just beyond my rock. I covered him with a pistol and then spoke. He had put down his rifle to lift the gear; and was at my mercy till the others came. We held a court at once; and after a while Hamed confessed that, he and Salem having had words, he had seen red and shot him suddenly. Our inquiry ended. The Ageyl, as relatives of the dead man, demanded blood for blood. The others supported them; and I tried vainly to talk the gentle Ali round. My head was aching with fever and I could not think; but hardly even in health, with all eloquence, could I have begged Hamed off; for Salem had been a friendly fellow and his sudden murder a wanton crime.

Then rose up the horror which would make civilized man shun justice like a plague if he had not the needy to serve him as a hangmen for wages. There were other Moroccans in our army; [Hamed the Moor was a Moroccan] and to let the Ageyl kill one in feud meant reprisals by which our unity would have been endangered. It must be a formal execution, and at last, desperately, I told Hamed that he must die for punishment, and laid the burden of his killing on myself. Perhaps they would count me not qualified for feud. At least no revenge could lie against my followers; for I was a stranger and kinless.

I made him enter a narrow gully of the spur, a dank twilight place overgrown with weeds. Its sandy bed had been pitted by trickles of water down the cliffs in the late rain. At the end it shrank to a crack a few inches wide. The walls were vertical. I stood in the entrance and gave him a few moments' delay which he spent crying on the ground. Then I made him rise and shot him through the chest. He fell down on the weeds shrieking, with the blood coming out in spurts over his clothes, and jerked about till he rolled nearly to where I was. I fired again, but was shaking so that I only broke his wrist. He went on calling out, less loudly, now lying on his back with his feet towards me, and I leant forward and shot him for the last time in the thick of his neck under the jaw. His body shivered a little, and I called the Ageyl; who buried him in the gully where he was. Afterwards the wakeful night dragged over me, till, hours before dawn, I had the men up and made them load, in my longing to be set free of Wadi Kitan. They had to lift me into the saddle.

—T. E. LAWRENCE: *Seven Pillars of Wisdom**

What is Lawrence's attitude toward Hamed? Toward the Arabs and their blood feuds? Most of all, toward himself? Is he ashamed of himself? Proud of himself? Complacent and untroubled about himself?

The incident is told with detachment and an almost studied dryness. But it is evident that Lawrence is not glossing over the incident casually and briefly. He develops it fully, giving us even minute details: e.g., "bullet through his temples", "as he stooped over his saddle-bags", "shot him for the last time in the thick of his neck under the jaw". Even the scene of the execution, the gully, is described carefully and precisely: "Its sandy bed had been pitted by trickles of water down the cliffs in the late rain."

* From *Seven Pillars of Wisdom* by T. E. Lawrence. Copyright 1925, 1935 by Doubleday & Company, Inc.

The narrator evidently remembers the whole incident vividly, and knows how to make the incident vivid to his reader. Why, then, is he not more explicit about his own feelings and attitudes? Would anything have been gained if Lawrence had added a long paragraph describing the feelings that passed through his mind as he decided that he must act as executioner? Would anything have been lost? Notice that Lawrence is willing to use the word "horror", but he does not write, "As a civilized man I was overwhelmed with horror", but rather, "Then rose up the horror which would make civilized man shun justice like a plague if he had not the needy to serve him as a hangman for wages." Why does Lawrence, in this most explicit account of his own feelings, prefer the generalized statement?

A little meditation on these questions is likely to result in some such conclusion as this: that Lawrence, far from remaining cool and detached, was indeed terribly shaken by the experience, but that, nevertheless, he preferred to make his *account* of the experience as detached and objective as was possible. He chose to give a restrained description of his actions, leaving his reader to infer from the actions themselves what his feelings must have been.

This restraint itself has an important effect on the tone: it implies a certain modesty (his own mental anguish is not allowed to dominate the story as if he thought his anguish the important thing in the episode) and it implies a certain confidence in the reader's maturity and sensitiveness—the reader need not be "told" what Lawrence was feeling. But the restraint here is of still further importance; the restraint manifested in Lawrence's *account* of his action is a reflection of, and a type of, the disciplined control which he imposed on his followers and on himself in the desert. The man who relates the action is the man who acted, and his manner of writing about the event suggests his attitude toward the event itself.

This discussion of understatement and restraint should not prevent the student from writing on occasion as vividly as he can about exciting experiences. But the first things should come first, and underplaying certain aspects of a composition may be a necessary way of putting certain other aspects into proper focus. Understatement is, among other things, a means of bringing about a proper proportioning of the various elements of the composition.

Some practical don'ts

The problem of tone, then, is most important. There are obviously too many shadings of tone for us to be able to set down elaborate rules for achieving the proper tone. But it is possible to set down a few "don'ts" which have a very general application.

(1) Writing down. One must not "write down" to his audience. The sense of oversimple statement and painfully careful explanation can disgust the reader as quickly as any offense of which the writer is capable. Prose which is properly suited to an audience of eight-year-olds would prove completely tiresome or, on the other hand, unintentionally funny, to a mature audience. Take into account your reader's lack of special knowledge of your subject, but never underestimate your reader's intelligence.

(2) False enthusiasm. The reader is also likely to resent any hint of synthetic breeziness and false camaraderie. It is a fault into which modern advertising is tending to press the whole civilization. Bug-eyed young matrons oo-la-la-ing over the purchase of sheets or toothbrushes, and the all-too-infectious joviality of supersalesmen more and more fill the advertisements. The student obviously wishes to gain a kind of liveliness and warmth in his style, but an artificial concoction of informality and sprightliness can be more depressing than a rather painful dryness.

(3) Sentimentality. The third fault is hardly likely to appear in most simple expository writing, but as we have seen in earlier chapters, there is very little writing which is "simply expository". Sentimentality may show itself as pure gushiness or as a kind of hair-trigger emotional sensitiveness. But whatever form it takes, sentimentality always involves an implied demand on the part of the writer for more emotional response than the situation warrants; and it implies, on the part of the sentimental reader, a willingness to respond emotionally when the response is not actually justified.

THE SPECIAL AUDIENCE AND
THE IDEAL AUDIENCE

Earlier in this chapter we spoke of tone as reflecting the author's attitude toward his audience *and* toward his material, but the student may well ask: "When should attitude toward the audience dominate, and when attitude toward the material?"

Writing which demands that the author take into account his particular audience is, as we have seen, always "practical" writing—writing designed to effect some definite purpose. The advertiser is trying to persuade the housewife to buy something. The politician hopes that his speech will induce citizens to vote for him. Or, to take a more exalted case (for there need be no self-interest), a statesman urges a nation (through his writing and his speeches) to adopt a certain course of action. Yet these cases all have one thing in common: they are designed to secure a practical end. An audience is to be won to agreement or urged to action.

If such writing is to be effective, the author must, of course, keep his specific audience constantly in mind. An approach calculated to win the suffrage of one audience may very well repel another. The age, the intelligence, the amount of education, the interests, the habits and prejudices of the audience, must all be taken into account. The skillful management of such problems is an aspect of rhetoric, and for many people rhetoric has come to mean largely the art of persuasion. The pure scientist may be thought to escape the need for using rhetoric. The scientist writing strictly as a scientist does not persuade his reader, he "just tells him". The facts speak for themselves, and in purely technical writing they are allowed to speak for themselves. But they speak fully only to a specially trained audience.

But what about the student who has no special audience in view? Addressing himself to a general rather than a specific reader, he may find that the problem of tone becomes difficult simply because he lacks a definite target at which to aim. Yet all good writing is addressed to a reader, even though that reader is an ideal reader, not a limited and special one. One could argue, in fact, that because the ideal reader is ideal, his intelligence, his sensitivity, his general discrimination, are to be honoured and respected all the more. This is to say what has been said earlier—that we do not evade the problem of tone by addressing ourselves to the reader-in-general rather than to Tom, Dick or Harry. Actually, the problem of tone here becomes more important, not less important.

Yet the student, even though he agrees with what has just been argued, may find that the ideal reader remains too shadowy to furnish him something definite at which to aim. In that case it may be useful for him to imagine himself writing for some particular person —the most intelligent and discriminating person that he knows. If he can please that person and be convincing to that person, the problem of tone will probably have been taken care of quite adequately.

There is another practical way of considering the problem: The author writes for a particular audience, but he also writes for himself. There is his own sense of fitness that must be satisfied. The writer himself becomes the audience at which he aims. The question which he asks himself is not, "Have I made this convincing to Tom, or to Dick, or to Harry?" but rather, "Have I made this convincing to myself?" or, to put the matter more succinctly still, "Have I made this convincing?"

TONE AND OTHER COMPONENTS OF STYLE

It should be apparent that a particular tone is achieved by the interplay of various elements. Sentence structure, diction, and metaphor are only a few of those involved. Indeed, in discussing tone we have dealt in one way or another with nearly all the components of literary style. The only notable exception is that of rhythm. Since the tone of a work, taken in the deepest sense, most nearly embodies the organizing intelligence of a work—the "spirit" of a work—a brief discussion of rhythm would go far toward rounding out a simple account of the whole notion of literary style. (We shall mean by *style* the organization of meaning through form. Style represents "how" a thing is said, and how it is said goes far to determine what is said.)

Rhythm

In discussing tone we pointed out that in actual conversation the tone of voice, gesture, and facial expression supplement the words and do much to set the particular tone which the speaker intends— playfulness, seriousness, irritability, and so on. If we use the written word, however, the "tone" has to be established by the choice of words and the patterning of those words. But it will have occurred to the student that in moving from actual conversation to the written word the speaker relinquishes still another very important element —the matter of emphasis. Consider the following simple sentence: "Are you going to town?" If we stress the word *are*, the sentence becomes an emphatic question; and if we stress it heavily, it may even suggest surprise. But if we stress *you*, the question becomes centred upon whether it is *you* who are going rather than someone else. If we stress *town*, we get a third variation; the question then emphasizes the destination.

Thus the rhythmic inflection of a sentence, with its various stresses on particular words, is a very important way in which we express our meanings. When we put the sentence on paper, we can, of course, indicate some of this stress by underlining the words to be emphasized. But mere underlining is a relatively crude substitute for the living voice, and it is the mark of a clumsy writer to have to rely upon constant underlining. The skilled writer, by his control of the rhythm of his sentences, suggests where the proper emphases are to fall; for emphasis is an element of rhythm.

Rhythm and Clarity of Meaning

Control of rhythm, then, is important for clarity of meaning. This fact is illustrated by the muddled and monotonous rhythm of technological jargon. Jargon is difficult to read for a variety of reasons: It is fuzzy, abstract, and dull; it lacks flavour. But it lacks clarity as well, for there are no natural emphases, no obvious points of primary stress.

Consider the following sentence:

Oriental luxury goods—jade, silk, gold, spices, vermilion, jewels— formerly had come by way of the Caspian Sea overland; and a few daring Greek sea captains, now that this route had been cut by the Huns, catching the trade winds, were sailing from Red Sea ports and loading up at Ceylon.

The sentence is passable, and is not perhaps noticeably unrhythmical. But if we read this sentence in the form in which Robert Graves actually wrote it, we shall find that it is not only clearer, it is much more rhythmical and much easier to read:

Oriental luxury goods—jade, silk, gold, spices, vermilion, jewels— had formerly come overland by way of the Caspian Sea and now that this route had been cut by the Huns, a few daring Greek sea captains were sailing from Red Sea ports, catching the trade winds and loading up at Ceylon.

Emphatic rhythms tend to accompany emotional heightening. It is no accident that eloquent prose—prose that makes a strong appeal to the feelings—tends to use clearly patterned rhythms, or that poetry is commonly written in the systematized rhythm which we call "verse". The association of formal rhythm with emotional power is based on a perfectly sound psychological fact. Fervent expression of grief, rage or joy tends to fall into rhythmic patterns—whether it be the sobbings of a grief-stricken woman or the cursing of an irate cab driver.

The student may feel, however, that rhythm is much too intricate an instrument for him to try to use *consciously*. It almost certainly is. We do not suggest that the student consciously try for rhythmic effects. Yet a very practical use of rhythm can be made; the student may learn to use rhythm in order to test his composition. As he re-reads it aloud, he should learn to listen for the break in the rhythm, the jangling discord, the lack of smoothness that signals to him that something in the sentence is awry. This comment applies particularly to the disposition of modifiers, prepositional phrases, and the like. The student may find that reading his composition aloud and listening to its rhythms proves to be one of the best practical means for spotting sentence elements that are not in the best order.

Style

The real difficulty in discussing style comes at this point. Style, as we have already had occasion to point out, is an over-all result. It is a result determined by the working together of sentence structure, vocabulary, figures of speech, rhythm, and many other elements. It is not always easy for a reader to pick out the element which is most important, or even largely important, in giving the style of the writer its special quality. It is quite impossible for a writer to produce a given quality of style by mechanically measuring out so much of this element and so much of that. A modern author has put the matter in this way: "Style is not an isolable quality of writing; it is writing itself."

Like tone, rhythm represents the harmonious interplay of many diverse elements. Style itself, of which tone and rhythm are aspects, represents such an interplay. That is why it is difficult to discuss a style *as such*. Yet there are a few general considerations with regard to style that are worth saying to the student. In the first place, style is never to be thought of as a mere veneer, a decorated surface laid over the content. In the second place, a writer's real difficulty in composition is to know what he really wants to say—not, as we are often tempted to think, merely how to say it. For in a good composition, form and content interpenetrate each other and are inseparable. In the third place, a bad style always reveals itself in some disharmony or cleavage between what is said and what we guess the author actually meant to say.* The discordant elements "stick out"—they call attention to themselves.

These last considerations bear upon another aspect of style: the originality of the writer. We properly take originality to be a symptom of good style. If we see that style is not a veneer, but is the result of thousands of decisions and discriminations made by the writer, we can understand why style is always indelibly impressed with the writer's personality. If the personality is commonplace, the style will be commonplace. But the student needs to be warned against any excessive striving for originality as such. It is not enough to urge him to be his unique self, for frequently he finds that true self only through a process of exploration. Originality, the impress of personality, fortunately can be left to take care of itself if the writer manages to take care of what he can consciously control in his composition.

■ Applications

I The following are general questions which the student should ask himself as he considers the passages quoted below.

1. What is the author's attitude toward the reader? In what way is this shown?

---

* Ironic effects may seem to invite confusion with bad style since irony always involves a discrepancy, a "disharmony", between what is apparently said and what is actually meant. But the confusion, if it occurs, is usually only momentary. The ironic discrepancy proves to be a device under the writer's control—not an ineptitude.

2. What is the author's attitude toward his material?

3. Are there any instances of sentimentality? In what way is sentimentality revealed? Are there any instances of other kinds of overstatement? Is the overstatement justified or unjustified?

4. Which of the passages, if any, makes use of understatement?

5. Do any of the passages make use of irony? Try to characterize the kind of irony in each case—sarcasm, light mocking irony, bitter irony, gay irony, and so on.

6. Are there any passages which are relatively toneless? Are there any which are confused in tone?

A [The mate] felt all the majesty of his great position, and made the world feel it, too. When he gave even the simplest order, he discharged it like a blast of lightning, and sent a long reverberating peal of profanity thundering after it. I could not help contrasting the way in which the average landsman would give an order with the mate's way of doing it. If the landsman should wish the gang-plank moved a foot farther forward, he would probably say: "James, or William, one of you push that plank forward please"; but put the mate in his place, and he would roar out: "Here, now, start that gang-plank for'ard! Lively, now! What're you about! Snatch it! There! There! Aft again! aft again! Don't you hear me? Dash it to dash! are you going to sleep over it! 'Vast heaving. 'Vast heaving, I tell you! Going to heave it clear astern! *Where're you* going with that barrel! for'ard with it 'fore I make you swallow it, you dash-dash-dash-*dashed* split between a tired mud-turtle and a crippled hearse-horse!" I wished I could talk like that.

—SAMUEL L. CLEMENS: *Life on the Mississippi*

Characterize the tone of the mate's speech. Characterize the author's attitude toward the mate. Be as specific as you can.

B It wasn't the bully amateur's world any more. Nobody knew that on armistice day, Theodore Roosevelt, happy amateur warrior with the grinning teeth, the shaking forefinger, naturalist, explorer, magazine writer, Sunday school teacher, cowpuncher, moralist, politician, righteous orator with a short memory, fond of denouncing liars (the Ananias Club) and having pillowfights with his children, was taken to the Roosevelt hospital gravely ill with inflammatory rheumatism.

Things weren't bully any more;

T. R. had grit;

he bore the pain, the obscurity, the sense of being forgotten as he had borne the grilling portages when he was exploring the River of Doubt, the heat, the fetid jungle mud, the infected abscess in his leg.

and died quietly in his sleep

at Sagamore Hill,

on January 6, 1919

and left on the shoulders of his sons

the white man's burden.

—JOHN DOS PASSOS: "The Happy Warrior", *1919**

C No man could have been more bitter against opponents, or more unfair to them or more ungenerous. In this department, indeed, even so gifted a specialist in dishonorable controversy as Dr. (Woodrow) Wilson has seldom surpassed him. He never stood up to a frank and chivalrous debate. He dragged herrings across the trail. He made seductive faces to the gallery. He capitalized on his enormous talents as an entertainer, his rank as a national hero, his public influence and consequence. The two great lawsuits in which he was engaged were screaming burlesques upon justice. He tried them in the newspapers before ever they were called; he befogged them with irrelevant issues; his appearances in court were not the appearances of a witness standing on a level with other witnesses, but those of a comedian sure of his crowd. He was, in his dealings with concrete men as in his dealings with men in the mass, a charlatan of the very highest skill—and there was in him, it goes without saying, the persuasive charm of the charlatan as well as the daring deviousness, the humanness of naivete as well as the humanness of chicane. He knew how to woo—and not only boobs. He was, for all his ruses and ambuscades, a jolly fellow.

—H. L. MENCKEN: "Roosevelt: An Autopsy",
Prejudices: Second Series†

Both Dos Passos and Mencken exhibit definite attitudes toward Theodore Roosevelt; compare and contrast them. How

---

* From *1919*, second volume of *U.S.A.* by John Dos Passos. Published by Houghton Mifflin Company.

† From "Roosevelt: An Autopsy" by H. L. Mencken. Reprinted from *Prejudices: Second Series* by H. L. Mencken, by permission of Alfred A. Knopf, Inc. Copyright 1920 by Alfred A. Knopf, Inc. Copyright 1948 by H. L. Mencken.

does the attitude in each case colour the writer's account? Cite specific instances.

II A The worst experience I ever had was being trapped in a cave. The idea of being all alone and in the dark and unable to move is enough to make most grown men afraid, and I was only fourteen. Even though the chances were I'd be found soon, I couldn't be dead sure. But I kept my head and this probably saved me from serious injury. The doctor said later that if I had tried to pull my foot loose I probably would have injured it severely. It was bad enough as it was, and the sprained ankle kept me on crutches for several weeks. My friends began kidding me about them after a while, but I think it's better to be safe than sorry. The doctor had told me to use the crutches as long as I wanted to.

B Getting trapped in a cave is no fun, but it's not the worst thing that can happen to you if you keep your head. After telling myself over and over "Keep your head, now", it struck me that it wasn't my head I was in danger of losing, it was my foot. I had to laugh, even in the fix I was in, and started telling myself, "Keep your foot, now." It sort of cheered me up and kept me from doing anything stupid.

When it was all over, people kept saying, "I'll bet you were scared to death." And my mother, after she got over her crying spell, would say, "Jimmie's not scared of anything." They were both wrong. I was scared, all right, but I kept seeing the funny side of it.

How would you characterize the tone of the first version? Of the second? Finish the account of the experience, continuing the tone of the first or the second version. Attempt to rewrite this account, giving it still another tone—say one that might be used by a much younger child, or by a philosophical old man.

III Review the following examples of tone given in this chapter— the excerpts from "Farewell, My Lovely", *Flowering Earth, Life on the Mississippi,* and Mencken's "Roosevelt: An Autopsy". In each case analyze the author's use of tone and style. Then write a theme of 500 to 700 words, imitating the style of one of these excerpts. The imitation should not be slavish, but the student should attempt to apply to his own writing all that he can learn from his model.

PART TWO
Some Functions of Discourse

CHAPTER FIVE

Language and Mankind

When someone shouts at you, "Look out!" and you jump just in time to avoid being hit by an automobile, you owe your escape from injury to the fundamental co-operative act by which most of the higher animals survive, namely, communication by means of noises. You did not see the car coming: nevertheless, someone did, and he made certain *noises to communicate* his alarm to you. In other words, although your nervous system did not record the danger, you were unharmed because another nervous system did. You had, for the time being, the advantage of someone else's nervous system in addition to your own.

Indeed, most of the time when we are listening to the noises people make or looking at the black marks on paper that stand for such noises, we are drawing upon the experience of others in order to make up for what we ourselves have missed. Obviously the more an individual can make use of the nervous systems of others to supplement his own, the easier it is for him to survive. And, of course, the more individuals there are in a group co-operating by making helpful noises at each other, the better it is for all—within the limits, naturally, of the group's talents for social organization. Birds and animals congregate with their own kind and make noises when they find food or become alarmed. In fact, gregariousness as an aid to survival and self-defense is forced upon animals as well as upon men by the necessity of uniting nervous systems even more than by the necessity of uniting physical strength. Societies, both animal and human, might almost be regarded as huge co-operative nervous systems.

While animals use only a few limited cries, however, human beings use extremely complicated systems of sputtering, hissing, gurgling, clucking, cooing noises called *language*, with which they express and report what goes on in their nervous systems. Language is, in addition to being more complicated, immeasurably more flexible than the animal cries from which it was developed—so flexible indeed that it can be used not only to report the tremendous variety of things that go on in the human nervous system but also *to report those reports*. That is, when an animal yelps, he may cause a second animal to yelp in imitation or alarm; the second yelp, however, is not *about* the first yelp. But when a man says, "I see a river", a second man can say, "He says he sees a river"—which is a statement about a statement. About this statement-about-a-statement further statements can be made—and about these, still more. *Language, in short, can be about language.* This is a fundamental way in which human noisemaking systems differ from the cries of animals.

The Pooling of Knowledge

In addition to having developed language, man has also developed means of making, on clay tablets, bits of wood or stone, skins of animals, and paper, more or less permanent marks and scratches which *stand for* language. These marks enable him to communicate with people who are beyond the reach of his voice, both in space and in time. There is a long course of evolution from the marked trees that indicated Indian trails to the metropolitan daily newspaper, but they have this in common: they pass on what one individual has known to other individuals, for their convenience or, in the broadest sense, instruction. Many of the lopstick trails in the Canadian woods, marked by Indians long since dead, can be followed to this day. Archimedes is dead, but we still have his reports on what he observed in his experiments in physics. Keats is dead, but he can still tell us how he felt on first reading Chapman's Homer. From our newspapers and radios we learn with great rapidity facts about the world we live in. From books and magazines we learn how hundreds of people whom we shall never be able to see have felt and thought. All this information is helpful to us at one time or another in throwing light on our own problems.

A human being, then, is never dependent on his own experience alone for his information. Even in a primitive culture he can make use of the experience of his neighbours, friends, and relatives, which they communicate to him by means of language. Therefore, instead of remaining helpless because of the limitations of his own experience and knowledge, instead of having to discover what others have already discovered, instead of exploring the false trails they explored and repeating their errors, he can *go on from where they left off*. Language, that is to say, makes progress possible.

Indeed, most of what we call the human characteristics of our species are expressed and developed through our ability to co-operate by means of our systems of making meaningful noises and meaningful scratches on paper. Even people who belong to backward cultures in which writing has not been invented are able to exchange information and to hand down from generation to generation considerable stores of traditional knowledge. There seems, however, to be a limit both to the amount and to the trustworthiness of knowledge that can be transmitted orally.* But when writing is invented, a tremendous step forward is taken. The accuracy of reports can be checked and rechecked by successive generations of observers. The amount of knowledge accumulated ceases to be limited by people's ability to remember what has been told them. The result is that in any literate culture of a few centuries' standing, human beings accumulate vast stores of knowledge—far more than any individual in that culture can read in his lifetime, let alone remember. These stores of knowledge, which are being added to constantly, are made widely available to all who want them through such mechanical processes as printing and through such distributive agencies as the book trade, the newspaper and magazine trade, and library systems. The result is that all of us who can read any of the major European or Asiatic languages are potentially in touch with the intellectual resources of centuries of human endeavour in all parts of the civilized world.

* This is so despite the fact that preliterate people often exhibit remarkable feats of memory, such as the ability to remember every landmark and detail of a journey that may extend for hundreds of miles, or the ability to recall verbatim folk tales and sagas that may take days to recite. Literate people, who rely on notebooks and reference books, have relatively very poor memories.

A physician, for example, who does not know how to treat a patient suffering from a rare disease can look up the disease in the *Index Medicus,* which will send him in turn to medical journals published in all parts of the world. In these he may find records of similar cases as reported and described by a physician in Rotterdam, Holland, in 1913, by another physician in Bangkok, Siam, in 1935, and by still other physicians in Kansas City in 1954. With such records before him, he can better handle his own case. Again, if a person is worried about ethics, he is not limited to the advice of the pastor of the Elm Street Baptist Church; he may go to Confucius, Aristotle, Jesus, Spinoza, and many others whose reflections on ethical problems are on record.

Language, that is to say, is the indispensable mechanism of human life—of life such as ours that is molded, guided, enriched, and made possible by the accumulation of the *past* experience of members of our own species. Dogs and cats and chimpanzees do not, so far as we can tell, increase their wisdom, their information, or their control over their environment from one generation to the next. But human beings do. The cultural accomplishments of the ages, the invention of cooking, of weapons, of writing, of printing, of methods of building, of games and amusements, of means of transportation, and the discoveries of all the arts and sciences come to us as *free gifts from the dead.* These gifts, which none of us has done anything to earn, offer us not only the opportunity for a richer life than our forebears enjoyed but also the opportunity to add to the sum total of human achievement by our own contributions, however small they may be.

To be able to read and write, therefore, is to learn to profit by and take part in the greatest of human achievements—that which makes all other achievements possible—namely, the pooling of our experiences in great co-operative stores of knowledge, available (except where special privilege, censorship, or suppression stand in the way) to all. From the warning cry of primitive man to the latest newsflash or scientific monograph, language is social. Cultural and intellectual co-operation is the great principle of *human* life.

In our modern civilization, however, the flow of words has become a Niagara assailing each individual every day of his life from the first morning news report on radio to the late-late movie on TV; from the morning newspaper to the bedtime magazine or novel. By one means or another, editors, politicians, salesmen, disc jockeys, columnists, speechmakers, friends and family compete for his attention giving him little chance to think about language, which alone makes this communication possible.

This part of the book is devoted, then, to the study of the relationships between language, thought, and behaviour. We shall examine language and people's linguistic habits as they reveal themselves in thinking (at least nine-tenths of which is talking to oneself), speaking, listening, reading, and writing.

■ Applications

I In what circumstances might you become aware of the following messages? Discuss possible reactions to them, taking into account the occasions on which they might occur.

1. Please be seated.
2. Take the weight off your feet, Mac.
3. Remember viewers, when you purchase zesty "Creeps" you are saying "Thank you" to the sponsor of all the wonderful talent in this show.
4. Watch out! Rocks!
5. LIONS MASSACRE ESKIMOS.
6. Sweet Helen, make me immortal with a kiss.
7. Trespassers will be prosecuted.
8. We hold these truths to be self-evident, that all men are created equal.

II Write an essay in which you attempt an answer to the question, "What constitutes my daily Niagara of words?" Consider these specific points: To whom do you listen from day to day? What newspapers and magazines do you read? What plays and movies do you see? What radio and TV programs do you hear? Which of these do you attend to carefully, and to which do you expose yourself only to kill time?

What important communications come to you from the past? What advertisements do you give special attention to? How do you *select* what to listen to or to read out of all the words directed at you by all the many channels of communication to which you are exposed? What do your choices reveal about the kind of person you are?

CHAPTER SIX
Symbols

The Symbolic Process

Animals struggle with each other for food or for leadership, but they do not, like human beings, struggle with each other for things that *stand for* food or leadership: such things as our paper symbols of wealth (money, bonds, titles), badges of rank to wear on our clothes or low-slung sports cars, supposed by some people to stand for social precedence. For animals, the relationship in which one thing *stands for* something else does not appear to exist except in very rudimentary form.

The process by means of which human beings can arbitrarily make certain things *stand for* other things may be called the *symbolic process*. Whenever two or more human beings can communicate with each other, they can, by agreement, make anything stand for anything. For example, here are two symbols:

$$X \qquad\qquad Y$$

We can agree to let X stand for buttons and Y stand for bows: then we can freely change our agreement and let X stand for the B.C. Lions and Y for the Hamilton Ti-Cats; or let X stand for Chaucer and Y for Shakespeare, X for Alberta, and Y for Saskatchewan. *We are, as human beings, uniquely free to manufacture and manipulate and assign values to our symbols as we please.* Indeed, we can go further by making symbols that stand for symbols. If necessary we can, for instance, let the symbol M stand for all the X's in the above example (buttons, Lions, Chaucer, Alberta) and let N stand for all the Y's (bows, Ti-Cats, Shakespeare, Saskatchewan). Then we can make another symbol, T, stand for M and N, which would be an instance of a symbol of symbols of symbols. This freedom to create symbols of *any* assigned value and to create *symbols that stand for symbols* is essential to what we call the symbolic process.

Everywhere we turn, we see the symbolic process at work. Feathers worn on the head or stripes on the sleeve can be made to stand for military rank; cowrie shells or rings of brass or pieces of paper can stand for wealth; crossed sticks can stand for a set of religious beliefs; buttons, elks' teeth, ribbons, special styles of ornamental haircutting or tattooing can stand for social affiliations. The symbolic process permeates human life at the most primitive and the most civilized levels alike. Warriors, medicine men, policemen, doormen, nurses, cardinals, and kings wear costumes that symbolize their occupations. American Indians collected scalps, college students collect membership keys in honorary societies, to symbolize victories in their respective fields. There are few things that men do or want to do, possess or want to possess, that have not, in addition to their mechanical or biological value, a symbolic value.

All fashionable clothes are highly symbolic: materials, cut, and ornament are dictated only to a slight degree by considerations of warmth, comfort or practicability. The more we dress up in fine clothes, the more we restrict our freedom of action. But by means of delicate embroideries, easily soiled fabrics, starched shirts, high heels, long and pointed fingernails, and other such sacrifices of comfort, the wealthy classes manage to symbolize, among other things, the fact that they don't have to work for a living. On the other hand, the not-so-wealthy, by imitating these symbols of wealth, symbolize their conviction that, even if they do work for a living, they are just as good as anybody else.

With changes in Canadian life since the nineteenth century, many changes have taken place in our ways of symbolizing social status. Except for evening and party wear, fashionable clothes nowadays are often designed for outdoor life and therefore stress comfort, informality, and, above all, freedom from the conventions of business life—hence the gaily coloured sports shirts for men and capri pants for women.

In the past, a deeply tanned skin was indicative of a life spent in farming and other outdoor labour, and women then went to a great deal of trouble shielding themselves from the sun with parasols, wide hats, and long sleeves. Today, however, a pale skin is indicative of confinement in offices and factories, while a deeply tanned skin suggests a life of leisure—of trips to Florida, Sun Valley, and Hawaii. Hence, a sun-blackened skin, once considered ugly because it symbolized work, is now considered beautiful because it symbolizes leisure, and pallid people in New York, Chicago, and Toronto who cannot afford midwinter trips to the West Indies find comfort in browning themselves with drugstore tanning solutions.

Food, too, is highly symbolic. Religious dietary regulations, such as those of the Catholics, Jews, and Mohammedans, are observed in order to symbolize adherence to one's religion. Specific foods are used to symbolize specific festivals and observances in almost every country—for example, cherry pie on George Washington's birthday; haggis on Burns' Nicht. And eating together has been a highly symbolic act throughout all of man's known history: "companion" for instance, means one with whom you share your bread.

The white Southerner's apparently illogical attitude toward Negroes can also be accounted for on symbolic grounds. People from outside the South often find it difficult to understand how so many white Southerners accept close physical contact with Negro servants and yet become extremely upset at the idea of sitting beside Negroes in restaurants or buses. The attitude of the Southerner rests on the fact that the ministrations of a Negro servant—even personal care, such as nursing—have the symbolic implication of social inequality; while admission of Negroes to buses, restaurants, and nonsegregated schools has the symbolic implication of social equality.

We select our furniture to serve as visible symbols of our taste, wealth, and social position. We often choose our residences on the basis of a feeling that it "looks well" to have a "good address". We trade in a perfectly good car for a later model, not always to get better transportation, but to give evidence to the community that we can afford it.

Such complicated and apparently unnecessary behaviour leads philosophers, both amateur and professional, to ask over and over again, "Why can't human beings live simply and naturally?" Often the complexity of human life makes us look enviously at the relative simplicity of such lives as dogs and cats lead. But the symbolic process, which makes possible the absurdities of human conduct, also makes possible language and therefore all the human achievements dependent upon language. The fact that more things can go wrong with motorcars than with wheelbarrows is no reason for going back to wheelbarrows. Similarly, the fact that the symbolic process makes complicated follies possible is no reason for wanting to return to a cat-and-dog existence. A better solution is to understand the symbolic process so that instead of being its victims we become, to some degree at least, its masters.

Language as Symbolism

Of all forms of symbolism, language is the most highly developed, most subtle, and most complicated. It has been pointed out that human beings, by agreement, can make anything stand for anything. Now, human beings have agreed, in the course of centuries of mutual dependency, to let the various noises that they can produce with their lungs, throats, tongues, teeth, and lips systematically stand for specified happenings in their nervous systems. We call that system of agreements *language*. For example, we who speak English have been so trained that, when our nervous systems register the presence of a certain kind of animal, we may make the following noise: "There's a cat." Anyone hearing us expects to find that, by looking in the same direction, he will experience a similar event in his nervous system—one that will lead him to make an almost identical noise. Again, we have been so trained that when we are conscious of wanting food, we make the noise "I'm hungry."

There is, as has been said, *no necessary connection between the symbol and that which is symbolized.* Just as men can wear yachting costumes without ever having been near a yacht, so they can make the noise "I'm hungry" without being hungry. Furthermore, just as social rank can be symbolized by feathers in the hair, by tattooing on the breast, by gold ornaments on the watch chain, or by a thousand different devices according to the culture we live in, so the fact of being hungry can be symbolized by a thousand different noises according to the culture we live in: *"J'ai faim"*, or *"Es hungert mich"*, or *"Ho appetito"*, or *"Hara ga hetta"*, and so on.

However obvious these facts may appear at first glance, they are actually not so obvious as they seem except when we take special pains to think about the subject. Symbols and things symbolized are independent of each other; nevertheless, we all have a way of feeling as if, and sometimes acting as if, there were necessary connections. For example, there is the vague sense we all have that foreign languages are inherently absurd: foreigners have such funny names for things, and why can't they call things by their right names? This feeling exhibits itself most strongly in those tourists who seem to believe that they can make the natives of any country understand English if they shout loud enough. Like the little boy who was reported to have said, "Pigs are called pigs because they are such dirty animals", they feel that the symbol is inherently connected in some way with the thing symbolized. Then there are the people who feel that since snakes are "nasty, slimy creatures" (incidentally, snakes are *not* slimy), the word "snake" is a *nasty, slimy word.*

The Pitfalls of Drama

Naïveté regarding the symbolic process extends to symbols other than words, of course. In the case of drama (stage, movies, television), there appear to be people in almost every audience who never quite fully realize that a play is a set of fictional, symbolic representations. An actor is one who symbolizes other people, real or imagined. In a movie some years ago, Fredric March enacted with great skill the role of a drunkard. Florence Eldridge (Mrs. March) reports that for a long time thereafter she got letters of advice and sympathy from women who said that they too were married to alcoholics. Also some years ago it was reported that when Edward G. Robinson, who used to play gangster roles with extraordinary vividness, visited Chicago, local hoodlums would telephone him at his hotel to pay their professional respects.

One is reminded of the actor, playing the role of a villain in a travelling theatrical troupe, who, at a particularly tense moment in the play, was shot by an excited cowpuncher in the audience. But this kind of confusion does not seem to be confined to unsophisticated theatregoers. In recent times, Paul Muni, after playing the part of Clarence Darrow in *Inherit the Wind*, was invited to address the American Bar Association; Ralph Bellamy, after playing the role of Franklin D. Roosevelt in *Sunrise at Campobello,* was invited by several colleges to speak on Roosevelt. Also, there are those astonishing patriots who rushed to the recruiting offices to help defend the nation when, on October 30, 1938, the United States was "invaded" by an "army from Mars" in a radio dramatization.

The Word Is Not the Thing

The above, however, are only the more striking examples of confused attitudes toward words and symbols. There would be little point in mentioning them if we were *uniformly and permanently aware* of the independence of symbols from things symbolized. But we are not. Most of us have, in some area or other of our thinking, improper habits of evaluation. For this, society itself is often to blame: most societies systematically encourage, concerning certain topics, the habitual confusion of symbols with things symbolized.

The habitual confusion of symbols with things symbolized, whether on the part of individuals or societies, is serious enough at all levels of culture to provide a perennial human problem. But with the rise of modern communications systems, the problem of confusing verbal symbols with realities assumes peculiar urgency. We are constantly being talked at by teachers, preachers, salesmen, public-relations counsels, governmental agencies, and moving-picture sound tracks. The cries of the hawkers of soft drinks, detergents, and laxatives pursue us into our homes, thanks to radio and television—and in some houses the sets are never turned off from morning to night. The mailman brings direct-mail advertising. Billboards confront us on the highway, and we even take portable radios with us to the seashore.

We live in an environment shaped and largely created by hitherto unparalleled semantic influences: mass-circulation newspapers and magazines which are given to reflecting, in a shocking number of cases, the weird prejudices and obsessions of their publishers and owners; radio programs, both local and network, almost completely dominated by commercial motives; public-relations counsels who are simply highly paid craftsmen in the art of manipulating and reshaping our semantic environment in ways favourable to their clients. It is an exciting environment, but fraught with danger: it is only a slight exaggeration to say that Hitler conquered Austria by radio. Today, the full resources of advertising agencies, public-relations counsels, radio, television, and slanted news stories are brought to bear in order to influence our decisions in election campaigns.

Citizens of a modern society need, therefore, more than that ordinary "common sense" which has been defined as that which tells you that the world is flat. They need to be systematically aware of the powers and limitations of symbols, especially words, if they are to guard against being driven into complete bewilderment by the complexity of their semantic environment. The first of the principles governing symbols is this: The symbol is NOT the thing symbolized; the word is NOT the thing; the map is NOT the territory it stands for.

Maps and Territories

There is a sense in which we all live in two worlds. First, we live in the world of happenings which we know at first hand. This is an extremely small world, consisting only of that continuum of the things that we have actually seen, felt or heard—the flow of events constantly passing before our senses. So far as this world of personal experience is concerned, Africa, South America, Asia, Ottawa, New York or Los Angeles, do not exist if we have never been to these places. Lyndon B. Johnson is only a name if we have never seen him. When we ask ourselves how much we know at first hand, we discover that we know very little indeed.

Most of our knowledge, acquired from parents, friends, schools, newspapers, books, conversation, speeches, and television, is received *verbally*. All our knowledge of history, for example, comes to us only in words. The only proof we have that the Battle of Waterloo ever took place is that we have had reports to that effect. These reports are not given us by people who saw it happen, but are based on other reports: reports of reports of reports, which go back ultimately to the first-hand reports given by people who did see it happening. It is through reports, then, and through reports of reports, that we receive most knowledge: about government, about what is happening in Viet Nam, about what picture is showing at the downtown theatre—in fact, about anything that we do not know through direct experience.

Now this verbal world ought to stand in relation to the world of experience as a *map* does to the *territory* it is supposed to represent. If a child grows to adulthood with a verbal world in his head which corresponds fairly closely to the world that he finds around him in his widening experience, he is in relatively small danger of being shocked or hurt by what he finds, because his verbal world has told him what, more or less, to expect. He is prepared for life. If, however, he grows up with a false map in his head—that is, with a head crammed with error and superstition—he will constantly be running into trouble, wasting his efforts, and acting like a fool. He will not be adjusted to the world as it is; he may, if the lack of adjustment is serious, end up in a mental hospital.

Some of the follies we commit because of false maps in our heads are so commonplace that we do not even think of them as remarkable. There are those who protect themselves from accidents by carrying a rabbit's foot. Some refuse to sleep on the thirteenth floor of hotels—a situation so common that most big hotels, even in the capitals of our scientific culture, skip "13" in numbering their floors. Some plan their lives on the basis of astrological predictions. Some play fifty-to-one shots on the basis of dream books. Some hope to make their teeth whiter by changing their brand of tooth paste. All such people are living in verbal worlds that bear little, if any, resemblance to the world of actuality.

We all inherit a great deal of useless knowledge, and a great deal of misinformation and error (maps that were formerly thought to be accurate), so that there is always a portion of what we have been told that must be discarded. But the cultural heritage of our civilization that is transmitted to us—our socially pooled knowledge, both scientific and humane—has been valued principally because we have believed that it gives us accurate maps of experience. The analogy of verbal worlds to maps is an important one and will be referred to elsewhere in this book. It should be noticed at this point, however, that there are two ways of getting false maps of the world into our heads; first, by having them given to us; second, by creating them ourselves when we misread the true maps given to us.

■ Applications

1. What makes a map "good" or "bad"? If an outline map of Canada had the following cities arranged in this fashion (the left standing for the west):

   Winnipeg   Montreal   Vancouver

   people would say that the map was incorrect. What should be done to correct it? Is it simply a matter of putting the names in the "right" places? How do we know what the "right" places are?

2. In George Orwell's novel *1984,* society has accepted three slogans:

   WAR IS PEACE
   FREEDOM IS SLAVERY
   IGNORANCE IS STRENGTH

   Discuss the possible meanings of these paradoxical statements. Cite a number of slogans current in our society and consider their implications; e.g., victory or death.

3. Select a word which has a strong emotional charge (negative or positive), such as "spider", "math", "blonde", "Negro", and write a paper describing the feelings which you associate with the term. To what extent are they based on personal experience and to what extent on verbal reports?

CHAPTER SEVEN

Reports, Inferences, Judgments

For the purposes of the interchange of information, the basic symbolic act is the *report* of what we have seen, heard or felt: "There is a ditch on each side of the road." "You can get those at Smith's hardware store for $2.75." "There aren't any fish on that side of the lake, but there are on this side." Then there are reports of reports: "The longest waterfall in the world is Victoria Falls in Rhodesia." "The Battle of Hastings took place in 1066." "The papers say that there was a smash-up on Highway 41 near Evansville." Reports adhere to the following rules: first, they are *capable of verification*; second, they *exclude*, as far as possible, *inferences* and *judgments*.

Verifiability

Reports are verifiable. We may not always be able to verify them ourselves, since we cannot track down the evidence for every piece of history we know, nor can we all go to Evansville to see the remains of the smash-up before they are cleared away. But if we are roughly agreed on the names of things, on what constitutes a "foot", "yard", "bushel", and so on, and on how to measure time, there is relatively little danger of our misunderstanding each other. Even in a world such as we have today, in which everybody seems to be quarrelling with everybody else, *we still to a surprising degree trust each other's reports*. We ask directions of total strangers when we are travelling. We follow directions on road signs without being suspicious of the people who put them up. We read books of information about science, mathematics, automotive engineering, travel, geography, the history of costume, and other such factual matters, and we usually assume that the author is doing his best to tell us as truly as he can what he knows. And we are safe in so assuming most of the time. With the interest given today in the discussion of biased newspapers, propagandists, and the general untrustworthiness of many of the communications we receive, we are likely to forget that we still have an enormous amount of reliable information available and that deliberate misinformation, except in warfare, is still more the exception than the rule. The desire for self-preservation that compelled men to evolve means for the exchange of information also compels them to regard the giving of false information as profoundly reprehensible.

At its highest development, the language of reports is the language of science. By "highest development" we mean greatest general usefulness. Presbyterian and Catholic, workingman and capitalist, East German and West German, *agree* on the meanings of such symbols as *2 × 2 = 4, 100° C., HNO₃, 3:35 a.m., 1940* A.D., *1000 kilowatts, Quercus agrifolia,* and so on. But how, it may be asked, can there be agreement about even this much among people who disagree about political philosophies, ethical ideas, religious beliefs, and the survival of my business *versus* the survival of yours? The answer is that circumstances *compel men to agree,* whether they wish to or not.

The language of reports, then, including the more accurate reports of science, is "map" language, and because it gives us reasonably accurate representations of the "territory", it enables us to get work done. Such language may often be dull or uninteresting reading: one does not usually read logarithmic tables or telephone directories for entertainment. But we could not get along without it. There are numberless occasions in the talking and writing we do in everyday life that *require that we state things in such a way that everybody will be able to understand and agree with our formulation.*

Inferences

We rely in everyday life and in science as much on *inferences* as on reports; in some areas of thought—for example, geology, paleontology, and nuclear physics—reports are the foundations, but inferences (and inferences upon inferences) are the main body of the science. An inference, as we shall use the term, is *a statement about the unknown made on the basis of the known.* We may *infer* from the material and cut of a woman's clothes her wealth or social position; we may *infer* from the character of the ruins the origin of the fire that destroyed the building; we may *infer* from a man's calloused hands the nature of his occupation; we may *infer* from a senator's vote on an armaments bill his attitude toward Russia; we may *infer* from the structure of the land the path of a prehistoric glacier; we may *infer* from a halo on an unexposed photographic plate that it has been in the vicinity of radioactive materials; we may *infer* from the sound of an engine the condition of its connecting rods. Inferences may be carelessly or carefully made. They may be made on the basis of a broad background of previous experience with the subject matter, or no experience at all. For example, the inferences a good mechanic can make about the internal condition of a motor by listening to it are often startlingly accurate, while the inferences made by an amateur (if he tries to make any) may be entirely wrong. But the common characteristic of inferences is that they are statements about matters which are not directly known, statements made on the basis of what has been observed. When we say, "He was angry", we are not reporting; we are making an inference from such observable facts as the following: "He pounded his fist on the table; he swore; he threw the telephone directory at his stenographer." In this particular example, the inference appears to be fairly safe; nevertheless, it is important to remember, especially for the purposes of training oneself, that it is an inference. Such expressions as "He thought a lot of himself", "He was scared of girls", and "He has an inferiority complex", made on the basis of casual social observation, are highly inferential. We should keep in mind their inferential character and, in reports, should substitute for them such statements as "He rarely spoke to subordinates in the plant", "I saw him at a party, and he never danced except when one of the girls asked him to", and "He wouldn't apply for the scholarship although I believe he could have won it easily."

In spite of the exercise of every caution in avoiding inferences and reporting only what is seen and experienced, we all remain prone to error, since the making of inferences is a quick, almost automatic process. We may watch a car weaving as it goes down the road and say, "Look at that *drunken driver*", although what we *see* is only *the irregular motion of the car*.

All this is not to say that we should never make inferences, however. The inability to make inferences is itself a sign of mental disorder as alienists have discovered. Hence the question is not whether or not we make inferences; the question is whether or not we are aware of the inferences we make.

Judgments

By judgments, we mean *all expressions of the writer's approval or disapproval of the occurrences, persons or objects he is describing.* For example, a report cannot say, "It was a wonderful car", but must say something like this: "It has been driven 50,000 miles and has never required any repairs." Again statements such as "Jack lied to us" must be suppressed in favour of the more verifiable statement, "Jack told us he didn't have the keys to his car with him. However, when he pulled a handkerchief out of his pocket a few minutes later, a bunch of car keys fell out." Also a report may not say, "The M.L.A. was stubborn, defiant, and unco-operative", or "The M.L.A. courageously stood by his principles"; it must say instead, "The M.L.A.'s vote was the only one against the bill."

Many people regard statements such as the following as statements of "fact": "Jack *lied* to us", "Jerry is a *thief*", "Tommy is *clever*." As ordinarily employed, however, the word "lied" involves first an inference (that Jack knew otherwise and deliberately misstated the facts) and second a judgment (that the speaker disapproves of what he has inferred that Jack did). In the other two instances, we may substitute such expressions as "Jerry was convicted of theft and served two years in prison", and "Tommy plays the violin, leads his class in school, and is captain of the debating team." After all, to say of a man that he is a "thief" is to say in effect, "He has stolen *and will steal again*"—which is more of a prediction than a report. Even to say, "He has stolen", is to make an inference (and simultaneously to pass a judgment) on an act about which there may be difference of opinion among those who have examined the evidence upon which the conviction was obtained. But to say that he was "convicted of theft" is to make a statement capable of being agreed upon through verification in court and prison records.

Scientific verifiability rests upon the external observation of facts, not upon the heaping up of judgments. If one person says, "Peter is a deadbeat", and another says, "I think so too", the statement has not been verified. In court cases, considerable trouble is sometimes caused by witnesses who cannot distinguish their judgments from the facts upon which those judgments are based. Cross-examinations under these circumstances go something like this:

WITNESS: That dirty double-crosser Jacobs ratted on me.
DEFENSE ATTORNEY: Your honour, I object.
JUDGE: Objection sustained. (Witness's remark is stricken from the record.) Now, try to tell the court exactly what happened.
WITNESS: He double-crossed me, the dirty, lying rat!
DEFENSE ATTORNEY: Your honour, I object!
JUDGE: Objection sustained. (Witness's remark is again stricken from the record.) Will the witness try to stick to the facts.
WITNESS: But I'm telling you the facts, your honour. He did double-cross me.

This can continue indefinitely unless the cross-examiner exercises some ingenuity in order to get at the facts behind the judgment. To the witness it is a "fact" that he was "double-crossed". Often patient questioning is required before the factual bases of the judgment are revealed.

Many words, of course, simultaneously convey a report and a judgment on the fact reported. For the purposes of a report as here defined, these should be avoided. Instead of "sneaked in", one might say "entered quietly"; instead of "politicians", "M.L.A.'s" or "aldermen" or "candidates for office"; instead of "bureaucrat", "public official"; instead of "tramp", "homeless unemployed"; instead of "dictatorial set-up", "centralized authority"; instead of "crackpots", "holders of nonconformist views". A newspaper reporter, for example, is not permitted to write, "A crowd of suckers came to listen to Senator Smith last evening in that rickety firetrap and ex-dive that disfigures the south edge of town." Instead he says, "Between seventy-five and a hundred people heard an address last evening by Senator Smith at the Evergreen Gardens near the South Side city limits."

Snarl-Words and Purr-Words

Throughout this book, it is important to remember that we are not considering language as an isolated phenomenon. Our concern, instead, is with language in action—language in the full context of the nonlinguistic events which are its setting. The making of noises with the vocal organs is a muscular activity and, like other muscular activities, often involuntary. Our responses to a powerful stimuli, such as to things that make us very angry, are a complex of muscular and physiological events: the contracting of fighting muscles, the increase of blood pressure, a change in body chemistry, clutching of our hair, *and* the making of noises, such as growls and snarls. We are a little too dignified, perhaps, to growl like dogs, but we do the next best thing and substitute series of words, such as "You dirty double-crosser!", "The filthy scum!" Similarly, if we are pleasurably agitated, we may, instead of purring or wagging the tail, say things like "She's the sweetest girl in all the world!"

Speeches such as these are, as direct expressions of approval or disapproval, judgments in their simplest form. They may be said to be human equivalents of snarling and purring. "She's the sweetest girl in all the world" is not a statement about the girl; it is a purr. This seems to be a fairly obvious fact; nevertheless, it is surprising how often, when such a statement is made, both the speaker and the hearer feel that something has been said about the girl. This error is especially common in the interpretation of utterances of orators and editorialists in some of their more excited denunciations of "Reds", "greedy monopolists", "Wall Street", "radicals", "foreign ideologies", and in their more fulsome dithyrambs about "our way of life". Constantly, because of the impressive sound of the words, the elaborate structure of the sentences, and the appearance of intellectual progression, we get the feeling that something is being said about something. On closer examination, however, we discover that such utterances only tell us about the feelings of those who make them; they are not reports describing conditions in the world.

Of course, we should not dismiss such statements as unimportant. We should simply be careful to allocate their meaning correctly by seeing them as revelations of states of mind: judgments in fact.

How Judgments Stop Thought

A judgment ("He is a fine boy", "It was a beautiful service", "Baseball is a healthful sport", "She is an awful bore") ought to be a conclusion, summing up a large number of previously observed facts. The reader is probably familiar with the fact that students almost always have difficulty in writing themes of the required length because their ideas give out after a paragraph or two. The reason for this is that those early paragraphs contain so many judgments that there is little left to be said. When the conclusions are carefully excluded, however, and observed facts are given instead, there is never any trouble about the length of papers; in fact, they tend to become too long, since inexperienced writers, when told to give facts, often give far more than are necessary, because they lack discrimination between the important and the trivial.

Still another consequence of judgments early in the course of a written exercise—and this applies also to hasty judgments in everyday thought—is the temporary blindness they induce. When, for example, a description starts with the words, "He was a real Madison Avenue executive", or "She was a typical sorority girl", if we continue writing at all, we must make all our later statements consistent with those judgments. The result is that all the individual characteristics of this particular "executive" or this particular "sorority girl" are lost sight of; and the rest of the account is likely to deal not with observed facts but with the writer's private notion (based on previously read stories, movies, pictures, and so forth) of what "Madison Avenue executives" or "typical sorority girls" are like. The premature judgment, that is, often prevents us from seeing what is directly in front of us, so that clichés take the place of fresh description.

Slanting

In the course of writing reports of personal experiences, it will be found that in spite of all endeavours to keep judgments out, some will creep in. An account of a man, for example, may go like this: "He had apparently not shaved for several days, and his face and hands were covered with grime. His shoes were torn, and his coat, which was several sizes too small for him, was spotted with dried clay." Now, in spite of the fact that no judgment has been stated, a very obvious one is implied. Let us contrast this with another description of the same man. "Although his face was bearded and neglected, his eyes were clear, and he looked straight ahead as he walked rapidly down the road. He seemed very tall; perhaps the fact that his coat was too small for him emphasized that impression. He was carrying a book under his left arm, and a small terrier ran at his heels." In this example, the impression about the same man is considerably changed, simply by the inclusion of new details and the subordination of unfavourable ones. The process of selecting details favourable and unfavourable to the subject being described may be termed *slanting*. Slanting gives no explicit judgments, but it differs from reporting in that it makes certain judgments inescapable.

How, then, can we ever give an impartial report? The answer is, of course, that we cannot attain complete impartiality while we use the language of everyday life. Even with the very impersonal language of science, the task is sometimes difficult. Nevertheless, we can, by being aware of the favourable or unfavourable feelings that certain words and facts can arouse, attain enough impartiality for practical purposes. Such awareness enables us to balance the implied favourable and unfavourable judgments against each other and so redress the balance.

On the other hand, slanting may be employed with the deliberate aim of damaging reputations. One-sided or biased slanting of this kind, not uncommon in private gossip, and all too common in the interpretative reporting of newspapers and newsmagazines, can be described as a technique of lying without actually telling any lies.

Nevertheless, the writer who is neither an advocate nor an opponent avoids slanting, except when he is seeking special literary effects. The avoidance of slanting is not only a matter of being fair and impartial; it is also a matter of making good maps of the territory of experience. The individual with genuine skill in writing, one who has imagination and insight, can look at the same subject from a number of points of view in the interests of fullness and solidity as the following example shows:

Adam turned to look at him. It was, in a way, as though this were the first time he had laid eyes on him. He saw the strong, black shoulders under the red-check calico, the long arms lying loose, forward over the knees, the strong hands, seamed and calloused, holding the reins. He looked at the face. The thrust of the jawbone was strong, but the lips were heavy and low, with a piece of chewed straw hanging out one side of the mouth. The eyelids were pendulous, slightly swollen-looking, and the eyes bloodshot. Those eyes, Adam knew, could sharpen to a quick, penetrating, assessing glance. But now looking at that slack, somnolent face, he could scarcely believe that.

—ROBERT PENN WARREN: *Wilderness*

■ Applications

I Here are a number of statements which the reader may attempt to classify as judgments, inferences or reports. Since the distinctions are not always clear-cut, a one-word answer will not ordinarily be adequate. Note that we are concerned here with the nature of the statements, not the truth or falsity of them; for example, the statement, "Water freezes at 10° centigrade", is, although inaccurate, a report.

1. It is raining.
2. It must be raining.
3. He is a typical bureaucrat.
4. Look at her red hair; she must have a quick temper.
5. Research scientists have proved that *Snifflego* destroyed 84% of bacteria with which it came in contact. Get some today for the relief of *your* cold.
6. Once a thief, always a thief.
7. The freak weather we have had is caused by atomic explosions.
8. Earth has not anything to show more fair:
   Dull would he be of soul who could pass by
   A sight so touching in its majesty:

   WILLIAM WORDSWORTH

9. The dog is man's best friend.
10. Our antiquated and inefficient jury system allows all sorts of criminals to escape the penalties for their misdeeds.

II "A youth and a man were killed and three teenagers seriously injured early today in two auto accidents." Write:

1. A *report* of these accidents, inventing names and places.
2. A *slanted report* for a newspaper campaigning for stricter laws against juvenile delinquency. (Be sure to use factual statements only, letting your reader make his own inferences and judgments.)

CHAPTER EIGHT

The Language of Social Feelings

Noises as Expression

What above all complicates the problems of interpretation is the fact that informative uses of language are intimately fused with older and deeper functions of language, so that only a small proportion of utterances in everyday life can be described as purely informative. We have every reason to believe that the ability to use language for strictly informative purposes was developed relatively late in the course of linguistic evolution. Long before we developed language as we now know it, we probably made, like the lower animals, all sorts of cries, expressive of such internal conditions as hunger, fear, loneliness, desire, and triumph. We can recognize a variety of such noises and the conditions of which they are symptoms in our domestic animals. Gradually such noises seem to have become more and more differentiated; consciousness expanded. Grunts and gibberings became language. Therefore, although we have developed language in which accurate reports may be given, we almost universally tend to *express* our internal conditions *first*, then to follow up with a report if necessary: "Ow! (expression) My tooth hurts (report)." Many utterances are, as we have seen with regard to "snarl-words" and "purr-words", vocal equivalents of expressive gestures, such as crying in pain, baring the teeth in anger, nuzzling to express friendliness, dancing with delight, and so on. When words are used as vocal equivalents of expressive gestures, we shall say that language is being used in *presymbolic* ways. These presymbolic uses of language coexist with our symbolic systems, and the talking we do in everyday life is a thorough blending of symbolic and presymbolic.

Indeed, the presymbolic factors in everyday language are always most apparent in expressions of strong feeling of any kind. If we carelessly step off a curb when a car is coming, it doesn't much matter whether someone yells, "Look out!" or "Kiwotsuke!" or "Hey!" or "Prends garde!" or simply utters a scream, so long as whatever noise is made is uttered loudly enough to alarm us. It is the fear expressed in the *loudness* and *tone* of the cry that conveys the necessary sensations, and not the words. Similarly, commands given sharply and angrily usually produce quicker results than the same commands uttered tonelessly. The quality of the voice itself, that is to say, has a power of expressing feelings that is almost independent of the symbols used. We can say, "I hope you'll come to see us again", in a way that clearly indicates that we hope the visitor never comes back.

Very small infants understand the love, the warmth or the irritation in a mother's voice long before they are able to understand her words. Most children retain this sensitivity to presymbolic elements in language. It even survives in some adults; they are the people credited with "intuition" or "unusual tact". Their talent lies in their ability to interpret tones of voice, facial expressions, and other symptoms of the internal condition of the speaker: they listen not only to *what* is said, but to *how* it is said. On the other hand, people who have spent much of their lives in the study of *written* symbols (scientists, intellectuals, bookkeepers) tend to be relatively deaf to everything but the surface sense of the words.

Noise for Noise's Sake

Sometimes we talk simply for the sake of hearing ourselves talk; that is, for the same reason that we play golf or dance. The activity gives us a pleasant sense of being alive. Children prattling, adults singing in the bathtub, are alike enjoying the sound of their voices. Sometimes large groups make noises together, as in group singing, group recitation, or group chanting, for similar presymbolic reasons. In all this, the significance of the words used is almost completely irrelevant. We may, for example, chant the most lugubrious words about a desire to be carried back to a childhood home in old Virginny, when in actuality we have never been there and haven't the slightest intention of going.

What we call social conversation is again largely presymbolic in character. When we are at a tea or dinner party, for example, we all have to talk—about anything: the weather, the performance of the B.C. Lions, James Michener's latest book, or Natalie Wood's recent picture. Rarely, except among very good friends, are the remarks made during these conversations important enough to be worth making for their informative value. Nevertheless, it is regarded as rude to remain silent. Indeed, in such matters as greetings and farewells—"Good morning"—"Lovely day"—"And how's your family these days?"—"It was a pleasure meeting you"—"Do look us up the next time you're in town"—it is regarded as a social error not to say these things even if we do not mean them. There are numberless daily situations in which we talk simply because it would be impolite not to. From these social practices it is possible to state, as a general principle, that *the prevention of silence is itself an important function of speech*, and that it is completely impossible for us in society to talk only when we "have something to say".

This presymbolic talk for talk's sake is, like the cries of animals, a form of activity. We talk together about nothing at all and thereby establish friendships. The purpose of the talk is not the communication of information, as the symbols used would seem to imply ("I see the Dodgers are out in the lead again"), but the establishment of communion. Human beings have many ways of establishing communion among themselves: breaking bread together, playing games together, working together. But talking together is the most easily arranged of all these forms of collective activity. The *togetherness* of the talking, then, is the most important element in social conversation; the subject matter is only secondary.

There is a principle at work, therefore, in the selection of subject matter. Since the purpose of this kind of talk is the establishment of communion, *we are careful to select subjects about which agreement is immediately possible*. Consider, for example, what happens when two strangers feel the necessity or the desire to talk to each other:

"Nice day, isn't it?"
"It certainly is." (Agreement on one point has been established. It is safe to proceed.)
"Altogether, it's been a fine summer."

"Indeed it has. We had a nice spring too." (Agreement on two points having been established, the second party invites agreement on a third point.)

"Yes, it was a lovely spring." (Third agreement reached.)

The togetherness, therefore, is not merely in the talking itself, but in the opinions expressed. Having agreed on the weather, we go on to further agreements—that it is nice farming country around here, that it certainly is scandalous how prices are going up, that Toronto is certainly an interesting place to visit but it would be awful to have to live there, and so on. *With each new agreement, no matter how commonplace or how obvious, the fear and suspicion of the stranger wears away, and the possibility of friendship enlarges.* When further conversation reveals that we have friends or political views or artistic tastes or hobbies in common, a friend is made, and genuine communication and co-operation can begin.

Maintenance of Communication Lines

Such presymbolic uses of language not only establish new lines of communication, but keep old lines open. Old friends like to talk even when they have nothing especially to say to each other. In the same way that long-distance telephone operators, ship radio officers, and army signal corps outposts chatter with each other even when there are no official messages to communicate, so do people who live in the same household or work in the same office continue to talk to each other even when there is nothing much to say. The purpose in both cases seems to be partly to relieve tedium, but partly, and more importantly, to keep the lines of communication open. And how does one know that the lines of communication are still open unless one keeps them at work? When a sound engineer says into a microphone, "One . . . two . . . three . . . four . . . testing . . ." he isn't saying anything much. But it is nevertheless important at times that he say it.

Language in Ritual

Sermons, political caucuses, conventions, pep rallies, and other ceremonial gatherings illustrate the fact that all groups—religious, political, patriotic, scientific, and occupational—like to gather together at intervals for the purpose of sharing certain accustomed activities, wearing special costumes (vestments in religious organizations, regalia in lodges, uniforms in patriotic societies, and so on), eating together (banquets), displaying the flags, ribbons or emblems of their group, and marching in processions. Among these ritual activities is always included a number of speeches, either traditionally worded or specially composed for the occasion, whose principal function is *not* to give the audience information it did not have before, *not* to create new ways of feeling, but something else altogther.

Let us look at what happens at a pep rally such as precedes college football games. The members of "our team" are "introduced" to a crowd that already knows them. Called upon to make speeches, the players mutter a few incoherent and often ungrammatical remarks, which are received with wild applause. The leaders of the rally make fantastic promises about the mayhem to be performed on the opposing team the next day. The crowd utters "cheers", which normally consist of animalistic noises arranged in extremely primitive rhythms. *No one comes out any wiser or better informed than he was before he went in.*

To some extent religious ceremonies are equally puzzling at first glance. The priest or clergyman in charge utters set speeches, *often in a language incomprehensible to the congregation* (Hebrew in orthodox Jewish synagogues, Latin in the Roman Catholic churches, Sanskrit in Chinese and Japanese temples), with the result that, as often as not, no information whatsoever is communicated to those present.

If we approach these linguistic events from a detached point of view, and if we also examine our own reactions when we enter into the spirit of such occasions, we cannot help observing that, whatever the words used in ritual utterance may signify, we often do not think very much about their signification during the course of the ritual. As children we are taught to repeat such sets of words before we can understand them, and many of us continue to say them for the rest of our lives without bothering about their signification. Only the superficial, however, will dismiss these facts as "simply showing what fools human beings are". We cannot regard such utterances as "meaningless", because they have a genuine effect upon us. We may come out of church, for example, with no clear memory of what the sermon was about, but with a sense nevertheless that the service has somehow "done us good".

What is the "good" that is done us in ritual utterances? It is the *reaffirmation of social cohesion*: the Christian feels closer to his fellow-Christians, the Elk feels more united with his brother Elks, the American feels more American, and the Frenchman more French, as the result of these rituals. Societies are held together by such bonds of common reactions to sets of linguistic stimuli.

Ritualistic utterances, therefore, whether made up of words that have symbolic significance at other times, of words in foreign or obsolete tongues, or of meaningless syllables, may be regarded as consisting in large part of presymbolic uses of language: that is, *accustomed sets of noises* which convey no information, but to which feelings (often group feelings) are attached. Such utterances rarely make sense to anyone not a member of the group. The abraca-dabra of a lodge meeting is absurd to anyone not a member of the lodge. When language becomes ritual, that is to say, its effect be-comes to a considerable extent independent of whatever significa-tion the words once possessed.

To understand the presymbolic elements that enter into our everyday language is extremely important. We cannot restrict our speech to the giving of factual information and to the asking of questions; we cannot confine ourselves strictly to statements that are literally true, or we should often be unable to say even "Pleased to meet you" when the occasion demanded. The intellectually per-snickety often tell us that we ought to say what we mean and mean what we say, and talk only when we have something to talk about. These are, of course, impossible prescriptions.

Ignorance of the existence of these presymbolic uses of language is not so common among uneducated people (who often perceive such things intuitively) as it is among the educated. The educated often listen to the chatter at teas and receptions, and conclude from the triviality of the conversation that all the guests (except them-selves) are fools. They may discover that people often come away from church services without any clear memory of the sermon and conclude that churchgoers are either fools or hypocrites. Listening to political oratory, they may wonder "how anybody can believe such rot", and then conclude that people in general are so unintelligent that democracy is unworkable. Almost all such gloomy conclusions about the stupidity or hypocrisy of our friends and neighbours are unjustifiable on such evidence, because they usually come from applying the standards of symbolic language to linguistic events that are either partly or wholly presymbolic in character.

One further illustration may make this clearer. Let us suppose that we are on the roadside struggling with a flat tire. A not-very-bright-looking but friendly youth comes up and asks, "Got a flat tire?" If we insist upon interpreting his words literally, we will regard this as an extremely silly question and our answer may be, "Can't you see I have, you dumb ox?" If we pay no attention to what the words say, however, and understand his meaning, we will return his gesture of friendly interest by showing equal friendliness, and in a short while he may be helping us to change the tire.* In a similar way, many situations in life demand that we pay no attention to what the words say, since the meaning may often be a great deal more intelligent and intelligible than the surface *sense* of the words themselves. A great deal of our pessimism about the world, about humanity, and about democracy probably derives from the fact that unconsciously we apply the standards of symbolic language to presymbolic utterances.

■ Applications

I Comment on the meaning of the following utterances. In your assessment, take into account both informational and psychological aspects.

1. I'm delighted to meet you.

* Dr. Karl Menninger, in *Love Against Hate* (1942), comments on this passage and offers the following translation of "Got a flat tire?" in terms of its psychological meaning: "Hello—I see you are in trouble. I'm a stranger to you but I might be your friend now that I have a chance to be if I had any assurance that my friendship would be welcomed. Are you approachable? Are you a decent fellow? Would you appreciate it if I helped you? I would like to do so but I don't want to be rebuffed. This is what my voice sounds like. What does your voice sound like?" Why does not the youth simply say directly, "I would be glad to help you"? Dr. Menninger explains: "But people are too timid and mutually distrustful to be so direct. *They want to hear one another's voices. People need assurance that others are just like themselves.*" (Italics added.)

2. Lovely weather, isn't it?
3. Twas brillig and the slithy toves
   Did gyre and gimble in the wabe;
   All mimsy were the borogroves
   And the mome raths outgrabe
4. How do you like my new hat? Charming, isn't it?
5. Fore!
6. Good morning; nasty weather we're having.
7. Oremus. Flectamus genua. Levate.
   Protector noster aspice, Deus.
8. Rah! Rah! Rah!
   Zizz boom bah!
   Chuck-a-lack-a Chuck-a-lack-a
   Motor-car.

II In a carefully organized paper discuss the kinds of utterance employed by the members of any group of whom you have first-hand knowledge. Try to go beyond the surface meaning of the statements to their social implications.

CHAPTER NINE

The Language of Social Control

Making Things Happen

The most interesting and perhaps least understood relationship between words and the world is that between words and future events. When we say, for example, "Come here!" we are not describing the world about us, nor are we merely expressing our feelings; we are trying to *make something happen*. What we call "commands", "pleas", "requests", and "orders" are the simplest ways we have of making things happen by means of words.

There are, however, more roundabout ways. When we say, for example, "Our candidate is a great man", we are of course making an enthusiastic purr about him, but we may also be influencing other people to vote for him. Again, when we say, "Our war against the enemy is God's war. God wills that we must triumph", we are saying something which, though unverifiable, may influence others to help in the prosecution of the war. Or if we merely state as a fact, "Milk contains vitamins", we may be influencing others to buy milk.

Consider, too, such a statement as "I'll meet you tomorrow at two o'clock in front of the Palace Theatre." Such a statement about *future* events can only be made, it will be observed, in a system in which symbols are independent of things symbolized. The future, like the recorded past, is a specifically human dimension. To a dog, the expression "hamburger *tomorrow*" is meaningless—he will look at you expectantly, hoping for the extensional meaning of the word "hamburger" to be produced *now*. Squirrels, to be sure, store food for "next winter", but the fact that they store food regardless of whether or not their needs are adequately provided for demonstrates that such behaviour (usually called "instinctive") is governed neither by symbols nor by other interpreted stimuli. Human beings are unique in their ability to react meaningfully to such expressions as "next Saturday", "on our next wedding anniversary", "twenty years after date I promise to pay", "some day, perhaps five hundred years from now". That is to say, maps can be made, even though the territories they stand for are not yet actualities. Guiding ourselves by means of such maps of territories-to-be, we can impose a certain predictability upon future events.

With words, therefore, we influence and to an enormous extent *control future events*. It is for this reason that writers write; preachers preach; employers, parents, and teachers scold; propagandists send out news releases; statesmen give addresses. All of them, for various reasons, are trying to influence our conduct—sometimes for our good, sometimes for their own. These attempts to control, direct or influence the future actions of fellow human beings with words may be termed *directive uses of language*.

Now it is obvious that if directive language is going to direct, it cannot be dull or uninteresting. If it is to influence our conduct, it *must* make use of every effective element in language: dramatic variations in tone of voice, rhyme and rhythm, purring and snarling, words with strong affective connotations, endless repetition. If meaningless noises will move the audience, meaningless noises must be made; if facts move them, facts must be given; if noble ideals move them, we must make our proposals appear noble; if they will respond only to fear, we must scare them stiff.

The nature of the affective means used in directive language is limited, of course, by the nature of our aims. If we are trying to direct people to be more kindly toward each other, we obviously do not want to arouse feelings of cruelty or hate. If we are trying to direct people to think and act more intelligently, we obviously should not use subrational appeals. If we are trying to direct people to lead better lives, we use affective appeals that arouse their finest feelings. Included among directive utterances, therefore, are many of the greatest and most treasured works of literature: the Christian and Buddhist scriptures, the writings of Confucius, Milton's *Aeropagitica*, and Lincoln's Gettysburg Address.

There are, however, occasions when it is felt that language is not sufficiently affective by itself to produce the results wanted. We supplement directive language, therefore, by *nonverbal affective appeals* of many kinds. We supplement the words "Come here" by gesturing with our hands. Advertisers are not content with saying in words how beautiful their products will make us; they supplement their words by the use of coloured inks and by pictures. Newspapers are not content with saying that communism is a menace; they supply political cartoons depicting communists as criminally insane people placing sticks of dynamite under magnificent buildings labelled "American way of life". The affective appeal of sermons and religious exhortations may be supplemented by costumes, incense, processions, choir music, and church bells. A political candidate seeking office reinforces his speech-making with a considerable array of nonverbal affective appeals: brass bands, flags, parades, picnics, barbecues, and free cigars. Often a candidate's smile may itself be a powerful influence upon the voter.

Now, if we want people to do certain things and if we are indifferent as to *why they do them,* then no effective appeals need be excluded. Some political candidates want us to vote for them regardless of our reasons for doing so. Therefore, if we hate the rich, they will snarl at the rich for us; if we dislike strikers, they will snarl at the strikers; if we like clambakes, they will throw clambakes; if the majority of us like hillbilly music, they may say nothing about the problems of government, but travel among their constituencies with hillbilly bands. Again, many business firms want us to buy their products regardless of our reasons for doing so; therefore, if delusions and fantasies will lead us to buy their products, they will seek to produce delusions and fantasies; if we want to be popular with the other sex, they will promise us popularity; if we like pretty girls in bathing suits, they will associate pretty girls in bathing suits with their products, whether they are selling shaving cream, automobiles, summer resorts, ice-cream cones, house paint or hardware. Only the law keeps them from presenting pretty girls without bathing suits. The records of the Federal Trade Commission, as well as the advertising pages of many magazines, show that some advertisers will stop at practically nothing.

The Promises of Directive Language

Almost all directive utterances say something about the future. They are "maps", either explicitly or by implication, of *"territories" that are to be.* They direct us to do certain things with the stated or implied promise that if we do these things, certain consequences will follow: "If you adhere to the Bill of Rights, your civil rights too will be protected." "If you vote for me, I will have your taxes reduced." "Live according to these religious principles, and you will have peace in your soul." "Read this magazine, and you will keep up with important current events." "Take Lewis's Licorice Liver Pills and enjoy that glorious feeling that goes with regularity." Needless to say, some of these promises are kept, and some are not. Indeed, we encounter promises daily that are obviously incapable of being kept.

There is no sense in objecting as some people do to advertising and political propaganda—the only kind of directives they worry about—on the ground that they are based on "emotional appeals". Unless directive language has affective power of some kind, it is useless. We do not object to campaigns that tell us, "Give to the Community Chest and enable poor children to enjoy better care", although that is an "emotional appeal". Nor do we resent being reminded of our love of home, friends, and nation when people issue moral or patriotic directives at us. The important question to be asked of any directive utterance is: "Will things happen as promised if I do as I am directed to do? If I accept your philosophy, shall I achieve peace of mind? If I vote for you, will my taxes be reduced? If I use Lifeguard Soap, will my boy friend really come back to me?"

Directive utterances undertake to tell us how we can bring about certain desirable events and how we can avoid undesirable events. If we can rely upon what they tell us about the future, the uncertainties of life are reduced. When, however, directive utterances are of such a character that things do *not* happen as predicted—when, after we have done as we were told, the peace in the soul has not been found, the taxes have not been reduced, the boy friend has not returned, there is disappointment. Such disappointments may be trivial or grave; in any event, they are so common that we do not even bother to complain about some of them. They are, nevertheless, all serious in their implications. *Each of them serves, in greater or*

lesser degree, to break down that mutual trust that makes co-opera-
tion possible and knits people together into a society.

Every one of us, therefore, who utters directive language, with its
concomitant promises, stated or implied, is morally obliged to be as
certain as he can, since there is no absolute certainty, that he is
arousing no false expectations. Politicians promising the immediate
abolition of poverty, national advertisers suggesting that tottering
marriages can be restored to bliss by a change in the brand of
laundry detergent used in the family, newspapers threatening the
collapse of the nation if the party they favour is not elected—all such
utterers of nonsense are, for the reasons stated, menaces to the social
order. It does not matter much whether such misleading directives
are uttered in ignorance and error or with conscious intent to de-
ceive, because the disappointments they cause are all similarly
destructive of mutual trust among human beings.

The Foundations of Society

But propaganda, no matter how persuasive, does not create society.
We can, if we wish, ignore its directives. We come now to *directive*
utterances that we cannot ignore if we wish to remain organized in
our social groups.

What we call society is a vast network of mutual agreements. We
agree to refrain from murdering our fellow citizens, and they in turn
agree to refrain from murdering us; we agree to drive on the right-
hand side of the road, and others agree to do the same; we agree to
deliver specified goods, and others agree to pay us for them; we
agree to observe the rules of an organization, and the organization
agrees to let us enjoy its privileges. This complicated network of
agreements, into which almost every detail of our lives is woven and
upon which most of our expectations in life are based, consists essentially of *statements about future events which we are supposed, with*
our own efforts, to bring about. Without such agreements, there
would be no such thing as society. We would all be huddling in
miserable and lonely caves, not daring to trust anyone. With such
agreements, and a will on the part of the vast majority of people to
live by them, behaviour begins to fall into relatively predictable
patterns; co-operation becomes possible; peace and freedom are
established.

Therefore, in order that we shall continue to exist as human beings, we *must* impose patterns of behaviour on each other. We must make citizens conform to social and civic customs; we must make husbands dutiful to their wives; we must make soldiers courageous, judges just, priests pious, and teachers solicitous for the welfare of their pupils. In early stages of culture the principal means of imposing patterns of behaviour was, of course, physical coercion. But such control can also be exercised, as human beings must have discovered extremely early in history, by *words*—that is, by directive language. Therefore, directives about matters which society as a whole regards as essential to its own safety are made especially powerful, so that no individual in that society will fail to be impressed with a sense of his obligations. To make doubly sure, society further reinforces the directives by the assurance that punishment, possibly including imprisonment and death, may be visited upon those who fail to heed the words.

Directives with Collective Sanction

These directive utterances with collective sanction, which try to impose patterns of behaviour upon the individual in the interests of the whole group, are among the most interesting of linguistic events. Not only are they usually accompanied by ritual; they are usually the central purpose of ritual. There is probably no kind of utterance that we take more seriously, that affects our lives more deeply, that we quarrel about more bitterly. Constitutions of nations and of organizations, legal contracts, and oaths of office are utterances of this kind; in marriage vows, confirmation exercises, induction ceremonies, and initiations, they are the essential constituent. Those terrifying verbal jungles called *laws* are simply such directives, accumulated, codified, and systematized through the centuries. In its laws, society makes its mightiest collective effort to impose predictability upon human behaviour.

Directive utterances made under collective sanction may exhibit any or all of the following features:

1. Such language is almost always phrased in *words that have affective connotations,* so that people will be appropriately impressed and awed. Archaic and obsolete vocabulary or stilted phraseology quite unlike the language of everyday life is employed. For example:

"Wilt thou, John, take this woman for thy lawful wedded wife?" "This lease, made this tenth day of July, A.D. One Thousand Nine Hundred and Sixty-three, between Samuel Smith, hereinafter called the Lessor, and Jeremiah Johnson, hereinafter called Lessee, WITNESSETH, that Lessor, in consideration of covenants and agreements hereinafter contained and made on the part of the Lessee, hereby leases to Lessee for a private dwelling, the premises known and described as follows, to wit. . . ."

2. Such directive utterances are often accompanied by *appeals to supernatural powers,* who are called upon to help us carry out the vows, or to punish us if we fail to carry them out. An oath, for example, ends with the words, "So help me God." Prayers, incantations, and invocations accompany the utterance of important vows in practically all cultures, from the most primitive to the most civilized. These further serve, of course, to impress our vows on our minds.

3. The *fear of direct punishment* is also invoked. If God does not punish us for failing to carry out our agreements, it is made clear either by statement or implication that our fellow men will. For example, we all realize that we can be imprisoned for desertion, nonsupport or bigamy; sued for "breach of contract"; "unfrocked" for activities contrary to priestly vows; "cashiered" for "conduct unbecoming an officer"; "impeached" for "betrayal of public trust"; "hanged" for "treason".

4. The formal and public utterance of the vows may be preceded by *preliminary disciplines* of various kinds: courses of training in the meaning of the vows one is undertaking; fasting and self-mortification, as before entering the priesthood, initiation ceremonies involving physical tortures, as before induction into the warrior status among primitive peoples or membership in college fraternities.

5. The utterance of the directive language may be accompanied by other *activities or gestures calculated to impress the occasion on the mind.* For example, everybody in a courtroom stands up when a judge is about to open a court; huge processions and extraordinary costumes accompany coronation ceremonies; academic gowns are worn for commencement exercises; for many weddings, an organist and a soprano are procured and special clothes are worn.

6. The uttering of the vows may be immediately followed by

feasts, dancing, and other joyous manifestations. Again the purpose seems to be to reinforce still further the effect of the vows. For example, there are wedding parties and receptions, graduation dances, banquets for the induction of officers and, even in the most modest social circles, some form of "celebration" when a member of the family enters into a compact with society. In primitive cultures, initiation ceremonies for chieftains may be followed by feasting and dancing that last for several days or weeks.

7. In cases where the first utterance of the vows is not made a special ceremonial occasion, the effect on the memory is usually achieved by *frequent repetition*. The Lord's Prayer, for instance, is repeated daily in most schools. Mottoes, which are briefly stated general directives, are repeated frequently; sometimes they are stamped on dishes, sometimes engraved on a warrior's sword, sometimes inscribed in prominent places such as on gates, walls, and doorways, where people can see them and be reminded of their duties.

The common feature of all these activities that accompany directive utterances, as well as of the affective elements in the language of directive utterances, is the deep effect they have on the memory. Every kind of sensory impression from the severe pain of initiation rites to the pleasures of banqueting, music, splendid clothing, and ornamental surroundings may be employed; every emotion from the fear of divine punishment to pride in being made the object of special public attention may be aroused. This is done in order that the individual who enters into his compact with society—that is, the individual who commits himself to the "map" of the not-yet-existent "territory"—shall never forget to try to bring that "territory" into existence.

For these reasons, such occasions as when a cadet receives his commission, when a Jewish boy has his *bar mitzvah,* when a priest takes his vows, when a foreign-born citizen is sworn in as a citizen of Canada, or when a Governor-General takes his oath of office— these are events one never forgets. Even if, later on, a person realizes that he has not fulfilled his vows, he cannot shake off the feeling that he should have done so. All of us, of course, use and respond to these ritual directives. The phrases and speeches to which we respond reveal our deepest religious, patriotic, social, professional, and political allegiances more accurately than do the citizenship papers or membership cards that we may carry in our pockets or the badges that we may wear on our coats. A man who has changed his religion after reaching adulthood will, on hearing the ritual he was accustomed to hearing in childhood, often feel an urge to return to his earlier form of worship. In such ways, then, do human beings use words to reach out into the future and control each other's conduct.

What Are "Rights"?

Directive language in everyday life is used, as we have seen, in one or other of two main contexts: persuasion toward a particular course of action or compulsion by society on its members. In the latter instance, the individual becomes most aware of social pressures on him in the matter of what are called "personal possessions". What, for instance, is the meaning of the word "my" in such expressions as "my real estate", "my book", "my automobile"? Certainly the word "my" describes no characteristics of the objects named. A cheque changes hands and "your" automobile becomes "mine" but no change in the automobile. What has changed?

The change is, of course, in *our social agreements covering our behaviour* toward the automobile. Formerly, when it was "yours", you felt free to use it as you liked, while I did not. Now that it is "mine", I use it freely and you may not. The meaning of "yours" and "mine" lies not in the external world, but in *how we intend to act*. And when society as a whole recognizes my "right of ownership" (by issuing me, for example, a certificate of title), it agrees to protect me in my intentions to use the automobile and to frustrate, by police action if necessary, the intentions of those who may wish to use it without my permission. Society makes this agreement with me in return for my obeying its laws and paying my share of the expenses of government.

Are not, then, all assertions of ownership and statements about "rights" directives? Cannot, "This is *mine*", be translated, "I am going to use this object; you keep your hands off"? Cannot, "Every child has a *right* to an education", be translated, "*Give* every child an education"? And is not the difference between "moral rights" and "legal rights" the difference between agreements which people believe *ought* to be made, and those which, through collective, legislative sanction, *have been* made?

"Ownership", then, may be defined as a set of directive agreements recognized by society as to who may enjoy the use of certain goods and services. The freedom to use and enjoy what is "mine" is, however, limited according to the kind of property: e.g., I may drive "my" automobile only if it is duly registered and if I have a driver's licence, and I may build a house on "my" real estate lot only if the plans are approved by the appropriate authority.

In Conclusion

A few cautions may be added on the subject of directive language. Firstly, it must be remembered that the words of such directives are no more than indications of what may come to pass some time in the future and often the future will bear no relation to the predictions. Directive utterances cannot impose a pattern on events that are yet to happen; they suggest possibilities or probabilities; they do not indicate certainties. Realization of this fact saves us from having impossible expectations and therefore from suffering needless disappointments.

Secondly, one should distinguish between directive and informative utterances, which often look alike. Such statements as "A boy scout is clean and chivalrous and brave" or "Policemen are defenders of the weak" *set up goals* and do not necessarily describe the present situation. This is extremely important, because all too often people understand such definitions as descriptive and are then shocked and disillusioned when they encounter a boy scout who is not chivalrous or a policeman who is a bully. They decide that they are "through with the boy scouts" or "disgusted with all policemen", which, of course, is nonsense. They have, in effect, inferred an informative statement from what is to be taken only as a very general directive.

A third source of disappointment and disillusionment arising from the improper understanding of directives results from reading into them promises that they did not make, or from believing that their promises are more specific and concrete than they really are. A common instance is provided by advertisements of the antiseptics, patent medicines, and toilet preparations which people buy under the im-

158

pression that cure or prevention of some illness, physical disability or social handicap was promised. To avoid trouble with the law, the writers of these advertisements are careful to avoid saying that their preparations will prevent or cure anything. Instead, they say that they "help reduce the severity of the infection", or "help release the natural oils in the skin", or "destroy bacteria". Politicians, likewise, phrase their promises in such vague terms that it is easy for a hearer to confuse levels of abstraction by applying them to his specific situation and assuming that it alone is meant.

■Applications

I Explain the differences in the meanings of the word "my" in the following expressions:

1. *my* house
2. *my* hotel room
3. *my* electric iron
4. *my* teacher
5. *my* friend.

II The following statements, in the contexts in which they are usually found, are directives. Which of these directives have collective sanction and which have not? What rewards (if any) are promised to those who follow the directives, and what punishments (if any) are threatened to those who do not? What is the likelihood, in each case, of the consequences following as promised?

1. Trespassers will be prosecuted.
2. Support your Red Feather campaign.
3. Drink Blotto's coffee for refreshing, fuller flavour.
4. Thou shalt not kill.
5. The performance will begin at 8:30 sharp.
6. Give your child better grades by Christmas. Start his school year off right with a Jones Galaxy portable typewriter. For typing improves grades . . . and report cards prove it. When students start typing assignments, school work (and grades) start to improve almost immediately. Educators acknowledge it. Classroom tests have proved it. But for truly first-

class work, a student needs a portable that is easy to type on, easy to learn on . . . a Jones Galaxy.

—Advertisement

7. Know then thyself, presume not God to scan;
   The proper study of mankind is man.

—Alexander Pope

8. No admission to those under eighteen years of age.
9. Dogs must be kept on a leash.
10. Fire alarm; penalty for improper use, $25.

III Analyze a group of advertisements in one field; for example, cosmetics, cigarettes, television sets, movies, automobiles or clothing. Comment on the chief forms of directive utterance used and give particular attention to the words used by the copywriters.

CHAPTER TEN

The Language of Literature

Bearing the Unbearable

Animals know their environment by direct experience only; man crystallizes his knowledge and his feelings in phonetic symbolic representations; by written symbols he accumulates knowledge and passes it on to further generations of men. Animals feed themselves where they find food, but man, co-ordinating his efforts with the efforts of others by linguistic means, feeds himself abundantly and with food prepared by a hundred hands and brought great distances. Animals exercise but limited control over each other, but man, again by employing symbols, establishes laws and ethical systems, which are linguistic means of imposing order and predictability upon human conduct. Acquiring knowledge, securing food, establishing social order—these activities make sense to the biologist because they contribute to survival. For human beings, each of these activities involves a symbolic dimension—a dimension of which lower animals have no inkling.

But there is one area of human activity where the symbolic dimension is all-important: that is, in literature. A frustrated or unhappy animal can do relatively little about its tensions. A human being, however, with an extra dimension (the world of symbols) to move around in, not only undergoes experience, but also *symbolizes his experience to himself*. Our states of tension—especially the unhappy tensions—*become tolerable* as we manage to *state what is wrong— to get it said*—whether to a sympathetic friend, or on paper to a hypothetical sympathetic reader, or even to oneself. From the point of view of the utterer, one of the most important functions of the utterance is the relieving of *tensions*. We have all known the relief that comes from uttering a long and resounding series of impolite vocables under the stress of great irritation. The same releasing of psychological tensions—Aristotle called it *catharsis*—appears to be effected at all levels of affective utterance, if we are to believe what writers themselves have said about the creative process. The novel, the drama, the poem, like the oath or the expletive, arise, at least, in part, out of internal necessity when the organism experiences a serious tension, whether resulting from joy, grief, disturbance or frustration. And as a result of the utterances made, the tension is, to a greater or lesser degree—perhaps only momentarily—mitigated.

If, however, our symbolizations are adequate and sufficiently skillful, our tensions are brought *symbolically under control*; that is, we reclassify experiences to make them easier to bear. But as we all know, language is social, and for every speaker there may be hearers. An utterance that relieves a tension for the speaker can relieve a similar tension, should one happen to exist, in the hearer. And because human experience remains fairly constant, this process is possible even when speaker and hearer are separated by centuries or by different cultures.

William Ernest Henley, for instance, confronted the fact of his chronic invalidism—he had been ill since childhood and had spent long periods of his life in hospitals—by stating, in his well-known poem "Invictus", his refusal to be defeated:

> Out of the night that covers me,
>   Black as the pit from pole to pole,
> I thank whatever gods may be
>   For my unconquerable soul.
>
> In the fell clutch of circumstance
>   I have not winced nor cried aloud.
> Under the bludgeonings of chance
>   My head is bloody, but unbowed.
>
> Beyond this place of wrath and tears
>   Looms but the horror of the shade,
> And yet the menace of the years
>   Finds, and shall find me, unafraid.
>
> It matters not how strait the gate,
>   How charged with punishments the scroll,
> I am the master of my fate:
>   I am the captain of my soul.

How, at a different time and under different circumstances, other people can use Henley's utterance to take arms against a different sea of troubles is shown by the fact that this poem is one of the favourite poems of American Negroes and is sometimes recited or sung chorally by Negro organizations. The extra meaning of the word "black" in the second line when the poem is said by Negroes makes it perhaps an even more pointed utterance for the Negro reader than it was for the original author. Indeed, the entire poem takes on different meanings depending on what a reader, putting himself into the role of the speaker of the poem, projects into the words "the night that covers me".

What Literature Is For

From what has been said, our first and most obvious conclusion is that since the expression of individual feelings is central to literature, affective elements are of the utmost importance in all literary writing. In the evaluation of a novel, poem, play or short story, as well as in the evaluation of sermons, moral exhortations, political speeches, and directive utterances generally, the usefulness of the given piece of writing as a "map" of actual "territories" is often secondary—sometimes quite irrelevant. If this were not the case, *Gulliver's Travels, Alice in Wonderland, The Scarlet Letter* or Emerson's *Essays* would have no excuse for existence.

Secondly, when we say that a given piece of affective writing is true, we do not mean "scientifically true". We may merely mean that we agree with the sentiment; we may also mean that we believe that an attitude has been accurately expressed; again, we may mean that the attitudes evoked seem such as will lead us to better social or personal conduct.

The word "true" has many meanings. People who feel that science and literature or science and religion are in necessary conflict do so because they habitually think in opposites of black and white, true and false, good and evil. To such people, if science is "true", then literature or religion is nonsense; if literature or religion is "true", science is merely "pretentious ignorance". What should be understood when people tell us that certain statements are "scientifically true" is that they are useful and verifiable formulations, suitable for the purposes of organized co-operative workmanship. What should be understood when people tell us that the plays of Shakespeare or the poems of Milton or Dante are "eternally true" is that they produce in us attitudes toward our fellow men, an understanding of ourselves, or feelings of deep moral obligation that are valuable to humanity under any conceivable circumstances.

Thirdly, let us consider an important shortcoming of the language of reports and of scientific writing. John Smith in love with Mary is not William Brown in love with Jane; William Brown in love with Jane is not Henry Jones in love with Anne; Henry Jones in love with Anne is not Robert Browning in love with Elizabeth Barrett. Each of these situations is unique; no two loves are exactly alike—in fact, no love even between the same people is *exactly* the same from day to day. Science, seeking as always laws of the widest possible applicability and the greatest possible generality, would abstract from these situations *only what they have in common*. But each of these lovers is conscious only of the *uniqueness* of his own feelings: each feels, as we all know, that he is the first one in the world ever to have so loved. Literature creates the sense of what life feels like in the living.

How is that sense of difference conveyed? It is here that affective uses of language play their most important part. The infinity of differences in our feelings toward all the many experiences that we undergo are too subtle to be reported; they must be expressed. And we express them by the complicated manipulation of tones of voice, of rhythms, of connotations, of affective facts, of metaphors, of allusions, of every affective device of language at our command.

Frequently the feelings to be expressed are so subtle or complex that a few lines of prose or verse are not enough to convey them. It is sometimes necessary, therefore, for authors to write entire books, carrying their readers through numbers of scenes, situations, and adventures, pushing their sympathies now this way and now that, arousing in turn their fighting spirit, their tenderness, their sense of tragedy, their laughter, their superstitiousness, their cupidity, their sensuousness, their piety. Sometimes it is only in such ways that the *exact* feelings an author wants to express can be recreated in his readers. This, then, is the reason that novels, poems, dramas, stories, allegories, and parables exist: to convey such propositions as "Life is tragic" or "Susanna is beautiful", not by telling us so, but by putting us through a whole series of experiences that make us feel toward life or toward Susanna as the author did. *Literature is the most exact expression of feelings, while science is the most exact kind of reporting.* Poetry, which condenses all the affective resources of language into patterns of infinite rhythmical subtlety, may be said to be *the language of expression at its highest degree of efficiency.*

Symbolic Experience

In a very real sense, then, people who have read good literature have lived more than people who cannot or will not read. To have read *Gulliver's Travels* is to have had the experience, with Jonathan Swift, of turning sick at one's stomach at the conduct of the human race; to read *Huckleberry Finn* is to feel what it is like to drift down the Mississippi River on a raft; to have read Byron is to have suffered with him his rebellions and neuroses and to have enjoyed with him his nose-thumbing at society; to have read *Native Son* is to know how it feels to be frustrated in the particular way in which many Negroes in Chicago are frustrated. This is the great task that affective communication performs: it enables us to feel how others felt about life, even if they lived thousands of miles away and centuries ago. It is not true that we have only one life to live; if we can read, we can live as many more lives and as many kinds of lives as we wish.

In the enjoyment and contemplation of a work of literary or dramatic art—a novel, a play, a moving picture—*we find our deepest enjoyment when the leading characters in the story to some degree symbolize ourselves.* As we identify ourselves with the people in the story, the dramatist or the novelist puts us through *organized sequences of symbolic experiences.*

The differences between actual and symbolic experiences are great—one is not scarred by watching a moving-picture battle, nor is one nourished by watching people in a play having dinner. Furthermore, actual experiences come to us in highly disorganized fashion: meals, arguments with the landlady, visits to the doctor about one's fallen arches, and so on, interrupt the splendid course of romance. The novelist, however, *abstracts* only the events relevant to his story and then *organizes* them into a meaningful sequence. This business of abstracting (selecting) events and organizing them so that they bear some meaningful relationship to each other and to the central theme of a novel or play constitutes the storyteller's art. Plot construction, development of character, narrative structure, climax, denouement, and all the other things one talks about in technical literary criticism have reference to this organizing of symbolic experiences so that the whole complex of symbolic experiences (i.e., the finished story or play) will have the desired impact on the reader.

All literary and dramatic enjoyment, whether of nursery tales in childhood or of moving pictures later on or of "great literature", appears to involve to some degree the reader's imaginative identification of himself with the roles portrayed and his projection of himself into the situations described in the story. Whether a reader is able to identify himself with the characters of a story depends both on the maturity of the story and the maturity of the reader. If a mature reader finds difficulty identifying himself with the hero of a cowboy story, it is because he finds the hero too simple-minded a character to serve as an acceptable symbol for himself, and the villains and the events too improbable to serve as symbols for his own enemies and his own problems.

However, the simple-mindedness of the people and the improbability of the events of cowboy and western movies contribute much to their popularity on television. We live in a complex civilization, in which the vast majority of us lead peaceful, unaggressive lives. When we are troubled by problems—when sales fall off or profits decline or our jobs are threatened or shipments do not arrive on time or customers complain—many, many things may be to blame: manufacturers, middlemen, the stock market, the labour unions, high taxes, high rentals, the railroads, the government, local zoning regulations or the problems of communication inevitable in large and complex societies. There is as a rule no single villain or group of villains, no one agency, that can be the object of our wrath when things go wrong. Hence, the world of the television western is comforting to come home to when the day's work is done: the "good guys" (in white hats) and the "bad guys" (in black hats) are clearly distinguishable, and all troubles are dissolved in a happy ending when the "bad guys" are defeated or dead after a heroic gun-fight.

(Pictures in which the "good guys" wear black hats are known as "adult westerns".)

One of the reasons for calling some people immature is that they are incapable of confronting defeat, tragedy or unpleasantness of any kind. Such persons usually cannot endure an "unhappy ending" *even in a set of symbolic experiences.* Hence the widespread passion for happy endings in popular literature, so that even stories about unhappy events have to be made, in the end, to "come out all right". The immature constantly need to be reassured that everything will always come out all right.

Readers who mature as they grow older, however, steadily increase the depth and range and subtlety of their symbolic experiences. Under the guidance of skilled writers who have accurately observed the world and have been able to organize their observations in significant ways, the mature reader may symbolically experience murder, guilt, religious exaltation, bankruptcy, the loss of friends, the discovery of gold mines or new philosophical principles, or the sense of desolation following a locust invasion on the Prairies. Each new symbolic experience means the enrichment of his insight into people and events.

But for all of us who read, whether mature or not, some enlivening of the spirit results from reading works of literature in which language is the means of providing symbolic experience arranged in a pattern of order. This imposition of order upon our pictures of the world is, it appears, what we mean by "understanding". When we say that a scientist "understands" something, does it not mean that he has ordered his observations at the objective, descriptive, and higher inferential levels of abstraction into a workable system in which all levels are related to other levels in terms of a few powerful generalizations? When a great religious leader or philosopher is said to "understand" life, does it not mean that he has also ordered his observations into a set of attitudes, often crystallized into exceedingly general and powerful directives? And when a novelist is said to "understand" the life of any segment of humanity (or humanity as a whole), has he not also ordered his observations at many different levels of abstraction—the particular and concrete, the general, and the more general? However, the novelist presents that order not in a scientific, ethical or philosophical system of highly abstract generalizations, but in a set of symbolic experiences at the descriptive level of affective reports, involving the reader's feelings through the mechanism of identification. And these symbolic experiences, in the work of any competent novelist, are woven together to frame a consistent set of attitudes, whether of scorn or compassion or admiration of courage or sympathy with the downtrodden or a sense of futility, depending on his outlook.

Some of the ways of organizing a set of experiences for literary purposes are purely mechanical and external: these are the "rules" governing the proper construction of the novel, the play, the short story, the sonnet, and so on. But more important are the ways of organization suggested by the materials of the literary work—the experiences which the writer wishes to organize. When the materials of a story do not fit into the conventional pattern of a novel, the novelist may create a new organization altogether, more suited to the presentation of his experiences than the conventional patterns. In such a case, critics speak of the materials as "creating their own form". In such a case, too, the order may seem like disorder at first—one thinks of Laurence Sterne's *Tristram Shandy* and James Joyce's *Ulysses*—because the principles of organization, being new, have to be discovered in the course of reading. The reason a poem, novel or play assumes the shape it ultimately does is the concern of the technical literary critic. He studies the interplay of external and internal demands which finally shape the materials into a "work of art".

To symbolize one's experiences adequately and then to order them into a coherent whole constitute an integrative act. The great novelist or dramatist or poet is one who has successfully integrated and given coherence to vast areas of human experience. Literary greatness requires, therefore, great awareness of the first-hand range of human experience as well as great powers of ordering that experience meaningfully. This is why the discipline of the creative artist is endless: there is always more to learn, both about human experience (which is the material to be ordered) and about the techniques of his craft (which are the means of ordering).

From the point of view of the reader, the fact that language is social is again of central importance. The ordering of experiences and attitudes accomplished linguistically by the writer produces, in the reader, some ordering of his own experiences and attitudes. The reader becomes, as a result of this ordering, somewhat better organized himself. That's what art is for.

Its effects, however, go beyond the individual, for the better organized he is, the more easily he comes to see the community of interest that exists between him and his fellow men. This the language of science cannot achieve; it enables mankind to co-operate by the exchange of information and the pooling of observations. Literature, on the other hand, enlarges individual sympathies and makes man willing to co-operate with his fellows.

■ Applications

I Comment on the following statement:

> The end of writing is to instruct; the end of poetry is to instruct by pleasing.
>
> —SAMUEL JOHNSON

II Study the following poems to see:
- (a) what tensions of his own the author seems to be trying to resolve;
- (b) what methods he employs;
- (c) whether his resolution might be applicable to other people;
- (d) whether he has ordered his experiences into a coherent, meaningful whole.

1.   Ozymandias

I met a traveller from an antique land
Who said: Two vast and trunkless legs of stone
Stand in the desert. Near them, on the sand,
Half sunk, a shattered visage lies, whose frown,
And wrinkled lip, and sneer of cold command,
Tell that its sculptor well those passions read
Which yet survive, stamped on these lifeless things,
The hand that mocked them and the heart that fed;
And on the pedestal these words appear:
"My name is Ozymandias, king of kings:
Look on my works, ye Mighty, and despair!"
Nothing beside remains. Round the decay
Of that colossal wreck, boundless and bare
The lone and level sands stretch far away.

—PERCY BYSSHE SHELLEY

2.   My Life Closed Twice . . . .
            My life closed twice before its close;
                It yet remains to see
            If Immortality unveil
                A third event to me,

            So huge, so hopeless to conceive,
                As these that twice befell.
            Parting is all we know of heaven,
                And all we need of hell.

                                    ——EMILY DICKINSON

3.   Sonnett CXXX
            My mistress' eyes are nothing like the sun;
            Coral is far more red than her lips' red:
            If snow be white, why then her breasts are dun;
            If hairs be wires, black wires grow on her head.
            I have seen roses damask'd red, and white,
            But no such roses see I in her cheeks
            And in some perfumes is there more delight
            Than in the breath that from my mistress reeks.
            I love to hear her speak, yet well I know
            That music hath a far more pleasing sound;
            I grant I never saw a goddess go;
            My mistress, when she walks, treads on the ground.
            And yet, by heaven, I think my love as rare
            As any she belied with false compare.

                                    ——WILLIAM SHAKESPEARE

III Select a piece of literature in any genre that has had an effect
on your feelings. Analyze the effect and discuss the means used
by the writer to appeal to your emotions.

CHAPTER ELEVEN

Some Qualities of Affective Language

Connotations

Report language, as we have seen, is instrumental in getting work done; but as we have also seen, language is frequently used for the direct expression of the feelings of the speaker or writer as well as for giving information. Considering language from the point of view of the hearer or reader, we can say that report language informs us but that these expressive uses of language (for example, judgments, what we have called presymbolic functions, directives, and litera-ture) *affect* our feelings. When language is *affective,* it has the char-acter of a kind of force. A spoken insult, for instance, provokes a return insult, just as a blow provokes a return blow; a loud and forceful command compels, just as a push compels; talking and shouting are as much a display of energy as the pounding of the chest. And the first of the affective elements in speech, as we have seen, is the tone of voice, its loudness or softness, its pleasantness or unpleasantness, its variations in volume and intonation during the course of the utterance.

Another affective element in language is rhythm. *Rhythm* is the name we give to the effect produced by the repetition of auditory (or kinesthetic) stimuli at fairly regular intervals. From the boom-boom of a childish drum to the subtle nuances of cultivated poetry and music, there is a continuous development and refinement of man's responsiveness to rhythm. To produce rhythm is to arouse attention and interest; so affective is rhythm, indeed, that it catches our attention even when we do not want our attention distracted. *Rhyme* and *alliteration* are, of course, ways of emphasizing rhythm in language, through repetition of similar sounds at regular intervals.

Political-slogan writers and advertisers therefore have a special fondness for rhyme and alliteration: "Tippecanoe and Tyler Too", "Rum, Romanism, and Rebellion", "Keep Cool with Coolidge", "Order from Horder", "Better Buy Buick", "Take Tea 'n' See", "I Like Ike." These are totally absurd slogans so far as informative value is concerned, but by their sound they set up small rhythmic echoes in one's head that make them annoyingly difficult to forget.

In addition to tone of voice and rhythm, another extremely important affective element in language is the aura of feelings, pleasant or unpleasant, that surrounds many words. This quality is usually called, simply, *connotation*, but such a designation is hardly accurate enough if *denotation* is confined, as it ought to be, to a silent pointing at the object of which the corresponding word is a symbol and *connotation* used for the ideas and feelings suggested by the utterance of the word. With this in mind, we can divide connotation into two kinds, the *informative* and the *affective*.

Informative Connotations

The informative connotations of a word are its socially agreed upon, "impersonal" meanings, *insofar as meanings can be given at all by additional words*. For example, if we talk about a "pig" we cannot give the denotational meaning of the word unless there happens to be an actual pig for us to point to. But we can give its informative connotations: "pig" for English-speaking people means "domesticated mammalian quadruped of the kind generally raised by farmers to be made into pork, bacon, ham, lard. . . ."

Informative connotations may include both the *definition* of a term ("pig" as a "domesticated mammalian. . . .") and its *denotation* (by pointing to a pig or pigs). But some terms have a definition, yet lack denotation: for example, a "mermaid" exists by definition only ("a creature half woman and half fish"). The term has no denotation because an extensional mermaid is not to be found. Terms in mathematics which have "logical existence" but no extensional reference can also be said to have informative connotations, but no denotation.

Denotations would seem to offer few problems of interpretation, since we are dealing here with words apart from the personal feelings that they may arouse. But such is not the case, because the same word may denote different things to people in different occupations or in different parts of the English-speaking world. The names of birds, animals, and plants are an interesting example of confusion about denotations. The English "robin" is an entirely different species from the North American "robin". Many different and un-related kinds of fish are denoted by the word "bream" (pronounced "brim" in the southern United States). Belgian hares, we are told, are "really rabbits", while our jackrabbit is "really a hare". The term "crocus", as popularly used, refers in different parts of the country to different flowers. The writer has also heard from a bird-watcher that "The English sparrow is not a sparrow at all, but a weaver finch. House finches are often called linnets. The linnet is a European bird that we don't have in America."

Such differences in popular and regional terminology are among the reasons for establishing scientific names for plants and animals —names which are accepted and used by the entire international scientific community.

Affective Connotations

The affective connotations of a word, on the other hand, are the aura of personal feelings it arouses, as, for example, "pig": "Ugh! Dirty, evil-smelling creatures, wallowing in filthy sties", and so on. While there is no necessary agreement about these feelings—some people like pigs and others don't—it is the existence of these feel-ings that enables us to use words, under certain circumstances, *for their affective connotations alone*, without regard to their informa-tive connotations. That is to say, when we are strongly moved, we express our feelings by uttering words with the affective connotations appropriate to our feelings, without paying any attention to the informative connotations they may have. We angrily call people "rats", "wolves", "old bears", "skunks", or lovingly call them "honey", "sugar", "duck", and "sweetie pie". Indeed, all verbal expressions of feeling make use to some extent of the affective con-notations of words.

All words have, according to the uses to which they are put, some affective character. There are many words that exist more for their affective value than for their informative value; for example, we can refer to "that man" as "that gentleman", "that individual", "that person", "that gent", "that guy", "that hombre", "that bird", or "that bozo"—and while the person referred to may be the same in all these cases, each of these terms reveals a difference in our feelings toward him. Dealers in knickknacks frequently write "Gyfte Shoppe" over the door, hoping that such a spelling carries, even if their merchandise does not, the flavour of antiquity. Affective connotations suggestive of England and Scotland are often sought in the choice of brand names for men's suits and overcoats: "Glenmoor", "Regent Park", "Bond Street". Sellers of perfume choose names for their products that suggest France—"Mon Désir", "Indiscret", "Evening in Paris"—and expensive brands always come in "flacons", never in bottles. Consider, too, the differences among the following expressions:

I have the honour to inform Your Excellency . . .
This is to advise you . . .
I should like to tell you, sir . . .
I'm telling you, Mister . . .
Cheez, boss, git a load of dis . . .

How would you classify them in terms of their possible contexts?

A Note on Verbal Taboo

In every language there seem to be certain "unmentionables"— words of such strong affective connotations that they cannot be used in polite discourse. The fear of death carries over, for instance, into fear of the *words* having to do with death. Many people, therefore, instead of saying "died", substitute such expressions as "passed away", " gone to his reward", "departed", and "gone west".

Money is another subject about which communication is in some ways inhibited. It is all right to mention *sums* of money, such as "ten thousand dollars", or "two dollars and fifty cents". But it is considered in bad taste to inquire directly into other people's financial affairs, unless such an inquiry is really necessary in the course of business. When creditors send bills, they practically never mention money, although that is what they are writing about. There are many circumlocutions: "We beg to call your attention to what might be an oversight on your part." "We would appreciate your early attention to this matter." "May we look forward to an early remittance?"

Then there are words which have to do with sexual matters, the excretory processes, and parts of the anatomy connected with these. Such verbal taboos, though sometimes amusing, also produce serious problems—since they prevent frank discussion of sexual matters. Social workers, with whom the writer has discussed this question, report that young people of junior high school and high school age who contract venereal disease, become pregnant out of wedlock and get into other serious trouble of this kind, are almost always profoundly ignorant of the most elementary facts about sex and procreation. Their ignorance is apparently due to the fact that neither they nor their parents have a vocabulary in which to discuss such matters: the nontechnical vocabulary of sex is to them too coarse and shocking to be used, while the technical, medical vocabulary is unknown to them. The social workers find, therefore, that the first step in helping these young people is usually linguistic: they have to be taught a vocabulary in which they can talk about their problems before they can be helped further.

The stronger verbal taboos have, however, a genuine social value. When we are extremely angry and we feel the need of expressing our anger in violence, the uttering of these forbidden words provides us with a relatively harmless verbal substitute for going berserk and smashing furniture; that is, they act as a kind of safety valve in our moments of crisis.

It is difficult to explain why some words should have such powerful affective connotations while others with the same informative connotations do not. Some of our verbal reticences, especially the religious ones, have the authority of the Bible: "Thou shalt not take the name of the Lord thy God in vain; for the Lord will not hold him guiltless that taketh His name in vain" (Exodus 21:7). "Gee", "gee whiz", "gosh almighty", "gee whillikens", and "gosh darn" are ways of avoiding saying "Jesus", "God Almighty", and "God damn"; and carrying the biblical injunction one step further, we also avoid taking the name of the Devil in vain by means of such expressions as "the deuce", "the dickens", and "Old Nick". It appears that among all the people of the world, among the civilized as well as the primitive, there is a feeling that the names of the gods are too holy, and the names of evil spirits too terrifying, to be spoken lightly.

The primitive confusion of word with thing, of symbol with thing symbolized, manifests itself in some parts of the world in a belief that the name of a person is *part* of that person. To know someone's name, therefore, is to have power over him. Because of this belief, it is customary among some peoples for children to be given at birth a "real name" known only to the parents and never used, as well as a nickname or public name to be called by in society. In this way the child is protected from being put in someone's power. The story of Rumpelstiltskin is a European illustration of this belief in the power of names.

Words with Built-in Judgments

The fact that some words arouse both informative and affective connotations simultaneously gives a special complexity to discussions involving religious, racial, national, and political groups. To many people, the word "communist" means simultaneously "one who believes in communism" (informative connotations) *and* "one whose ideals and purposes are altogether repellent" (affective connotations). Words applying to occupations of which one disapproves ("pickpocket", "racketeer", "prostitute"), like those applying to believers in philosophies of which one may disapprove ("atheist", "heretic", "materialist", "Holy Roller"), likewise often communicate *simultaneously* a fact and a judgment on the fact. Where strong racial or national prejudices exist, too, variant names for members of the group concerned also acquire strongly affective force ("nigger", "Yid", "Hun", "Canuck", "Siwash").

Negroes, to take one example, having for a long time been victims of unfair persecution because of race, are often sensitive about racial appellations. It need hardly be said that Negroes suffer from the confusion of informative and affective connotations just as often as white people. Such Negroes, and those white sympathizers with the Negro cause who are equally naïve in linguistic matters, tend to feel that the entire coloured "race" is vilified whenever and wherever the word "nigger" occurs. They bristle even when it occurs in such expressions as "niggertoe" (the name of an herb; also a dialect term for Brazil nut), "niggerhead" (a type of chewing tobacco), "niggerfish" (a kind of fish found in West Indian and Floridan waters)— and even the word "niggardly" (of Scandinavian origin, unrelated, of course, to "Negro") has to be avoided before some audiences.

Such easily offended people sometimes send delegations to visit dictionary offices to demand that the word "nigger" be excluded from future editions, being unaware that dictionaries perform a historical, rather than legislative function. When racial discrimination against Negroes is done away with, the word will either disappear or else lose its present connotations. By losing its present connotations, we mean (1) that people who need to insult their fellow men will have found more interesting grounds on which to base their insults, and (2) that people who are called "niggers" will no longer fly off the handle any more than a person from New England does at being called a "Yankee".

One other curious fact needs to be recorded about words applied to such hotly debated issues as race, religion, political heresy, and economic dissent. Every reader is acquainted with certain people who, according to their own flattering descriptions of themselves, "believe in being frank" and like to "call a spade a spade". By "calling a spade a spade" they usually mean calling anything or anyone by the term which has the strongest and most disagreeable affective connotations. Why people should pin medals on themselves for "candour" for performing this nasty feat has often puzzled the writer. Sometimes it is necessary to violate verbal taboos as an aid to clearer thinking, but more often "calling a spade a spade" is to provide our minds with a greased runway down which we may slide back into old *and discredited* patterns of evaluation and behaviour.

Everyday Uses of Language

The language of everyday life, then, differs from "reports" such as those discussed in Chapter 7. As in reports, we have to be accurate in choosing words that have the informative connotations we want; otherwise the reader or hearer will not know what we are talking about. But in addition, we have to give those words the affective connotations we want in order that he will be interested or moved by what we are saying, and feel toward things the way we do. This double task confronts us in almost all ordinary conversation, oratory, persuasive writing, and literature. Much of this task, however, is performed intuitively; without being aware of it, we choose the tone of voice, the rhythms, and the affective connotations appropriate to our utterance. Over the informative connotations of our

utterances we exercise somewhat more conscious control. Improve-
ment in our ability to understand language, as well as in our ability
to use it, depends, therefore, not only upon sharpening our sense for
the informative connotations of words, but *also upon the sharpening
of our insight into the affective elements in language through social
experience, through contact with many kinds of people in many
kinds of situations, and through literary study.*

■ Applications

I The following words may be taken as neutral in their affective
connotations. For each, find two synonyms, one favourable,
the other unfavourable.

e.g. horse—thoroughbred, nag.
car, dance, speak, lawyer, teacher, girl, worker, house,
war, child.

II From the following advertisement select the words in parentheses which you think the copywriter might have adopted. Be
prepared to justify your choice.

Hong Kong is the (strange, weird, magic) island of (the
East, Asia, the Orient). And nowhere is the (spell, enchant-
ment) greater than in the Mandarin Hotel, with a standard
of (service, attention, care) that is (absolute, total, sheer)
wizardry. You have a choice of 4 (gourmet, superb, first-
rate) (restaurants, eating places, cafes); (sumptuous, regal,
delightful) bedrooms, each with its own private balcony.
Come and (savour, enjoy, appreciate) life at the Mandarin
—where the staff is ready to (grant, gratify, provide for)
your every wish.

III Using as many illustrations and examples as you can, write an
essay on one of the following topics:
The Meaning of Colour (or one single colour)
The Approving and Disapproving Terms of Music Criticism
(or Art Criticism or Literary Criticism)
The Language of Advertising
The Language of Political Persuasion

CHAPTER TWELVE

More Affective Qualities

The language of reports is instrumental in getting done the work necessary for life, but it does not tell us anything about what life feels like in the living. We can communicate scientific facts to each other without knowing or caring about each other's feelings; but before love, friendship, and community can be established among men so that we *want* to co-operate and become a society, there must be, as we have seen, a flow of sympathy between one man and another. This flow of sympathy is established, of course, by means of the affective uses of language. Most of the time, after all, we are not interested in keeping our feelings out of our discourse, but rather we are eager to express them as fully as we can. Let us examine, then, some more of the ways in which language can be made to work affectively.

The affective power of repetition of similar sounds, as in catchy titles and slogans, has already been mentioned. Somewhat higher on the scale are repetitions not only of sounds but of grammatical structures, as in:

First in war,
first in peace,
first in the hearts of his countrymen . . . .

Government of the people,
        by the people,
        for the people . . . .

Elements of discourse such as these are, from the point of view of scientific reporting, extraneous; but without them, these phrases would not have impressed people. Lincoln could have signified just as much for informative purposes had he said "government of, by, and for the people", or even more simply, "a people's government". But he was not writing a scientific monograph. He hammers the word "people" at us three times, and with each apparently unnecessary repetition he arouses deeper and more affecting connotations of the word. While this is not the place to discuss in detail the complexities of the affective qualities of language that reside in sound alone, it is important to remember that many of the attractions of literature and oratory have a simple phonetic basis—rhyme, alliteration, assonance, crossed alliteration, and all the subtleties of rhythm. All these sound-effects are used to reinforce, wherever possible, the other affective devices.

Another affective device is the *direct address* to the listener or reader, as: "Keep off the grass. This means YOU!" The most painful example of this device is, of course, the spurious friendliness and intimacy with which the announcer of television commercials "personally" addresses each of several million listeners. But direct appeal to an audience is by no means limited to the advertising poster and television announcer. It softens the impersonality of formal speeches, so that when a speaker or writer feels a special urgency about his message, he can hardly help using it. It occurs, therefore, in the finest rhetoric as well as in the simplest. An interesting variant of the "you" device occurs in the college classroom, when the learned professor says, "You will recall what Kropotkin says in his *Mutual Aid: A Factor in Evolution.* . . . " although he knows very well that Mr. Merkle, sprawling in his chair at the back of the class, has never even heard of Kropotkin before.

Almost as common as the "you" device is the "we" device. The writer in this case allies the reader with himself, in order to carry the reader along with him in seeing things as he does: "*We* shall now consider next . . .", "Let *us* take, for example . . .", "*Our* duty is to go forward . . . ." This device is particularly common in the politer forms of exhortation used by preachers and teachers, and it is found throughout this book. The "we" device is also often heard in kindergarten and the lower elementary grades, where teachers use it to sugar-coat their disciplinary directives: "Now, Ricky, now, Penny, we don't fight and call each other names here. We'll all say we're sorry and sit down and be friends again, *won't we*?" (Children usually believe that the word "co-operate" means "obey".)

In such rhetorical devices as the *periodic sentence* there is distortion of grammatical order for affective purposes. A periodic sentence is one in which the completion of the thought is, for the sake of the slight dramatic effect that can be produced by keeping the reader in suspense for a while, delayed. Then there are such devices as *antithesis,* in which strongly opposed notions are placed together or even laid side by side in parallel phonetic or grammatical constructions, so that the reader feels the contrast and is stirred by it: "Born a serf, he died a king", "The sweetest songs are those that tell of saddest thought", "The hungry judges soon the sentence sign,/ And wretches hang that jurymen may dine."

The Affectiveness of Metaphor and Simile

As we have seen, words have affective connotations in addition to their informative value, and this accounts for the fact that statements of the kind: "I've been waiting *ages* for you—you're an hour overdue!", "He's got *tons* of money!", "I'm so tired I'm simply *dead!*"— which are nonsensical if interpreted literally—nevertheless "make sense". The inaccuracy or inappropriateness of the informative connotations of our words are often irrelevant from the point of view of affective communication. Therefore we may refer to the moon as "a piece of cheese", "a lady", "a silver ship", "a fragment of angry candy", or anything else, so long as the words arouse the desired feelings toward the moon or toward the whole situation in which the moon appears. This, incidentally, is the reason literature is so difficult to translate from one language to another: a translation that follows informative connotations will often falsify the affective connotations, and *vice versa*, so that readers who know both the language of the original and the language of the translation are almost sure to be dissatisfied, feeling either that the "spirit of the original has been sacrificed" or else that the translation is "full of inaccuracies".

In translations, a further problem is presented by the fact that a well-understood metaphor in one culture may have entirely different meanings in another part of the world. The United Nations once made a short movie in which an owl was shown, to indicate wisdom. It completely misfired in certain Asiatic countries where the movie was shown, and the footage had to be re-shot. Why? Because in those countries it was found that the owl was a traditional image of stupidity and an object of amusement.

During the long time in which *metaphor* and *simile* were regarded as "ornaments" of speech—that is, as if they were like embroidery, which improves the appearance of our linen but adds nothing to its utility—the psychology of such communicative devices was neglected. We tend to assume that things that create in us the same responses are identical with each other. If, for example, we are revolted by the conduct of an acquaintance at dinner and we have had such a sense of revulsion before only when watching pigs at a trough, our first, unreflecting reaction is naturally to say, "He is a pig." So far as our feelings are concerned, the man and the pig are identical with each other. Again, the soft winds of spring may produce in us agreeable sensations; the soft hands of lovely young girls also produce agreeable sensations; therefore, "Spring has soft hands." This is the basic process by which we arrive at metaphor. Metaphors are not "ornaments of discourse"; they are direct expressions of evaluations and are bound to occur whenever we have strong feelings to express. They are to be found in special abundance, therefore, in all primitive speech, in folk speech, and in the speech of the unlearned, in the speech of children, and in the professional argot of theatre people, of gangsters, and of those in other lively occupations.

So far as our feelings are concerned, there is no distinction between animate and inanimate objects. Our fright *feels* the same whether it is a creature or object that we fear. Therefore, in the expression of our feelings, a car may "lie down and die", the wind "kisses" our cheeks, the waves are "angry" and "roar" against the cliffs, the roads are icy and "treacherous", and mountains "look down" on the sea, machine guns "spit", revolvers "bark", volcanoes "vomit" fire, and the engine "gobbles" coal. This special kind of metaphor is called *personification* and is ordinarily described in textbooks of rhetoric as "making animate things out of inanimate". It is better understood, however, if we describe it as *a reaction that does not distinguish between the animate and the inanimate.*

Simile

However, even at rudimentary stages of evaluation it becomes apparent that calling a person a pig does not take sufficiently into consideration the differences between the person and the pig. Further reflection compels one to say, in modification of the original statement, "He is *like* a pig." Such an expression is called a *simile* —the pointing out of the similarities in our feelings toward the person and the pig. The simile, then, is something of a compromise stage between the direct, unreflective expression of feeling and the report, but of course closer to the former than the latter.

Adequate recognition has never been given to the fact that what we call slang and vulgarism works on exactly the same principles as poetry does. Slang makes constant use of metaphor and simile: "sticking his neck out", "out like a light", "way out on a limb", "baloney (no matter how thin you slice it)", "punch-drunk", "slick chick", "keep your shirt on", "as phony as a three-dollar bill". Clarence "Pinetop" Smith, one of the founders of the boogie-woogie style of piano-playing, used to admonish his friends: "Take it easy, greasy; there's a long way to slide!"

The imaginative process by which phrases such as these are coined is the same as that by which poets arrive at poetry. In poetry, there is the same love of seeing things in scientifically outrageous but emotionally expressive language:

The snow doesn't give a soft white
damn Whom it touches.   —E. E. CUMMINGS

                    . . . the leaves dead
Are driven, like ghosts from an enchanter fleeing,
Yellow, and black, and pale, and hectic red,
Pestilence-stricken multitudes.   —PERCY BYSSHE SHELLEY

Sweet are the uses of adversity,
Which like the toad, ugly and venomous,
Wears yet a precious jewel in his head;
And this our life, exempt from public haunt,
Finds tongues in trees, books in the running brooks,
Sermons in stones, and good in everything.

                                        —WILLIAM SHAKESPEARE

I saw Eternity the other night
Like a great ring of pure and endless light.

                                        —HENRY VAUGHAN

What is called slang, therefore, might well be regarded as the poetry of everyday life, since it performs much the same function as poetry;

that is, it vividly expresses people's feelings about life and about the things they encounter in life.

Dead Metaphor

Metaphor, simile, and personification are among the most useful communicative devices we have, because by their quick affective power they often make unnecessary the inventing of new words for new things or new feelings. They are so commonly used for this purpose, indeed, that we resort to them constantly without realizing that we are doing so. For example, when we talk about the "head" of a cane, the "face" of a cliff, the "bowels" of a volcano, the "arm" of the sea, the "hands" of a watch, the "branches" of a river or an insurance company, we are using metaphor. A salesman "covers" an area; an engine "knocks"; people pass "rubber" cheques which "bounce"; a theory is "built up" and then "knocked down"; a government "drains" the taxpayers, and corporations "milk" the consumers. Even in so unpoetical a source as the financial page of a newspaper, metaphors are to be found: stock is "watered", shares are "liquidated", prices are "slashed" or "stepped up", markets are "flooded", the exchange is "bullish"; in spite of government efforts to "hamstring" business and "strangle" enterprise, there are sometimes "melons" to be "sliced"; although this is—but here we leave the financial page—"pure gravy" for some, others are left "holding the bag". The "rings" both of "political rings" and "hydrocarbon rings" are metaphorical, as are the "chains" in "chain stores" and "chain reactions".

Metaphors are so useful that they often pass into the language as part of its regular vocabulary. Metaphor is probably the most important of all the means by which language develops, changes, grows, and adapts itself to our changing needs. Sometimes, however, metaphors get overworked—"ball-and-chain" (wife), "head-shrinker", "a horse of a different colour", "a pretty kettle of fish"—so that they turn into linguistic deadwood (another metaphor!), or *clichés*.* When metaphors are successful, they "die"—that is, they become so much a part of our regular language that we cease thinking of them as metaphors at all.

* The word "cliché" conceals still another metaphor; see its etymology as given in *Webster's Third New International Dictionary.*

To object to arguments, as is often done, on the ground that they are based on metaphors or on "metaphorical thinking" is rarely just. The question is not whether metaphors are used, but whether the metaphors represent useful similarities.

Allusion

Still another affective device is *allusion*. If we say, for example, standing on a bridge in Vancouver, B.C., in the early morning:

> Earth has not anything to show more fair;
> Dull would he be of soul who could pass by
> A sight so touching in its majesty . . .

we are evoking, in the mind of anyone familiar with the poem, such feelings as Wordsworth expressed at the sight of London in the early morning light in September 1802, and we are applying them to Vancouver. Thus, by a kind of implied simile, we can give expression to our feelings. Allusion, then, is an extremely quick way of expressing and also of creating in our hearers shades of feeling. With a biblical allusion ("Hasten ye, O generation of vipers, and pay me heed") we can often arouse reverent or penitential attitudes; with a historical allusion, such as saying that New York is "the modern Babylon", we can say quickly and effectively that we feel New York to be a luxurious and extremely wicked city, doomed to destruction because of its sinfulness; by a literary allusion, we can evoke the exact feelings found in a given story or poem as a way of feeling toward the event before us.

But allusions work as an effective device only when the hearer is familiar with the history, literature, people or events alluded to. Family jokes (which are allusions to events or memories in the family's experience) have to be explained to outsiders; classical allusions in literature have to be explained to people not familiar with the classics. Nevertheless, whenever a group of people—the members of a single family or the members of a whole civilization—have memories and traditions in common, extremely subtle and efficient affective communications become possible through the use of allusion.

The foreigner, however well he may have studied English before coming to North America, will fail to detect the sources of the allusions in such expressions as, "He is a regular Lower Slobbovian" or, "That's a real Bennett buggy." The number of times we find it necessary to stop and explain things when we converse with foreigners indicates the degree to which we rely upon allusions in everyday discourse.

One of the reasons, therefore, that the young in every culture are made to study the literature and history of their own linguistic or national groups is that they may be able to understand and share in the communications of the group. Those who fail to understand passing allusions to well-known figures in European or American history, to well-known lines in Chaucer, Shakespeare, Milton, Wordsworth, or the King James version of the Bible, or to well-known characters in Dickens, Thackeray, or Mark Twain, may be said to be outsiders to an important part of the traditions of English-speaking people. The study of history and of literature, therefore, is not merely the idle acquisition of social polish, as practical men are fond of believing, but a necessary means both of increasing the efficiency of our communications with others and of increasing our understanding of what others are trying to communicate to us.

Irony, Pathos, and Humour

A somewhat more complex device, upon which much of humour, pathos, and irony depends, is the use of a metaphor, simile or allusion that is very obviously inappropriate to the subject at hand. The result of the incongruous comparison is a feeling of conflict, a conflict between our more obvious feelings toward that which we are talking about and the feelings aroused by the expression. In such a case, the conflicting feelings resolve themselves into a *third, new feeling*. Let us suppose, returning to our example above, that we are looking at an extremely ugly part of Vancouver, so that our obvious feelings are those of distaste. Then we arouse, with the Wordsworth quotation, the feeling of beauty and majesty. The result is a feeling suggested neither by the sight of the city alone nor by the allusion alone, but one that is a product of the *conflict* of the two—a sharp sense of incongruity that compels us either to laugh or to weep, depending on the rest of the context. There are many complex shades of feeling that can hardly be aroused in any other way. If a village poet is referred to as the "Mudville Milton", for example, the conflict between the inglorious connotations of "Mudville" and the glorious connotations of "Milton" produces an effect of the ludicrous, so that the poet is exposed to contempt. Irony is, of course, one of the means by which satirists shock their readers into awareness of some individual folly or weakness in society by showing up incongruities.

Another means of achieving the same end is *anticlimax* where the writer deliberately undercuts a statement by making its final item a trivial one by comparison with what has gone before. Thus, Alexander Pope achieves a comic effect by writing:

Not louder shrieks to pitying heav'n are cast
When husbands, or when lap dogs, breathe their last.

Understatement

The bald recital of details has, in itself, great power to stir the feelings of the reader; a skilled writer, then, will often employ report language—words with weak affective connotation—to convey the facts.

There is, however, one important difference between the affectiveness of facts and the other affective elements in language. In the latter, the writer or speaker is expressing his own feelings; in the former, he is "suppressing his feelings"—that is to say, stating things in a way that would be verifiable by all observers, regardless of one's feelings. Instead of telling the reader, "It was a ghastly accident!" *we can make the reader say it for himself.* The reader is, so to speak, *made to participate in the communicative act by being left to draw his own conclusions.* A skillful writer is often, therefore, one who is especially expert at selecting the facts that are sure to move his readers in the desired ways. We are more likely to be convinced by such descriptive and factual writing than by a series of explicit judgments, because the writer does not ask us to take his word for it that the accident was ghastly. Such a conclusion becomes, in a sense, our own discovery rather than his.

The prose style of Ernest Hemingway is perhaps the classic example of this technique—a highly sophisticated one, needless to say —of stating externally observable facts in the form of bare reports and of letting the reported facts have their impact on the reader. The following passage is the famous ending of *A Farewell to Arms:*

I went into the room and stayed with Catherine until she died. She was unconscious all the time, and it did not take her very long to die.

Outside the room, in the hall, I spoke to the doctor, "Is there anything I can do tonight?"

"No. There is nothing to do. Can I take you to your hotel?"

"No, thank you. I am going to stay here a while."

"I know there is nothing to say. I cannot tell you—"

"No," I said. "There's nothing to say."

"Good-night," he said. "I cannot take you to your hotel?"

"No, thank you."

"It was the only thing to do," he said. "The operation proved—"

"I do not want to talk about it," I said.

"I would like to take you to your hotel."

"No, thank you."

He went down the hall. I went to the door of the room.

"You can't come in now", one of the nurses said.

"Yes I can," I said.

"You can't come in yet."

"You get out," I said. "The other one too."

But after I had got them out and shut the door and turned off the light it wasn't any good. It was like saying good-by to a statue. After a while I went out and left the hospital and walked back to the hotel in the rain.

Conclusion

When affective devices like those described in the last two chapters are used with skill, they result in language which is in accord with the speaker's or writer's purpose: a stirring of feeling in the receiver of the message. Thus we may speak of the *tone* of an utterance when it affects the emotions of its hearers or readers symbolically, just as the original event or situation—whether actual or imagined— affected the orator or author. These devices, then, are not ornamental curlicues superimposed on language to dress it up; on the contrary, they are essential features of the various kinds of communication that govern our everyday lives.

In its highest form such affective expression is seen in poetry which of all forms of utterance has, or ought to have, the strongest appeal to our sympathies. This, of course, the language of science does not take into account, but the language of reports and inferences is only a small part of the total communicative process; the great majority of day-to-day utterances have only an indirect connection with the passing on of information and in these the emotional appeal is of more importance than the intellectual.

■ Applications

I The following allusions, drawn from a variety of sources, are frequently found in magazine articles or books. What sort of person or event might be described in them? What attitude to that person or event is suggested by their use? Check your findings from books of reference.

kill the fatted calf, Trojan horse, Lilliputian, a Beau Brummell, Oedipus complex, a Falstaffian figure, the handwriting on the wall, a pocket Hercules, a Hiroshima, an Ishmael, a bikini-clad figure, scorched-earth policy, a Titan of industry.

II Discuss the probable effect on the emotions of the following statements. Note particularly the use of affective qualities of language employed in each instance.

A On the twenty-ninth of July, in 1943, my father died. On the same day, a few hours later, his last child was born. Over a month before this, there had been, in Detroit, one of the bloodiest race riots of the century. A few hours after my father's funeral, a race riot broke out in Harlem. On the morning of August third we drove him to the graveyard through a wilderness of smashed plate glass.   —JAMES BALDWIN: *Notes of a Native Son*

B We have before us an ordeal of the most grievous kind. We have before us many, many long months of struggle and of suffering. You ask, What is our policy? I will say: "It is to wage war, by sea, land and air, with all our might and with all the strength that God can give us: to wage war against a monstrous tyranny, never surpassed in the dark, lamentable catalogue of human crime. That is our policy." You ask, What is our aim? I can answer in one word: Victory—Victory at all cost, victory in spite of all terror, victory however long and hard the road may be; for without victory there is no survival.   —WINSTON S. CHURCHILL

C As soon as she entered the hall, Emma felt the chill of damp plaster like a wet cloth upon her shoulders. The walls had been freshly white-washed, and the wooden treads of the staircase creaked. In the rooms on the first floor a pallid light came through the uncurtained windows. She could see the tops of trees, and, beyond them, the meadows half drowned in mist which wreathed like smoke in the moonlight along the course of the river. In the middle of the room stood a disorderly pile of assorted objects, drawers, bottles, curtain-rods, gilt bed-posts. Mattresses lay sprawled over chairs, basins littered the floor. The two men who had moved the furniture had left things just anyhow.

—GUSTAVE FLAUBERT: *Madame Bovary*, trans. Gerard Hopkins

D Englishwomen's shoes look as if they had been made by someone who had often heard shoes described, but had never seen any, and the problem of buying shoes in London is almost insoluble— unless you pay a staggering tariff on American ones. What provokes this outburst is that I have just bought a pair of English bedroom slippers and I not only cannot tell the left foot from the right, but it is only after profound deliberation that I am able to distinguish between the front and the back.

—MARGARET HALSEY: *With Malice Towards Some*

III Write a passage in the style of the Hemingway extract previously quoted in which you use restraint and simple statement of facts in appealing to the reader's emotions.

PART THREE

A Handbook for the Writer

THE CONCERNS OF THE WRITER

The average student finds it surprisingly easy to acquire the usual tricks of poor writing. To do a consistently poor job, however, one must grasp a few essential principles:

1. Ignore the reader.
2. Be verbose, vague, and pompous.
3. Do not revise.*

Everyone faced with an assignment in composition has four major concerns:

1. finding the material that will give *substance* to the main idea of the assignment,
2. arranging and expressing this substance in *appropriate language*,
3. making sure the *flow of ideas* in the whole composition from the first sentence to the last, is *continuous* and *apparent* to the intelligent reader,
4. *revising* every preliminary draft to make sure that the final draft fulfils the demands of 1, 2, and 3.

In short, the writer must find a subject and the material appropriate to it; give his writing a focus with a particular reader in mind; express his ideas in acceptable prose; and, finally, take the time to re-examine and revise what he has written. The following are some practical suggestions for the writer.

Concentrate on the main idea

The following points will help you concentrate on the main idea of the assignment:

1. list your ideas on the subject,
2. pick the one that interests you,
3. decide on the kind of reader for whom you plan to write,

* Paul Merrill, "The Principles of Poor Writing", from *Scientific Monthly,* January, (1947).

4. make sure that the idea can be developed within the limits of the assignment,

5. select and arrange appropriate material.

Begin by trying to express the main idea of your topic in one sentence. Then list the details that expand the topic in the direction suggested by this sentence. If the assignment calls for one paragraph, the first sentence can serve as the topic sentence. If the assignment is an essay, the same sentence can serve as a thesis statement for the whole composition, implying the method of development and the details that will have to be used. Although the thesis statement need not appear in the body of the composition, writing such a sentence helps you to determine the limits of your treatment of the topic.

Topic sentence or Thesis statement	Anyone planning to buy a used car should get expert advice.
	The obvious question the writer must now answer is "why"?
Topic sentence or Thesis statement	The prevailing tone in Housman's poetry is bitter and cold.
	The writer must now support this generalization with detailed evidence from Housman's poetry.
Topic sentence or Thesis statement	Finland is the sole remaining wilderness in Europe.
	Here the writer must set out specific details to prove his contention. He is not free to do anything else until he has made his point about Finland, clearly and logically. Only then can he move to something else; e.g., the architecture of Finland's cities or Helsinki in the grip of winter.

Check sentence structure and diction

Read your first draft as if someone else had composed it. Then take out every bit of awkwardness, every puzzling expression, every careless use of words. Check sentence structure by asking such questions as:

Could some sentences be combined without loss of meaning?

Are there any awkward or incomplete sentences?

Is there variety in sentence structure or are there too many short, simple sentences?

Check diction by asking such questions as:

Are all these adjectives necessary?
Are the adverbs correctly placed?
Are there any unnecessary words (deadwood)?
Are there any clichés?
What abstract words can be replaced by more concrete, exact words?

Check transition

Shifts in thought or in direction of the movement within a composition must be clearly indicated. An effective piece of writing, no matter how long, is like a road. There may be turns and changes in direction; sometimes, these are gradual, sometimes abrupt. A gradual bend in a road indicates what is to come, but an abrupt turn is marked by a sign; similarly, in writing, the transition from what you have said to what you are going to say must be natural and smooth. Therefore, any sharp change in direction must be marked by a transitional device.

Here are the opening sentences of three paragraphs in a sequence (they are taken from *Cider With Rosie* by Laurie Lee). Note how smoothly the writer links one paragraph to the next:

That was the day we came to the village, in the summer of the last year of the First World War.
I don't know where I lived before *then*.
But *on the first day* we were all lost.

Revise

Most effective writers accept the arduous task of revision because they have learned from experience that few first drafts meet Whitehead's definition of style: "The direct attainment of a foreseen end, simply and without waste." Even poets, usually credited with more than ordinary powers of inspiration and language, spend hours and sometimes years finding the right words for a single poem. Revision is the means the writer uses to re-examine his ideas and his expression of them. It is in this act of re-examination that he perfects what he wants to say.

Suggested Steps in Revision

1. Re-read your first draft. Set it aside and *rethink* the content of the assignment. Now rewrite quickly, concentrating only on the substance. If the assignment is fairly long, rewrite only the paragraphs that puzzle or trouble you.

2. If the assignment is short, examine your opening sentence. Ask yourself if it sets the tone, suggests the limits of your topic and the direction in which you are going to move. If the assignment is long, examine the introductory paragraph with the same questions in mind.

3. Now compare the two drafts and make a third out of the best elements in the first and second.

4. Read the revision aloud to discover unnecessary repetition, unpleasant sounds, gaps in development, illogical arrangement of sentences, and faulty references, and to make sure that the conclusion gives a sense of completeness.

5. Finally, ask yourself:

    a Have I used connectives logically? That is, should I have used *but* instead of *and*; *because* instead of *since* or *as*; or *until* instead of *when*?

    b How carefully have I used words like *never* or *always*? Should I have said *occasionally* or *seldom* or *usually*?

    c Have I used unnecessary modifiers? Can some modifiers be eliminated by a more precise choice of nouns or verbs?

    d What are my personal weaknesses as a writer? Are any of them here? This check may direct attention to spelling, flowery expression, clichés, etc.

FALLACIES IN THE EXPRESSION OF IDEAS

In utterances whose aim is persuasion, argument is employed. Sometimes, however, evidence is presented in such a way as to mislead, either by a faulty process of reasoning, or by an appeal to the emotions, or by trickery in the manipulation of words. The failure to conform to one or other of the rules of sound argument is called a *fallacy*; and such fallacies may be named and classified under three main types: material, psychological or logical.

Material Fallacies

A generalization may for instance be based on too few examples or on a non-representative sample of evidence—this is a fallacy of *over-generalization*. If you write "all" when you mean "many", you are guilty of this error. Very similar is the over-simplifying of the matter of argument into two clear-cut categories, good or bad, right or wrong. Such *black and white* reasoning is the kind employed by the dictator and the propagandist who announce that all who do not support them whole-heartedly are enemies to be destroyed. Over-simplification results, likewise, in attributing an effect to a single cause just because one event has preceded another in time. Thus, when you attribute your failure in a test to the fact that you forgot your lucky charm, you are guilty of the fallacy known as *post hoc ergo propter hoc* (after this, therefore because of this), or more simply, *post hoc*. Analogy, too, may be misused if you consider only the resemblances and ignore the differences between two objects of comparison. Such a *faulty analogy* occurs when you argue in the following manner: those who commit crimes of violence are no better than wild beasts; we destroy ferocious animals; we should, therefore, exterminate dangerous criminals.

Psychological Fallacies

Many appeals in an argument are directed at emotions or prejudices, and the question under consideration is ignored altogether. In this general category of psychological fallacies go pleas for support from individuals and groups or, on the other hand, abuse of an opponent. One common fallacy of the latter type is the *personal attack* in which argument is replaced by unpleasant remarks about the character and manners of the antagonist. This kind of verbal assault is often called *ad hominem,* from the Latin phrase meaning "against the man". Slightly more difficult to detect is the attempt to discredit by imputing *guilt by association*. In this instance, character is supposed to be established by noting the people with whom one associates and judging by them. A remark like: "Of course, he's bound to get into trouble, look at the crowd he hangs around with", is an example of this fallacy.

On the other hand, attempts to bolster a case by appeals to

authority are also suspect. In *appealing to famous men* you must ensure that they are authorities in the area of your appeal. The use of testimonials by advertisers frequently falls into this class—just because a man is a star hockey player he is not necessarily qualified as a judge of razor blades or hair cream. The *appeal to large numbers* is fallacious also, considered as support for an argument, and the statement which begins "Everyone thinks . . ." may be made valueless by citing a few contrary opinions. Part of the danger in such appeals is the pressure they put on the individual to conform; to get aboard the bandwagon and be like other plain folks as advertisers often suggest. Remember simply that these are not sound arguments for a proposition, and when you hear them, treat them with caution.

Logical Fallacies

Fallacies in logic involve support for an argument by various tricks in the use of words. Into this category go *equivocation, begging the question*, and *non sequitur*. The first of these involves the use of the same term in two different senses without making a distinction between the meanings. The Witches in *Macbeth* indulge in *equivocation* in their promises, as does the oracle in *Oedipus Rex* which set the king off on his tragic career. A more light-hearted example occurs in the following statement, "Nothing is more important than life. Holes in doughnuts are nothing. Therefore holes in doughnuts are more important than life."

Begging the question occurs when an arguer assumes something to be true which really needs proof. One way to beg the question is to smuggle into the original statement of the proposition what is really supposed to be at stake in the argument. Suppose that someone offers the proposition: "This ridiculous language requirement should be dropped." What we are expected to argue is that the requirement should be got rid of, but the word *ridiculous* in the original proposition poisons the argument before it starts. The same principle appears on a larger scale whenever we argue in a circle. For example:

A "No believer will ever die."
B "But X was one of your group and he died."
A "He wasn't a true believer."

B "Why not?"
A "He died, didn't he?"

Non sequitur means: "It does not follow." Such a fallacy is found where the evidence put forward does not lead to the stated conclusion. For instance, it may be argued: "William Brown doesn't drink or smoke, and so he ought to be a good husband." But it should be obvious that such a man may still be a poor husband. He may gamble, or loaf or beat his wife. Thus, a connection has been asserted which does not exist.

Fallacies and Refutation

An understanding of fallacies is useful in helping us to argue logically, but it is also useful in helping us to locate defects in an opposing argument. If we can point out a fallacy in an opposing argument, we can *refute* that argument, and refutation is a powerful secondary weapon for maintaining our own position. Even when we are not engaged in a debate and need not refute arguments made by an opponent but are simply writing a piece of argument, we often find that we have to refute certain arguments—arguments that we can anticipate or that occur to us in turning a question over in our minds.

It is not necessary to memorize a list of fallacies to discover defects in reasoning or to reason straight. Many people who have never heard the word *fallacy* can reason straight and can locate defects in the reasoning of another person. When we meet the example of a fallacy in cold type on the page of a textbook, we are inclined to say, "Nobody with common sense would commit such an error." That is true. But common sense is not, after all, so common, and sometimes we have to work for it.

■ Applications

Identify the unacceptable propositions or arguments among the following instances, and explain the fallacy, or fallacies, involved in each:

1. The holder of one hand in this poker game is bound to win. Jack holds one hand, and therefore is bound to win.
2. On the seacoast a dying man usually breathes his last just as the

tide begins to ebb because the going out of the water takes his strength with it.

3. You should not read the poetry of Byron, because his private life was immoral.
4. Telegrams bring bad luck.
5. The Irish love whisky, and so I am not going to hire Pat Mc-Goon.
6. After taking several bottles of Lightfoot's Liver Syrup, Mrs. Jones felt much better. So Mrs. Smith immediately bought a bottle.
7. This unjust tax should be repealed.
8. I would not trust him, his father was a Communist, you know.
9. Harry Thompson would make a good Member of Parliament because he belongs to the upper class.
10. All those who are not for us must be against us. Join our crusade today and show that you know the difference between right and wrong.

SENTENCE STRUCTURES AND SENTENCE FAULTS

The basic unit of meaning in written English is *the sentence,* an ordered group of words that usually makes a statement of fact or gives expression to the feelings of the writer, but can, by transformation, pose direct questions or make requests. In English, unlike some other languages, the meaning of the sentence is determined largely by word order, with the subject normally preceding the predicate verb to which it is linked by agreement. Eight basic patterns and two variations account for most of the declarative sentences written in English.

Basic Sentence Patterns

1. $N \longleftrightarrow V$
    Subject   Verb

    Dogs   bite.
    The boy   was playing.

2.   N ⟷ V   N
    Subject   Verb   Object

The student prepared his lesson.
Success will bring confidence.

3.   N ⟷ V   N   N
    Subject   Verb   Indirect   Direct
                    Object   Object

My friend gave the teacher his essay.
Frederick was showing the old man the way.

4.   N ⟷ LV   N
    Subject   Linking Verb   Complement (Noun)

John	is	a liar.
The play	has been	a success.
The manager	seemed	a pleasant person.

5.   N ⟷ LV   Adj.
    Subject   Linking Verb   Complement (Adjective)

John	is	tired.
The natives	appeared	hostile.
Giraffes	are	long-legged.

6.   N ⟷ LV   Adv.
    Subject   Linking Verb   Complement (Adverb)

Harry	is	here.
Our teams	are	ahead.
The principal	has been	away.

7.   N ⟷ V   N   N
    Subject   Verb   Direct   Object Complement
                    Object   (Noun)

The committee elected Smith secretary.
The general called the soldier a coward.
(Note the difference between this pattern and #3)

8.   N ⟷ V   N   Adj.
    Subject   Verb   Direct   Object Complement
                    Object   (Adjective)

The teacher called his students lazy.

Besides these patterns in normal subject-predicate order, English uses a structure word, *there*, to make yet another pattern.

There   LV⟵——————⟶ N
There   Linking Verb   Subject

There seems to have been an accident.
There were two men in the room.

In addition, *it* is sometimes used in a similar manner; the difference is that such a pattern never appears with a plural verb, so the agreement seems to exist between *it* and the verb rather than between the verb and the apparent subject which follows.

It   is   a fine day.
It   seems to have been raining.

Modifying the Basic Patterns

To enrich meaning or to give greater precision to statements, additional words, phrases, and subordinate clauses may be added to basic sentence structures in combination with noun or verb head-words. These elements make evaluations; tell what number were involved; give details of appearance, time, and place; tell what happened, how it happened, and why; or give the conditions under which something might occur. Such modification may be confined to words of the original pattern, but in more complicated structures, head-words in the modifiers are themselves qualified so that two or more layers of modification may be present.

In the following structures, note how the basic pattern, N⟵⟶V, is expanded, first by modifiers of the subject and the verb, then by other structures which modify words in the primary layer of modification.

       N   V
The students worked.

                  N   V
The two most industrious students/worked *hard in preparation for the examination.*

                         N
The two most industrious students *in the graduating class/*
   V
worked *hard in preparation for the government examination*

which would determine their standing if they wished to enter university.

In the third example, "graduating" modifies "class", which is itself part of a structure of modification; similarly, "government" modifies "examination", as does "which would determine their standing". The final clause modifies "would determine" and so forms a tertiary layer of modification.

The order of modifying elements in the sentence causes little difficulty to native speakers. Single-word modifiers of the noun usually precede their head-word, while phrases and clauses usually follow it. Noun modifiers may also be connected with their head-words by linking verbs when they form the complement of Sentence Pattern 5.

Though verb modifiers have somewhat more freedom of movement, they too are usually as close as possible to whatever they modify. Often, a faulty sentence may be improved simply by changing the position of a modifier to make clearer its relationship to its head-word.

AMBIGUOUS ORDER
What we read *deeply* affects our feelings.
The jury convicted the prisoner of second-degree murder *after arguing for several hours*.

CLEARER ORDER
What we read affects our feelings *deeply*.
After arguing for several hours, the jury convicted the defendant of second-degree murder.

Combining the Patterns

1. Two or more independent statements may be linked by connective words or by punctuation alone. Co-ordinators—*and, but, for, or, yet*—are the most commonly used conjunctive words though the correlatives, *either . . . or*, are also employed.

    We had intended to come this morning, *but* our car broke.
    Either Tom will collect the mail, *or* we can pick it up tomorrow.

2. Sometimes no conjunctive word is supplied; instead, two clauses are linked by a semicolon.

    John has a vivid imagination; he often seems to be living in a world of his own creation.

3. A semicolon is also conventional punctuation when sentence connectors (conjunctive adverbs) are used to link complete statements. The commonest of these connectives are *accordingly, also, however, hence, indeed, nevertheless, therefore.* These words are distinguished from co-ordinators by their freedom of movement within the second pattern of the two being combined.

> I wanted to visit Niagara; however, I felt I had no time.
> I wanted to visit Niagara; I had, however, no time.
> I wanted to visit Niagara; I had no time, however.

4. Often, too, statements may be combined by making one a subordinate clause and having it function as a modifier within the other, attached to a noun or to the predicate verb.

> John looked after the dog. He had found it.
> John looked after the dog *which he had found.*

> The alarm sounded. The students left.
> *When the alarm sounded,* the students left.

> People wanted to write to me. I met them on the trip.
> They learned I lived in Canada.
> People *whom I met on the trip* wanted to write to me *when they learned I lived in Canada.*

Transformations

By simple rearrangement of word order in sentences, sometimes accompanied by the insertion of appropriate function words, it is possible to change statements to questions or requests, or to put active sentences into the passive where the subject is acted on instead of acting.

1. Questions may be framed by shifting the auxiliary verb and the subject, supplying the appropriate form of *do* as an auxiliary if there is none in the original statement.

> He has worked well.
> *Has he* worked well?

> The natives seem friendly.
> *Do* the natives seem friendly?

> They go regularly.
> *Do* they go regularly?

Otherwise, appropriate interrogatory words are used to begin such transformed structures: *who, whom, whose, which, when, where, what, why, how*.

2. Requests or commands are formed by using the base form of the verb which frequently opens the transformed structure in the absence of a stated subject. Such patterns may also begin with *let's* or *please*.

> Give me some of these books.
> Let's give her the apples.
> Please buy Christmas seals.

3. Sentence Pattern 2 (and, more rarely, Sentence Patterns 3, 7, and 8) may be set in the passive by using the past participle of a transitive verb with some part of the auxiliary *be*. Sometimes, the original subject is retained in a phrase following the preposition *by*.

> The chorus sang the next number.
> The next number *was sung* by the chorus.
>
> He dug the well to a depth of 12 feet.
> The well *was dug* to a depth of 12 feet.
>
> Our team is defeating the opposing side.
> The opposing side *is being defeated* by our team.

Common Errors in Sentences

Mistakes in composing sentences may arise from ignorance or carelessness. The following list, arranged alphabetically for handy reference, deals with some of the commonest of these errors, suggesting correct forms and giving cross references where applicable.

Comma fault

When a comma is used to hold together two sentence patterns in a situation that requires a semicolon, the error is called a comma fault, and the sentence in which it occurs is called a *run-on sentence*. Such an error is a serious fault in written English since the resulting structure may be confusing to the reader. For example,

> John came home in the afternoon, Mary did not arrive till after supper.

Dangling modifier

A modifier is said to dangle when it is not firmly attached to the word it is supposed to modify or when no logical head-word is to be found.

> *Working at the bench,* the noise disturbed the *mechanic.*
> *Hurrying home,* his coat was lost.

In the first sentence, the apparent head-word is *noise,* whereas it should be *mechanic.* In the second sentence, the apparent head-word is *coat* and no alternative is supplied in the sentence as it stands. To revise the first, rearrange the statement so that *mechanic* becomes the subject and follows immediately after the modifier; to correct the second, supply a subject such as *he* and make the sentence active rather than passive.

> *Working at the bench, the mechanic* was disturbed by the noise.
> *Hurrying home, he* lost his coat.

Lack of agreement between subject and predicate verb

Certain parts of speech have variations in form depending on gender, person or number. When these stand in relationship to each other, they agree; a change in the form of one, therefore, involves a corresponding change in the other.

Subject and predicate verb must agree in number (The *boy is* tired. The *boys are* tired) and in person if the subject is a personal pronoun (*I leave* today. *He leaves* today). Mistakes in agreement usually result from failure to identify the subject so that the writer makes the verb agree with the wrong word.

1. Such an error may occur when a long phrase or clause containing a plural noun intervenes between a singular and its verb, or *vice versa.*

   > The *extent* of the player's injuries *has* not yet been discovered.
   > (The subject, *extent,* requires a singular verb form.)
   > The officers with the ship's captain *were* on deck.
   > (The subject, *officers,* requires a plural verb form.)

2. When the subject is compound, a plural verb form is normally used.

The boy and his sister *were* first to leave.
A band of peasants and one tired horse *were* coming towards us.

Only when the two elements of the compound refer to the same person or thing is the singular used.

The most respected teacher and the best scholar here *is* Dr. Jones.

3. Subjects connected by *or*, or *either . . . or*, or *neither . . . nor*, have a singular verb if both are singular but a plural verb if both are plural or if the subject nearer the verb is plural.

Jones *or* Brown *is* to be chosen.
Either John *or* Mary *is* to be chosen.
Neither the leader *nor* his five men *were* sure of the way.
Dogs *or* cats *were* the same to him.

4. When the elements of the subject are pronouns of differing persons, the verb is usually plural.

He and I *are* sure to go.
Neither you nor I *are* fit.

5. When the subject is an indefinite pronoun, *anybody, anyone, each, either, everybody, neither, nobody, no one, somebody,* the verb is generally singular in form.

Somebody has been here.
Each of them *makes* ten dollars a week.
Nobody in school *has* seen him.
Neither plan *has* succeeded.

6. *Any* and *none* as subjects take either singular or plural verbs, depending on the sense.

Are any of you going?
None are expected from that part of town.
None of this *is* suitable.

7. When the subject is a relative pronoun, the verb agrees with the antecedent in number.

He is one of the *men who deal* with us.
One of the *girls who work* in the office is leaving.
The *person who tries* hard will succeed.
People who try hard will succeed.

8. A subject may be plural in form but singular in intent. In this situation, the verb is usually singular.

> Ten thousand *dollars is* a large sum.
> Five *centuries is* a long time.

9. Titles take a singular verb.

> *The Times* is a famous London newspaper.
> *Under Western Eyes* is a novel by Joseph Conrad.

Note that the complement does not affect the agreement of the verb with the subject.

> Books are his chief delight.
> His chief delight is books.

Lack of agreement between pronouns and their antecedents

Pronouns agree with their antecedents in number, gender, and person.

> The *boy* has lost *his* way.
> The *girl* washed *her* hair.
> The *hurricane* changed *its* direction.
> The *men* fired *their* rifles.

1. When singular antecedents are joined by *and*, the pronoun reference to them is plural.

> John and Mike are searching for *their* books.
> Peter and I are leaving on *our* trip today.

2. When the antecedent is itself an indefinite pronoun, the singular is used.

> *Each* has *his* own task to perform.
> *Nobody* had *his* lesson prepared.
> Everybody was ready for *his* exam.

3. Since a pronoun draws its meaning from its antecedent, such a reference should be easily discoverable. For this reason, an unspecified or implied antecedent—often the idea contained in a complete clause—should be avoided.

> Employers have agreed to binding arbitration *which* pleased the negotiator.

In this case, the lack of a referent for *which* makes the pronoun unsuitable.

Shifted construction

Shifting from the normal subject-verb-complement pattern of the English sentence disrupts the structure, often causing the omission of essential elements.

1. A shift may lead to the disappearance of the subject, as in the following instance:

    For information concerning this matter may be located in the *International Index to Periodicals.*

2. Sometimes, the shift involves a change from one part of speech to another with elements that should be parallel. In the following example, the association of nouns with adjectives disturbs the flow of the sentence:

    The job seems *interesting* and *a well-paid position.*
    (Adjective paired with noun.)
    Anyone who has *character* or is *persistent* can do the job.

3. Sometimes the shift occurs from one clause to another and involves a change of structure or subject.

    After the method had been mastered, he had no difficulty in working the problem.
    (Passive construction followed by the active with subject *he.*)
    I looked from the window of the plant. Below you could hardly see the ground.
    (Shift from first to second.)

Wrong case of pronouns

Difficulties arise in this area of usage because in English only pronouns have kept distinct forms for the subjective and the objective case (I-me, he-him, she-her, we-us, they-them, who-whom). As a result, the form required is the one determined by its function as subject or object.

In written English, such difficulties are most likely to arise where two pronouns of different person are compounded, especially following a preposition like *between.* Usage of *who* and *whom*, however, also causes occasional difficulties.

Note these examples:

You and *I* are involved.
The case involved you and *me*.
Between you and *me*, I think he is wrong.
John divided the candy between *him* and *me*.
He asked me *whom* I meant.
He asked *who* had seen the whale.

Because of the power of English word order, *whom* has all but disappeared as the first word in an utterance. Here, *who* has taken over. *Whom* remains standard after the preposition, but it is nearly always incorrectly used elsewhere. For example:

Please submit the names of any persons *whom* you believe should be considered for the position.

The substitution of *him* or *them* in the above example would reveal that the use of *whom* is "not English".

The arguments over *It's me* hardly arise here since this construction occurs almost solely in spoken English where it has won full acceptance from such authorities as Fowler's *Modern English Usage*.

PUNCTUATION

A certain amount of punctuation is governed by convention and has to be learned as a matter of good manners in writing; the chief function of punctuation is, however, to provide a set of substitute signals for elements of speech that have no written equivalents. Thus the period, the comma, and the semicolon are visible indications of pitch patterns and pauses in spoken English. Some marks signal the end of sentences; others are internal and serve to separate elements or to show the relationship between them.

End punctuation

1. The *period* is by far the commonest signal of a sentence ending. It is standard at the conclusion of statements, of indirect questions, of polite requests, and of mild expressions of feeling.

   I asked if he had finished.
   Will you finish, please.
   What a pleasant spot this is.

2. The *question mark* denotes a direct question.

> How do you plan to finish that?
> She will come, won't she?
> You did say she would come, didn't you?

3. The *exclamation mark* follows a command or an expression of strong feeling. It should be used sparingly to keep its force. Note that it is a terminal mark and is followed by a capital letter.

> Stop! You are hurting that child.
> Look out! Timber!

Internal punctuation

Most problems in punctuating arise in connection with the two commonest marks of internal punctuation, the comma and the semicolon.

The comma

The *comma* has a variety of functions, some conventional or mechanical, others grammatical.

By convention, commas are used with dates, coming between the day of the month and the year:

> January 22, 1969.

They are also used with the salutation of friendly letters:

> Dear Fred,

With figures they group digits in threes:

> 1,035,672

In addresses, commas are used between the town or city and the province or country when these stand on the same line:

> Clinton, B.C.   Toronto, Ont.   Paris, France.

In a series of three or more items, commas separate the individual elements. Usage is divided on the question of inserting a comma before the last item of a series when a co-ordinator is present. Generally, it is safer to include it in such a position; but, whether you do or not, be consistent.

> The group consisted of ten men, three women, and five children.

A comma separates co-ordinate adjectives that modify the same noun. Adjectives are not co-ordinate when one of them modifies the noun while the other modifies both it and the noun as a unit.

Note the difference between "a bright, sunny day" and "a famous Canadian novelist".

Commas find their main grammatical uses as follows: after long introductory phrases or clauses to separate these from the main clause of the sentence; with parenthetical elements, including appositives and non-restrictive modifiers; and between the clauses of a compound sentence where these are linked by a co-ordinator.

With introductory modifiers, the writer has to decide whether the insertion of a comma will prevent misreading.

While eating, the baby became sick.
If you leave before morning, he will be offended.

Two commas are necessary to set off internal parenthetical elements, including non-restrictive modifiers which give information over and above what is necessary for the reader's understanding.

My aunt, Mrs. Brown, lives in the next block.
Jack, who had been asleep, suddenly leaped to his feet.

Note the difference between a restrictive modifier and one which is non-restrictive.

The students who come by bus were late.
(Restrictive: only those who came by bus were late.)
The students, who come by bus, were late.
(Non-restrictive: all the students were late and all come by bus.)

Between co-ordinate clauses connected by *but* or *for,* a comma is normal. A comma, likewise, emphasizes the distinction between two clauses linked by *and, or, nor, yet.*

The day was warm, yet the wind was blowing strongly.
This test is not exact, for the same result is given by other compounds.

The semicolon

The *semicolon*, unlike the comma, finds its main value as a marker for co-ordinate clauses closely linked in thought where no conjunctive word is used between them or where the linking word is one of a class called *sentence connectors*. These words differ from co-ordinators since they may be found in a variety of positions and are not restricted to the point of juncture. The commonest of these linking words are *therefore, moreover, however, consequently, further-*

more, still, then, likewise, instead; certain phrases function in the same way: *as a result, in the event, on the other hand* are examples.

I wish she would get ready; we are going to be late.
Day is the time for activity; night is the time for rest.
The weather was stormy; we stayed indoors, therefore.
John failed the test; Mary, on the other hand, passed with honours.

The colon

The *colon* serves a few conventional purposes in punctuation. It is used following the salutation in a formal letter; between hours and minutes in a statement of exact time; with an appositive series following a complete statement; as the introductory mark for a lengthy quotation, and with two co-ordinate clauses where the second explains the first.

Gentlemen: Dear Sir:
I must leave at 7:30.
The curriculum included these subjects: math, history, music, and art.
A statement by the *Bulletin of Statistics* tells the story: last year production rose by over 7,000 tons and . . . was the largest in the world.
I am now sure of one thing: first-aid saved my life.

The dash

The *dash* is useful to indicate an abrupt shift of thought; it should be employed sparingly in formal writing. A pair of dashes may set off internal appositives and modifiers when these contain commas.

I must tell you—but let's go somewhere quiet first.
To find the exit was our only hope—a faint one indeed.
My friends—John, Robert, and Thomas—were not at home.

Parentheses

Parentheses have one formal function: to mark off modifiers which interrupt the run of the text. They are used mostly in technical writing such as scientific papers, bibliographies, and textbooks.

Two players (probably Jones and Sadowski) will be dropped from the squad.
Bradbury, Ray. *The Martian Chronicles* (New York, 1950).

Brackets

Brackets, like parentheses, occur in pairs. Their use is highly specialized being confined to the insertion of a comment or correction in a piece of quoted material to show that the error existed in the original and was not the result of careless copying.

> Thomson wrote, "I left Fort St. John late in 1905 [1805] and travelled overland to Fraser Lake."
> Nelson's last letter begins, "I recieved [sic] your note yesterday."

Sic (Latin for *thus*) in brackets marks an error in mechanics which the reader can correct for himself.

Other marks

Quotation marks enclose direct speech or show that a word or group of words is being quoted. Normally, they are employed with other marks of punctuation; when the speech is introduced by a formula like *he said,* it is preceded by a comma before the first quotation marks. It is usual also to begin enclosed matter with a capital letter except where the quoted material is divided by the formula. Quotation marks also surround titles of poems, stories, and essays where these are not complete books or periodicals.

> The man shouted, "Let go at once."
> "Keep quiet or we'll be discovered", whispered a friend.
> "Go on", said Jack, "it's easy if you try."
> "Let's explore", Tom said. "We can leave at dawn."
> The speech begins, "Tomorrow, and tomorrow and tomorrow . . . ."
> The class had studied Pope's "Rape of the Lock" in their anthology.

The *apostrophe* is purely formal in function. It marks the possessive form of nouns and the omission of letters in contractions.

> John's book, the girls' exercises, he's tired, I can't do it

The *hyphen* is a mark of punctuation designed either to join or sometimes keep distinct two or more written units. Its most common use is to mark the division of a word at the end of a line. Otherwise, its employment is governed to a considerable extent by editors or by the degree of formality of the written material. Since usage with hyphens varies somewhat, it is a good plan to check with a reputable dictionary and follow the advice given there. Some standard uses may, however, be noted.

In compound words the hyphen marks an intermediate stage

between the wording of an expression as two words and its total fusion into one (foot ball, foot-ball, football).

The following are some conventional uses of the hyphen:

1. In numerals from twenty-one to ninety-nine and often with fractions:
   fifty-two, three hundred and ninety-seven, three-sixteenths, one twenty-fifth
2. In some compounds with *self*:
   self-contained, self-importance, self-government
3. In compounds consisting of a single letter and a noun:
   A-bomb, S-hook, T-bar, X-ray
4. The hyphen finds its chief use with compound modifiers when they precede a noun:
   first-class, heavy-handed, open-ended, well-made, slow-moving, three-year, eighteenth-century, high-scoring
5. A numeral as part of a modifier is hyphened:
   5-cents, 3 5-inch nails
6. Phrase modifiers are usually hyphened:
   on a pay-as-you-go basis
   a question-and-answer form
   a ninety-five-pound, three-foot-six midget
7. A hyphen carries the force of a modifier over to a later noun:
   first-, second-, and third-grade boys
   nineteenth- and twentieth-century inventions

Note that no hyphen is used when the first element of the compound ends in *ly*:

   a badly made bed
   a lightly cooked egg

Normally, no hyphen is used when the compound is in the predicate position:

The boy is well trained.
These goods are slow moving.

Hyphens occur between certain prefixes and the root words to which they are attached:

1. To avoid confusion between a prefix ending in a vowel and a root word beginning with the same vowel:
   re-elect, re-enter, pre-eminent.

2. Between a prefix and a proper noun:
   pro-Diefenbaker, ex-Senator Brown, anti-American.

Italic type is used by printers for various purposes. (In written or in typewritten script, underline the words that would appear in italics in a printed book.) Titles of complete works go in italics, as do foreign words or phrases or English words when they are being quoted as special examples.

> Have you read Shakespeare's *Julius Caesar?*
> I found the verse in *Poetry of our Time.*
> *Dolce far niente* means "the pleasure of doing nothing".
> You are confusing *there* and *their.*

THE RESEARCH PAPER

The research paper is a form of expository discourse. Its aim is to assemble facts and ideas from various sources so that by studying them, you may draw new conclusions or present the material in the light of a new interest. To do this adequately, you must be able to find a suitable topic, assemble available materials, organize them in a unified composition, and supply footnotes and a bibliography to indicate your authority for the various statements made and opinions put forward.

The first step toward making your paper systematic is to limit the topic so that the theme may be handled within the assigned length. You could, for instance, hardly write a research essay on "Winter Sports", but you could deal adequately with "Development in Skiing Techniques in the last Twenty Years". Next, you have to gather material and this has already been done for you in the form of books and articles in periodicals, some of which should be available in the library. To get at this material, you should ask help from the librarian in the use of the reference works which will lead you to relevant information.

References and Footnotes

When you refer to a work, you would be well advised to have a stock of 3 x 5 inch cards on which you may enter the following information:

For a book:

5″

> Strachey, Lytton, *Elizabeth and Essex,*
> London, Chatto & Windus, 1928

3″

For an article:

> Barrington, Margaret, "Censorship in
> Eire," *Commonweal,* XLVI (1947),
> 429-32.

Also on these cards should go any particularly telling facts or memorable expressions of opinion so that you will have this information at hand when you start to write the final draft of your paper from your rough outline.

Full credit must be given for the source of every fact or idea derived from another writer. Sometimes, you may be able to do this by introducing a statement by clear explanatory remarks such as these:

> As Sinclair Lewis shows in *Main Street*, the culture of the American small town is . . . .
> In *As For Me and My House,* Sinclair Ross depicts church life in Saskatchewan during . . . .

More often than not, however, you will have to state your authority in the form of a footnote which gives the data acknowledging your indebtedness. Every direct quotation must be so identified. Every statement of fact must also refer to its source, assuming that the information is available only in one authority, as must every opinion or interpretation drawn from another writer.

Within the text, the footnote number is placed at the end of the statement to which it refers and slightly above the line. The footnote appears at the bottom of the page, indented five spaces from the left margin. The footnote number is placed above the level of the line on which the required information is given. If a reference is to a page in the book by Lytton Strachey, the actual footnote entry may run as follows:

[1] Lytton Strachey, *Elizabeth and Essex* (London, 1928), p. 43.

Note that the author's name appears in direct form, not with the last name first as in a bibliography; that the title is underlined in typescript or writing to correspond with italics in print; that the place and date of publication are set in parentheses; and that a page number is given.

Should the reference be to an article in a periodical, the title of the article appears in quotation marks with the title of the publication italicized. Thus:

[2] Margaret Barrington, "Censorship in Eire", *Commonweal,* XLVI (1947), 432.

Other points to note are the inclusion of the volume number of the periodical, its year of issue, and the page reference without the abbreviation *p.*, omitted for periodicals after the volume number.

For later references to sources you have already mentioned, abbreviated forms may be used. When the source is the same as that indicated in a footnote *immediately preceding,* use *ibid.* (from the Latin, *ibidem*: in the same place). For example, a second reference to Margaret Barrington's article could read as follows:

[3] *Ibid.,* 430.

Notice that *ibid.* is capitalized when it begins a footnote, is in italics (underlined in typescript or handwriting), and is followed by both a period and a comma.

When the reference to be repeated does not immediately precede, the easiest method is to use a version of the original footnote containing only the author's last name, a shortened title, and the page reference. For example:

[4] Strachey, *Elizabeth,* p. 48.

Bibliography

The bibliography is a list of the works which you referred to in your essay. Such a list comes at the end of your essay, on a separate sheet, headed BIBLIOGRAPHY. The bibliography is arranged in alphabetical order according to the last name of the author or, if there is no author, by the main word of the title. The following are some examples of entries as they might appear in the bibliography of a paper on Woodrow Wilson:

Baker, Ray Stannard. "Our Next President and Some Others". *American Magazine*, LXXIV (June 1912).

Barnes, Harry Elmer. *The Genesis of the World War*. New York: Alfred A. Knopf, 1926.

Congressional Record, XLIX-LI, Washington: Government Printing Office, 1913-1914.

McAdoo, Eleanor R. W. *The Woodrow Wilsons*. New York: The Macmillan Company, 1937.

GLOSSARY

Abbreviations

In formal writing use standard forms such as:

Dr., Mr., Mrs., Messrs.

1066 A.D., 55 B.C.

In technical writing, legal documents, and personal notes, abbreviations save space. But even here it is a sound rule to use only recognized abbreviations, those listed in a comprehensive handbook or dictionary.

Ad—see Clipped Words

Adjectives

Adjectives should be used only to give greater precision to nouns. Two suggestions:

1. Never use an adjective to prop up a vague noun.
2. Use even the best adjectives sparingly to avoid redundance (e.g., *salty* ocean—*salty* is probably unnecessary).

Adverbs

The reservations about the use of the adjective apply to the adverb as well. Strong writing avoids both.

He shouted loudly.

Better: He shouted.

Read Hamlet's Soliloquy (Act III, Scene 1), and Chapter 13 of First Corinthians (King James Version), as examples of strong writing and the effective use of adjectives and adverbs.

Agreement

Lack of agreement is a problem for the following reasons:

1. Lack of agreement does not always destroy clarity, and in some dialects it goes unnoticed:

    He *don't* for He *doesn't* (Standard in early 19th Century)

    You *was* for You *were*

2. Often a noun of a different number comes between subject and predicate. Instead of:

    "This *kind* of apples *is* good for cooking"

    we may slip into:

    "This *kind* of apples *are* good for cooking."

3. Often the meaning is plural but the form is singular.

    The board is not free to pay one of *themselves*.

4. Custom and the idiom of the language take precedence over the logic of agreement. For example, in the sentence:

    More than one man has lost his money betting on the horses.

    more than one is certainly plural but we would not say:

    More than one man *have* lost *their* money betting on the horses.

All right

Alright, although widely used in advertising and popular literature, is still not so acceptable as *all right*.

Ambiguity

A statement that can be understood in two or more ways is said to be *ambiguous*. Ambiguity is often deliberately used in poetry to achieve multiple meaning, depth, and complexity. But ambiguity in prose writing is usually accidental, the result of misplaced modifiers and faulty reference of pronouns.

Mary phoned the man from the shop.

Was the phoning done from the shop or was the man she phoned an employee in the shop?

He paid his bill promptly by cheque, which is always good.

Is it the cheque that is good or the fact that he paid the bill promptly? Ambiguities tend to appear in most first draft writing. Revision is therefore the only way to make sure accidental (unintended) meanings do not appear in the finished draft.

Analogy

An *analogy* is a comparison of similarities in two or more things or situations. Though useful in explaining and suggesting unrecognized similarites, analogy cannot be used to prove anything.

In linguistics, analogy refers to the process by which new or less familiar words, spellings, pronunciations, and structures are made to conform with the pattern of more familiar (though often unrelated) words or constructions. For example, *energize* from energy by analogy with *apologize* from *apology; alright* (still not standard) by analogy with *already.*

Back formation

The process of forming a word from one that looks like its derivative is called *back formation.* Examples are the verb *beg* from *beggar, enthuse* from *enthusiasm, donate* from *donation, diagnose* from *diagnosis, opine* from *opinion.*

Some back formations like *to preach* and *to beg* are now accepted; others, like *to enthuse* and *to opine,* are questionable in all but informal usage.

Bad, badly

I feel *badly* is used by people who mistakenly think that a verb ought to be followed by an adverb. "I feel *badly*" is correctly used when the speaker is referring to his sense of touch. "I feel *bad*" is correctly used to mean "I don't feel well" or "I am upset."

Though today so common as to be almost standard, "I feel badly" was probably introduced by people who, according to the language scholar, Bergen Evans, thought they were speaking "extraly, specially finely".

Bombast

The term *bombast* refers to the use of high-sounding words, inappropriate to the occasion.

Cliché

Any overworked phrase that is no longer vivid and forceful is called a *cliché*. The term is also applied to over-used situations in the plots of second-rate stories, and to stock sounds in music. Sometimes, the cliché is used by writers to get ironic effects.

Clipped words

Clipped words like *prof* for *professor, gym* for *gymnasium, lit* for *literature, math* for *mathematics, home ec* for *home economics, dorm* for *dormitory, phone* for *telephone, ad* for *advertisement,* and *quote* for *quotation* are appropriate only in an informal context. Although a few, such as *taxi* for *taxicab* (itself a short form of *taximeter cabriolet*), have become standard, most clipped words are acceptable only in colloquial usage.

Colloquialism

A *colloquialism* is any expression acceptable in the informal talk of educated people; that is, any expression that educated people would use in informal speech and writing. It is neither incorrect nor illiterate but should be avoided in formal writing.

Conjunctive adverbs (*also called Sentence Connectors*)

The *conjunctive adverb* is a connecting device emphasizing the relationship between one sentence and another, or between elements within one sentence. Adverbs like *hence, nevertheless,* and *furthermore,* when used between independent clauses are preceded by a semicolon:

He arrived too late to help; nevertheless, he remained to give advice.

Like other transitional devices (personal and demonstrative pronouns) conjunctive adverbs show the movement of thought in a piece of writing.

Additional conjunctive adverbs are: *also, accordingly, besides, consequently, indeed, likewise, moreover, still, then, therefore, such as.*

Connotation — denotation

The term *connotation* refers to the emotional impact of a word, to the implications and suggestions that a word evokes. Examine the following sentences:

> He received the message while *sprawling* on the bed.
> He received the message while *reclining* on the bed.

In these sentences, *sprawling* and *reclining* have similar *denotative* or dictionary meanings, but their *connotative* meanings have different emotional impacts. Connotations may be *individual,* that is based on personal associations or *general,* based on cultural associations.

All first draft writing should be checked to make sure that the connotations used are appropriate.

Context

The term *context* is used to refer to the language or situation that surrounds a given word. By itself, a word may have many denotative meanings; in context, its meaning is made particular. For example, what does the word "duck" mean? A web-footed swimming bird? To stoop suddenly? A heavy cotton fabric? A military truck for amphibious use? In context, the particular meaning is made clear:

> We had roast *duck* for dinner.
> He patched the hole in the tent with *duck.*
> He tends to *duck* unpleasant tasks.

Context illustrates the complicated nature of the meaning of words. To quote *out of context* usually gives a wrong impression; to quote out of context deliberately is to use language cynically and dishonestly.

Dangling modifiers

In a sentence like the following, "Coming round the next turn in the road, Mount Eisenhower could be seen", the phrase, *Coming round the next turn in the road,* is called a *dangling modifier* because the word which the phrase is intended to modify is missing. The sentence should read, "Coming round the next turn in the road, we could see Mount Eisenhower."

The dangling modifier is often caused by unnecessary shifts to the passive form of the verb:

> To be a good student, many books must be read.
> Revised: To be a good student, *one* must read many books.

The word which a phrase is intended to modify should always be stated and placed as close to the phrase as possible.

Dialect

Each of us speaks a *dialect* which reflects his family speech habits, his neighbourhood, his education, his occupation, and many other things. A language is made up of a variety of dialects, mutually intelligible, but differing according to region, community, and occupational or social group. Central dialects of a language, like *standard spoken* or *standard written,* are written into dictionaries.

Different from — different than — different to

The commonest preposition after different is *from.* But *different to* is "found in writers of all ages" (O.E.D.), and is standard British. Fowler observes: "That *different* can only be followed by *from* and not by *to* is superstition."

Different than is still unacceptable to many, although this usage is centuries old and in some expressions saves us from saying *from what* or *from the way.* For example:

> This situation is different than I had expected.

Because *different than* is unacceptable to some people, use *different from* in all formal writing.

Double negative

Two negatives make a positive in algebra but not in English. "I didn't have no money" is certainly not acceptable English, but the sentence does not mean the same as "I had some money." Standard English avoids the *double negative* but occasionally one negative qualifies the other to express the weakest kind of positive, as in "I am not unhappy."

Due to

In strict usage *due to* is used only as an adjectival connective.

> The slippery roads were due to heavy rains.
> The roads had become slippery due to heavy rains.

In the second sentence, strict usage insists on *owing to* or *because of* instead of *due to*.

The distinction between the use of *due to* and *owing to* has all but disappeared, and there is every indication that the prepositional use will eventually gain general acceptance in formal usage. The phrase *due to the fact that* is always weak and should be replaced by the one word *because*.

> Due to the fact that I was absent, I did not get my marks.
> Better: Because I was absent, I did not get my marks.

Euphemism

A *euphemism* is the use of a mild, colourless or indirect term instead of its blunt or harsh synonym. Most polite references to bodily functions are *euphemistic*. At its best, the use of euphemisms is motivated by good taste, kindness, and a sense of decency. At its worst, it is an attempt to change unpleasant realities by means of words. The euphemist speaks of "unmentionables" rather than "underwear", "dentures" rather than "false teeth", "sanitary engineer" rather than "plumber", "strategic withdrawal" rather than "retreat".

Full words and function words

Full words are those words in the sentence that carry *primary* meaning. Full words can have typical inflections, or forms; they are therefore also called *form words*. Nouns, verbs, adverbs, and adjectives belong to this class. In the sentence, "The house was destroyed by fire", the primary meaning is in the string of full words: *house, destroyed, fire*. Full words are an "open class";

in other words, we are continually adding new nouns, verbs, adjectives, and adverbs to the language.

Function words are the words in a sentence used to hold form words together in a grammatical pattern, or structure. For this reason function words are also called *structure words*. Function words include auxiliary verbs, prepositions, and conjuctions. In the sentence, "The house was destroyed by fire", there are three function words: *the, was, by*. Function words are called a "closed class" for we rarely make a new function word.

Although auxiliary verbs can be inflected for tense (is, was; has, had, etc.), they are classed with function words because auxiliaries do not change the primary meaning in the main verb. There are only a few hundred function words in the language.

Functional shift

Functional shift is the term used to describe the ability of words to function as different parts of speech. Thus, the word *cut* may function as a noun (a deep cut), or a verb (to cut the grass), or as a modifier (a cut stem).

Gender

Gender is a term for classifying words grammatically as *masculine, feminine,* and *neuter*. Except for a few pronouns (he, she, it) English gender is *natural* rather than grammatical. The term *gender* is therefore not necessary in the discussion of English grammar. In German, for instance, it is important to know that grammatically the word for "table" (der Tisch) is masculine, the word for "door" (die Tür) is feminine, and the word for "window" (das Fenster) is neuter, because each gender has its special forms for the article and the adjective.

Gerund

Any "ing" verb that functions as a noun substitute is called a *gerund*. In the sentence, "Giving is often more fun than receiving", *Giving* and *receiving* are gerunds. In English, gerunds have the same form (-ing added to the base) as present participles. Notice the use of the possessive before the gerund:

I enjoy John's *singing.*
John's *singing* thrilled the audience.

We could say *Mary likes John singing* but this could mean *Mary likes John when he sings.* In general, the possessive before "ing" verbs is preferred.

Generalization

The inductive leap by which the mind moves from particular instances or evidence to a general conclusion is known as a *generalization.* Generalizations are often made hastily, based on too few instances or ignoring contrary evidence. The statement, "Thinking people are blood donors", is a generalization which has too many exceptions to be taken seriously. But much more dangerous are the hasty generalizations that result in racial, religious, and other kinds of prejudice. Even the most accurate generalization, because it is a leap from *some* to *all,* can never be more than a *probability.* "Heavy cigarette smoking is a major cause of lung cancer", may be a generalization without sufficient evidence, but it may be wise to accept it as a strong probability. The following are the tests for making a generalization:

1. A number of instances must be investigated.
2. The instances investigated must be typical and not special cases.
3. All negative instances must be accounted for.

Grammar

The word *grammar* can refer to three different things:

1. The *system* of the language; this has been defined as, "the formal patterns into which the words of a language are arranged to give larger meanings". In this sense, all those who speak a language are familiar with its grammar.
2. The *study of the system* of the language. This meaning of grammar refers to the scientific description and analysis of the language system.
3. The etiquette concerned with correctness and appropriateness in *language usage.* It is in this sense that "I ain't gonna

come" is referred to as *bad grammar,* and "I am not coming" is considered *good grammar.*

The term *grammar* causes confusion when these three meanings are mixed. Modern grammarians use the term for #1 and #2, but refer to #3 as *usage.* Most scholars of the language consider the terms "bad grammar" and "good grammar" too vague to be useful.

Head-word

Examine the italicized words in the following word groups:
1. The popular folk *singer* on the stage (noun cluster)
2. *Sang* with great feeling (verb cluster)

The italicized words *singer* and *sang* are called head-words because they are the key words in a *modification structure* (modifiers plus modified).

Head-word in 1: *singer*
Modifiers of head-word: The *popular* folk   *on the stage*
Head-word in 2: *sang*
Modifiers of head-word: *with great feeling*

Constructions in which the head-word is a noun are called *noun clusters*; constructions in which the head-word is a verb are called *verb clusters.* Nouns and verbs are the most common head-words in English.

Idiom

An *idiom* is an expression fixed by usage rather than by regular grammar and logic. *Idiomatic* expressions are subject only to the laws of what people using the language always say. For example, we say:

He did this *of his own accord.*
He did this *in accordance with* regulations.

There is no logical explanation for always using *of* with "his own accord" and *in* with "accordance with".

Some expressions appear to be idiomatic but can be grammatically explained. For example:

I have *a* cold.
I have *the* flu.

Because *cold* is often used in the plural as *colds,* we can consider it a *count noun* that can take the determiner "a". Because *flu* is seldom used in the plural, it follows the pattern of a *mass noun* that cannot take "a". For example: we cannot say, "I have *a* money." "I buy *a* rice." Similarly, we say:

> My name is John.
> Not: I call myself John.

Unless, of course, I mean that I am assuming the name John for the time being.

Imply—infer

To *imply* means to suggest; to *infer* means to draw a conclusion from evidence.

Irony

Irony is a subtle way of implying a comparison between *appearance* and *reality*. Irony is the contrast between what is said and what is meant, between what is expected and what is. The following are a few of the ways in which irony is classified:

1. *Verbal irony*   The writer's or speaker's *actual* meaning is the opposite of the *literal* meaning. (Jonathan Swift's *Modest Proposal* is a classic example.)

2. *Irony of situation*   The contrast between a series of actions and the outcome, between what happens and what the reader expects. (For example, Joseph and Charles Surface in Sheridan's *School for Scandal.*)

3. *Irony of understatement*   Saying less than what is actually true. "Last week I saw a woman flayed, and you will hardly believe how much it altered her appearance for the worse." (J. Swift)

4. *Dramatic irony*   Those words and actions of characters in a play or story that show them to be ignorant of the actual situation. An example is Macbeth's, "would he were here!" when Banquo's ghost was there all the time.

To comprehend the *irony* in a piece of writing requires intelligent and skilful reading. The subtler the irony, the easier it is to be taken in by the literal meaning and miss the writer's meaning.

Intensifiers

Words like *very, rather, somewhat* are called *intensifiers* because they intensify modifiers (adverb and adjective). Intensifiers are usually overworked to get obvious emphasis. Intensifiers may precede adjectives and adverbs but not verbs.

Intensification

Most *intensification* by means of such words as *significantly, tremendous, colossal,* and the slang words *super, keen, neat,* weakens rather than strengthens the desired emphasis.

Jargon

Linguistic transmogrification (*jargon*) is characterized by an optimum utilization of abstract terminology and the consequent break-down of intelligibility. You can see how easily this kind of language can hide lack of substance.

We would do well to remember Stendahl's words: "If I am not clear, the world around me collapses." Jargon is made up of the clichés of a trade or profession. It is acceptable only as shoptalk among initiates.

Language

Language is an arbitrary system of signs, verbal or written, with which people communicate meanings to one another. Language is man's greatest invention and a form of behaviour uniquely human.

Linguistics

The term *linguistics* refers to the scientific study of language. Branches of this study include the study of sounds and words; their history and changes in meaning; and the study of grammar. Note that grammar is only one of the many fields of study in the science of linguistics. Linguistics is the study and analysis of the systems comprising language.

Mass media

Mass media are the instruments used to send identical messages to large numbers of people who are physically separated. Each instrument is a special means of communicating information, ideas, and feelings, and each has its special effect on the receiver. According to Marshall McLuhan, "The medium is the message."

Mass media (or mediums) are usually classified as *print, film,* and *electronics.* Another system of classification is based on the degree of control exercised over the medium by the *receiver* of the message and the *sender* of the message. In this classification, *print* and some *film* are *receiver controlled* media because the initiative is largely with the receiver—he decides what to read, when and how to read it; and if he wishes, he can re-read or re-view. Television (an electronic medium) is, on the other hand, *sender-controlled.* Once the receiver has decided to watch a TV program, he is largely controlled by the sender, who makes all the decisions about the speed, style, amount of repetition, and the kind of emphasis the presentation is to have. The danger of this medium can be overcome only by the active and discriminating participation and judgment of the receiver. (For a detailed discussion of the effects of mass media see Austin Repath's *Mass Media and You,* Longmans Canada Limited, 1966.)

Point of view

The term *point of view* is applied in different ways:

1. In factual narration, point of view refers to the means the writer uses to maintain a consistent perspective. Here, point of view is apparent in the pronoun the writer uses when referring to himself. The questions, "Who tells the story? What is his relation to the story?" usually establish the identity of the writer and hence the point of view in the narrative.

   a *The "I" (first person) narrative* is the most natural way of narrating personal experience.

   b *The "you" (second person) narrative* is sometimes used to invite the participation of the reader. But the effective use of the "you" point of view depends on keeping the narrative impersonal, yet intimate. All but the best writers find this balance difficult to manage.

   c *The "he" narrative, or third person objective,* is used to tell a story from the outside. The writer is not in the minds of his characters; he reports actions and events and characters but does not interpret. "One" is sometimes used instead of "he" to suggest the point of view of people in general. But the use of "one" usually results in stilted and awkward sentence construction.

    d *The omniscient, omnipotent observer* is the term used to refer to the point of view in a narrative in which the writer is the all-knowing observer—inside the minds of his characters and capable of commenting on all events and actions.

2. In description, point of view refers to the *physical* point from which the observer looks at the thing he is describing.

3. In still another sense, point of view refers to the *tone* of what is said or written. Here, the point of view is psychological, revealing the writer's attitude to his subject.

Rhetoric

The term *rhetoric* has many meanings. To some people, rhetoric suggests flowery, insincere language, whose lack of substance is indicated by the phrase "empty rhetoric". To others, rhetoric is the name for the arts of oratory and persuasion. Aristotle defined rhetoric as, "The power to see the possible ways of persuading people about any given subject." At one time, rhetoric referred only to spoken discourse, but today the term refers to the *effective use* of language in speech and writing. The major concerns of rhetoric are:

1. the effective arrangement and organization of material,
2. the efficient construction of sentences and paragraphs,
3. the choice of appropriate words,
4. the effect upon the reader or audience.

Semantics

Semantics is the study of meanings, and changes in meaning, in a language. Semantics is concerned with the relations between the word and its *referents* and *context,* with *denotation* and *connotation.* Semantics is based on the realization that language is more than a code for the transmission of facts, it recognizes that many logical fallacies are the result of lack of concern with precise referents.

Syntax

Syntax is the part of grammar concerned with the order and relationship of words in a sentence. *Faulty modifiers, inconsistencies of tense* and *voice, lack of agreement,* and *sentence fragments* are structural failures caused by lack of attention to syntax.

Wordiness

Wordiness is the use of more words than are needed. Two kinds of wordiness are particularly annoying: *inflated writing* and *redundancy*. The first refers to language that is larger than the subject calls for, "He was inebriated by his own verbosity", is an inflated version of, "He was drunk with his own words." Redundancy refers to the needless repetition of ideas. The sentence, "Both Tom and Mary should have a mutual liking for each other", is a redundant version of, "Tom and Mary should like each other."

Index

236